Noble was the gesture into which patriotic passion surprised the people in a utilitarian time and country; yet
the glory of the war falls short of its pathos.

Herman Melville

Holbrook Press, Inc.
Boston

GLORY
and
PATHOS

Responses of Nineteenth-Century American Authors to the Civil War

edited by
RICHARD DILWORTH RUST
The University of North Carolina

CONTENTS

Doubters: North

Enthusiasts: South

Doubters: South

PREFACE

The emotional literature of a people is as necessary to the philosophical historian as the mere details of events in the progress of a nation. This is essential to the reputation of the Southern people, as illustrating their feelings, sentiments, ideas, and opinions—the motives which influenced their actions, and the objects which they had in contemplation, and which seemed to them to justify the struggle in which they were engaged.

William Gilmore Simms

The Civil War was a watershed in American life and letters, a fact felt keenly by nineteenth-century American authors. Although sometimes on the periphery of events, they often had the clearest perception of the larger issues and problems of the war. As authors they combined perceptiveness with imagination to go beyond the factual events of the war and seek its intellectual and emotional significance. Probing to the heart of things, they frequently asked questions about the Civil War which have universal applications: What is the essence of war? What causes it? How do men respond to it? What is its effect upon humanity?

The selections which follow illustrate vividly the scope and variety of these responses to the war. My criterion for choosing authors was that they have a place in the mainstream of American literature or, at the very least, receive some modern critical attention. The period covered by the responses is essentially that of the conflict of 1861–65. A broader definition of the Civil War could, of course, refer to political and economic developments of the 1840s and 1850s through the Reconstruction decade. Some responses in that period are abolitionist pronouncements of Bryant and Whittier, Thoreau's journal entries and speeches on John Brown, Harriet Beecher Stowe's *Uncle Tom's Cabin,* and writings by De Forest, Lanier, and Melville on Reconstruction.

There is a rich variety of points of view, forms, styles, and interests in the material in this anthology. Two approaches to it, suggested in Appendices A and B, are to consider the effect authors'
military involvement or noninvolvement had upon their responses
or to compare responses by genres. The approach suggested by the
organization of the selections is to examine the authors as enthusiasts or as doubters concerning the war. A dictionary definition of
an enthusiast is "one who is animated by an intense and eager interest in an activity, cause, etc." A doubter is "one who is uncertain
about, questions, or feels distrust of something." Actually, few authors were wholly one or the other throughout the war. For example,
an enthusiast such as Lowell at times had doubts about one phase
or another of war policies and practices, while a skeptic such as
Melville gave firm, if qualified, support to the Union side. The purpose of the arbitrary enthusiast-doubter categories is thus not so
much to "place" American authors during the Civil War as to call
attention to the kinds and degrees of their enthusiasm or skepticism
regarding the war.

The basic rationale of this book is documentary, most
of the selections have intrinsic literary merit. This is particularly
true of the fiction of De Forest, Bierce, and Twain and the poetry of
Dickinson, Melville, Timrod, and Whitman. It should also be noted
that though many selections come from larger works, they can be
examined as self-contained units (e.g., De Forest's fictional account
of the attack and repulse at Port Hudson).

The study questions and topics at the end of the book provide
a wide diversity of themes and allow individual interpretations. As
a whole they are designed to help one recognize the connections between authors' responses and understand better the attempt American authors made to come to terms with their country's greatest
crisis.

I wish to think the University of North Carolina Research
Council for a grant providing some of the materials for this project;
the staffs of the rare-book rooms of the University of North Carolina
and Duke University for permission to xerox materials from their
collections; and Professors William R. Taylor, Robert E. Spiller,
Lewis Leary, Daniel W. Patterson, Robert A. Bain, and William J.
Powers for their stimulation and encouragement.

Richard Dilworth Rust

ENTHUSIASTS
North

We look upon the war as our only means of salvation.

Orestes Brownson

There never was a nation great except through trial.

Ralph Waldo Emerson

The volcanic upheaval of the nation, after that firing on the flag at Charleston, . . . will remain as the grandest and most encouraging spectacle yet vouchsafed in any age, old or new, to political progress and democracy.

Walt Whitman

ORESTES BROWNSON

(1803–1876)

Orestes Brownson began his professional career in 1826 as a Universalist minister, became a Unitarian from 1832 to 1836, and then organized his own church. He became closely associated with the Transcendentalists in the 1840s and maintained this association after his conversion to Catholicism in October, 1844. For thirty years he edited quarterly reviews, first the Boston Quarterly Review, *which merged with the* Democratic Review, *and later* Brownson's Quarterly Review.

An eclectic truth-seeker, Brownson changed his opinions a number of times on the issues of the war. He was an advocate of states' rights, but argued strongly for integrity of the Union after the war came. During the war years he wrote many patriotic articles and was in demand as a lecturer. He was an antihumanitarian conservative who saw the war as a divine purgation and as a renewal of the American revolutionary spirit. The best discussion of Brownson's life and changing views is found in Arthur M. Schlesinger, Jr., Orestes A. Brownson: A Pilgrim's Progress *(1939)*.

from THE GREAT REBELLION*

. . . The cause of the Southern rebellion is not in the aggressions of the North, nor in the movements of Northern abolitionists. We must seek it in the fact that the Slaveholding States wished through the slave interest, or the interest of capital invested in slaves, to control the policy of the country and administer the Government in their own favor, and in the farther fact that they felt they could

*From [Orestes Brownson], "The Great Rebellion," *Brownson's Quarterly Review*, Third New York Series, II (July, 1861), 378–402.

have no adequate security for the capital so invested while the wealthier and more populous Section of the Union entertained opinions and convictions hostile to slavery. No modification of the Constitution, however favor- [383/384] able to slavery, would have satisfied them so long as they felt themselves the weaker party. Nothing would satisfy them but the conversion of the North to their views of slavery. They knew perfectly well that slavery could not long exist in a country unless it were its controlling interest. It can flourish only so long as it governs, and must die out when the supremacy passes from its hands. Hence these States made at first a desperate struggle through the Northern Democracy, which almost from the origin of the Government had been allied with them, to retain their supremacy. They made afterwards a still more desperate struggle to change the opinions of the North with regard to slavery itself. But, failing in both attempts, and seeing that power must pass from their hands, and henceforth be wielded by a party that would not consent to be governed by the interests of the capital invested in slaves, they felt that their only security lay in breaking up the Union, and forming a separate Confederacy of their own, based on slavery as its corner-stone. They would, whatever they pretended, accept no compromise, and the Free States had no option but to submit to their dictation, abdicate their own rights in the Union, and recognize slavery as a Christian institution, as existing by divine right, and as forming the basis of our Republic, or to assert their own manhood, their equal rights as members of the Union, form a really constitutional party, carry the elections, and administer the Government for the common interests of the whole country, and not for the special interest of a particular section, and that the slaveholding section. This they did in the last Presidential election. No intelligent man in the South believed that the success of the Republican party threatened directly the institution of slavery; but the whole South saw in it the fact that the political control of the Union had passed from Southern hands, and that henceforth the Slaveholding States would be obliged to be contented to stand on a footing of equality with the non-Slaveholding States. There was no fear that the slave interest would be deprived of any of its legal rights, but there was a certainty that henceforth it would not be supreme in the councils of the Union; that, however scrupulously it might be respected within the Slaveholding States themselves, the extension of slavery into new territory where it had no legal existence, would be effectually checked; that no more territory could be acquired and annexed to the Union in the interest of slavery; [384/385] that the flag of the Union would be no longer permitted to cover the piratical slave-trade, and that all hopes of reopening the African slave-trade must be abandoned. Here, in our judgment, is, in brief, the real cause of the present collision between the United States and the Southern Rebels. The cause, we repeat, is not in Northern aggression, but in Northern emancipation from Southern domination. . . . [385/386]

Well, it has come to this. The South has appealed from ballots to bullets, and forced upon the North an issue which the people of the Free States could not refuse to accept without abdicating their manhood, and standing branded in history as the most miserable cravens and dastards that the world has ever known. The war has come, and come none too soon. The issue had to be tried, whether the New World was to be a land of freedom, sacred to free institutions and self-government, or whether it was to be a land of slavery, where man was to be treated no longer as man, but as a mere chattel, with no soul, no reason, no conscience, no immortality. . . . [386/387]

The war now raging is no doubt to be deeply deplored, or rather the causes which have led to it; but in this war the United States are in the right and the Southern Rebels wholly in the wrong. The Rebels, by aid of their Democratic friends in the non-Slaveholding States, have had the administration of the Government, have shaped its general policy at home and abroad, and wielded its patronage, with hardly an interval of time, since the inauguration of Mr. Jefferson in 1801. They have had almost every thing their own way. The South have had no wrongs from the Government, and no grievances from the North to complain of. The Federal government has, from the first, faithfully performed all its duties with regard to the question of slavery. It has fully protected the rights of the slave-owner, and has enacted and executed the most stringent and offensive laws in his favor. The Southern section of the Union has had far more than its share of officers in the Army and Navy, as well as of the Diplomatic representatives of the [387/388] country. Of the two foreign wars in which we have been engaged since the adoption of the Federal Constitution, the

first was forced upon us by the South for the purpose of ruining the
commerce and influence of the Northern and Eastern States; and
the second, that against Mexico, was undertaken wholly in the
slaveholding interest of the South. Though more than three-fourths
of the revenues of the Federal government have been collected in
the ports of the Free States, nearly two-thirds have been expended
in and for the Slaveholding States, and these States have held their
slave property in security and been protected in their peculiar institutions, solely because they were regarded by foreign nations and by
the citizens of the Free States as integral parts of the great American
Republic. No portion of the United States have received so great
and so many benefits from the Federal Union. Of what, then, do
they complain? What grievance have they had, not of their own
creating? . . . [388/389] . . .

     . . . The only grievance the South has to complain of in us of
the non-Slaveholding States is, that we are not charmed with the
beauties of the slave system; that we do not regard slavery as a
Christian institution existing by divine right; that in fact we dislike
slavery, that we detest it and take the liberty to say so. Here is the
head and front of our offending. But even in this respect we only
retain and express the views and feelings entertained and expressed,
till quite recently, by the prominent statesmen and leading men of
the Slaveholding States themselves. It amounts, then, to this, that
the people of the Slaveholding States have rebelled against the
Federal government because the majority of the people of the non-
Slaveholding States differ with them in opinion on the subject of
slavery, and insist upon treat- [389/390] ing black men, as well as
white men, as belonging to the human family, in a word, as men
created with rational and immortal souls and redeemed by the Passion and Death of our Lord—because, in fact, we include them in
the great brotherhood of humanity. This is their grievance for
which they have seen proper to rebel against the Federal government, and attempt to efface from the map of the world the great
Republic of the United States.

     The Federal government is manifestly in the right; for whether
the Federal government derives its powers by delegation from
sovereign States, or directly from the people politically divided into
States, it is, within its constitutional sphere, a government with all
the rights and immunities of government, and, like every govern-

ment, must have that first of all rights, the right of self-preservation. The question as to the source of its powers is and can be of no practical importance, when once its powers are ascertained and defined. The people of the United States, in forming the Federal Union, did not form a mere league or confederacy of sovereigns; they formed a government, a government with limited powers indeed, but still a government, supreme, sovereign within its constitutional limits. They formed a union and not a confederacy. From this union no State, any more than an individual, has the right to secede; for they expressly ordain that the "Constitution, and the Laws of the United States which shall be made in Pursuance thereof; and all Treaties made, or which shall be made, under the authority of the United States, shall be the supreme Law of the Land; and the Judges in every State shall be bound thereby, any Thing in the Constitution or Laws of any State to the contrary notwithstanding." There is no getting over this: the Federal government, within its constitutional limits, is the supreme government of the land, and paramount to all State constitutions, authorities, or laws. Any act of secession by a State is an act of rebellion, and therefore null and void, not only as against the Union, but in relation to its own citizens; and the attempt of the people, or any portion of the people of any State by force of arms to carry such an act into effect, is manifestly a levying of war against the United States, and therefore an act of treason. Even if it were conceded that the sovereignty theoretically still vests in the States, its exercise within certain limits is delegated to the Union and incapable of being revoked without a mani- [390/391] fest breach of faith. Say that the Union is a "constitutional compact," it is one of those compacts in which all the parties are bound to each and each to all. Such a compact can be dissolved only by the unanimous consent of all the contracting parties, while from its very nature the parties remaining faithful to it must necessarily have the right to enforce its observance upon any party seeking to evade its provisions. So, whether we take the Northern or the Southern view of the Federal Union, secession is illegal, is in violation of the Constitution, nothing more or less than an act of rebellion, and as such the Federal government has not only the constitutional right, but the constitutional duty, to put it down, if it has or can command the means to do it. [391/401] . . .

The true way to regard this war is to regard it as a chastisement from the hand of Divine Providence, as a just judgment from God upon our nation for its manifold sins; but a judgment sent in mercy, designed not to destroy us, but to purify and save us, to render us a wiser, a better, a more virtuous, a more elevated, and a more powerful people. It is intended to try us, to inure us to hardship, to make us feel that all mere worldly prosperity is short-lived and transitory, and that no people that departs from God, neglects eternal goods, and fixes its affections only on the low and perishing goods of sense, can ever hope to be a great, a strong, and long-lived people. Let us then welcome the sufferings, the privations, the hardships, the toil, the loss of affluence, the poverty that this war is sure to bring upon no small portion of our population. Let us welcome them as a severe but necessary chastisement, and let us wish the chastisement to be severe enough to correct us and to ensure our amendment and our future progress. Unless such be the case, no cause of the war will be removed; its seeds will remain, and at the first favorable opportunity will germinate anew, grow up, blossom, and bear their deadly fruit. [401]

from THE STRUGGLE OF THE NATION FOR LIFE*

Many worthy people regard war, especially a civil war like that which is now raging in the American Union, as the greatest calamity that can befall a nation, and so great is their horror of war that they seem willing to purchase peace at any price, even by national dishonor and national degradation, yet war is rather the effect of evil than the evil itself. The real evil is in the causes that precede and lead to it. In our case it is the effort of the sound part of the nation to expel a disease long since contracted, and [113/ 114] which was gradually but steadily approaching the seat of life, and threatening us with complete dissolution. To the eye of enlightened patriotism our condition as a people is less deplorable today than it was four years ago before the war broke out.

*From [Orestes Brownson], "The Struggle of the Nation for Life," *Brownson's Quarterly Review*, Third New York Series, III (Jan., 1862) , 113–132.

War is never lawful for its own sake, and can be rightfully undertaken only for the sake of a true and lasting peace; but, when necessary to that end, it is not only justifiable, but sacred and obligatory. It is a severe remedy for a desperate disease, what physicians call an "heroic" remedy, therefore good, but one which in certain cases must be resorted to, if recovery is not to be despaired of. Without it, we had no chance of prolonging our national life. With the slave interest in full power in nearly one half of the Union, and by its combinations ruling the councils of the nation; with Young America, reckless and destitute of principle, managing our politics at the North under the lead of Fernando Woods and New York Heralds; with the laxity of morals becoming almost universal in politics and business, in public life and private; with the growing tastes and habits of luxury and extravagance prevalent throughout the land, we were well nigh a lost people; our destruction as a nation was, if no change came, only a question of time, and thoughtful and far-seeing men were beginning to despair of the Republic. The impending ruin, in the ordinary providence of God, could be averted only by the war which has broken out, and is now raging. We deplore with all our heart the causes which made the war necessary and inevitable, but we do not and cannot grieve that it has come, or lament the sacrifices it compels us to make.

War is a less calamity to a nation than the effeminate and luxurious tastes and habits generated by a long peace and its attendant exterior prosperity. It can never be so fatal to a nation as the loss of virtue, courage, manliness, and love of glory, which we had suffered during the thirty years preceding the outbreak of the present Rebellion, and which renders it yet doubtful whether we have the moral qualities requisite to restore the Union, and preserve our national existence. What is the loss of blood or treasure in comparison with the loss of country or of national life? What are all the losses war can occasion in comparison with the possession of our manhood, and of those self-denying and self-sacrificing virtues which war demands and seldom fails [114/115] to develop? Indeed, we look upon the war as our only means of salvation, as sent in mercy to a privileged people to enable them to be a living people, a great, heroic, and chivalric nation, fitted to receive and fulfil the holy mission of proving what is the nobility of man when and where he is free to be himself. . . .

WILLIAM CULLEN BRYANT

(1794–1878)

Although William Cullen Bryant was sixty-six years old when the Civil War began, he nevertheless was active in support of the Union cause. As editor of the New York Evening Post*— a position he held for almost fifty years—he had frequently voiced his opposition to slavery. In 1856 he allied his newspaper with the new Republican organization and, after the war began, sided with the radical element of the Republican party. Thus when secession was announced, he opposed any type of compromise or moderation. In both his editorials and his poetry, Bryant continued to be a spokesman for American idealism until his death in 1878.*

NOT YET*

O country, marvel of the earth!
  O realm to sudden greatness grown!
The age that gloried in thy birth,
  Shall it behold thee overthrown?
Shall traitors lay that greatness low?
No, land of Hope and Blessing, No!

And we, who wear thy glorious name,
  Shall we, like cravens, stand apart,
When those whom thou hast trusted aim

---

*From William Cullen Bryant, *Poetical Works of William Cullen Bryant* (New York: D. Appleton and Co., 1878) . Written in July, 1861.

The death-blow at thy generous heart?   10
Forth goes the battle-cry, and lo!
Hosts rise in harness, shouting, No! [377/378]

And they who founded, in our land,
    The power that rules from sea to sea,
Bled they in vain, or vainly planned
    To leave their country great and free?
Their sleeping ashes, from below,
Send up the thrilling murmur, No!

Knit they the gentle ties which long
    These sister States were proud to wear,   20
And forged the kindly links so strong
    For idle hands in sport to tear?
For scornful hands aside to throw?
No, by our fathers' memory, No!

Our humming marts, our iron ways,
    Our wind-tossed woods on mountain-crest,
The hoarse Atlantic, with its bays,
    The calm, broad Ocean of the West,
And Mississippi's torrent-flow,
And loud Niagara, answer, No!   30

Not yet the hour is nigh when they
    Who deep in Eld's dim twilight sit,
Earth's ancient kings, shall rise and say,
    "Proud country, welcome to the pit!
So soon art thou, like us, brought low!"
No, sullen group of shadows, No!

For now, behold, the arm that gave
    The victory in our fathers' day,
Strong, as of old, to guard and save—
    That mighty arm which none can stay—   40
On clouds above and fields below,
Writes, in men's sight, the answer, No! [378]

EMANCIPATION AND THE WAR*

There is but one way of ending the war. Blow upon blow, battle
after battle, conquest upon conquest, the capture of all the rebel
seaports, the occupation of all the rivers in the rebel territory, no
delay, no pause in the course of victory, till every one of their
strongholds, and every one of their towns, from Manassas to Fort
Pickens, and from the Potomac to the Sabine, is ours. Then, when
we have subdued the insurrection, we will make our own terms—
terms such as shall seem to us just and fair, and so devised as best to
avoid the danger of a future insurrection of the class who have
caused all this strife and bloodshed. . . .

A peace purchased by receding from the policy of emancipation
will be but a hollow truce, in the womb of which would lurk other
insurrections and rebellions, ready to break out in civil war whenever an occasion like that of 1861 should arise. Suffer the rebel
States to return to the Union with the right of slavery acknowl-
edged, and you proclaim to them that they can at any time rebel at
their good pleasure, and, if unsuccessful in their revolt, take their
old place in the Union until a more auspicious moment shall arrive
for forming a new confederacy. You restore to their old station a
class of men whose sole occupations are politics and the use of fire-
arms and the lash; a rest- [203/204] less, ambitious, overbearing,
arbitrary class, with whom we have never lived in harmony except
by submitting to their will, and with whom we can never live in
peace hereafter, except by new submissions—a class of men bent on
embroiling our country with foreign nations, except when a quarrel
with a foreign government might bring the institution of slavery
into danger. By continuing the slave-holding class in existence, we
shall keep alive the vexed question of slavery, the curse of our
politics, the cause of infinite national disgrace, the source of indescribable barbarities, the occasion of this dreadful Civil War with
all its calamities and all its crimes. By adhering to the policy of the
proclamation we blot out this fierce controversy forever, and put in

*From Parke Godwin, *A Biography of William Cullen Bryant, with Extracts
from His Private Correspondence* (New York: D. Appleton and Co., 1883) , Vol. II.
First published in the New York *Evening Post*, July 1863.

its place eternal peace. On questions of expenditure, of trade, of internal improvements, of foreign policy, we may differ, we may dispute, we may form parties; but on this great, gloomy, fearful question, which, after years of stormy discussion, has been submitted to the frightful arbitrament of war, we shall have perpetual silence. We shall then be a homogeneous people—a people with the same interests and institutions as well as origin, from the Atlantic to the Pacific, and from our northernmost to our southernmost limit. Our parties will no longer be local and geographical, but, as in other countries, formed upon differences of opinion as to the proper province and powers of legislation. [204]

from LETTER TO CATHARINE M. SEDGWICK*

ROSLYN, JUNE 26, 1865

I have for some time past thought of writing to you, by way of congratulating you on the suppression of the rebellion and the close of our bloody Civil War. And yet I have nothing to say on the subject which is not absolutely commonplace. All that can be said of the terrible grandeur of the struggle which we have gone through, of the vastness and formidable nature of the conspiracy against the life of our republic, of the atrocious [227/228] crimes of the conspirators, of the valor and self-sacrificing spirit and unshaken constancy of the North, and of the magnificent result which Providence has brought out of so much wickedness and so much suffering, has been said already over and over.

Never, I think, was any great moral lesson so powerfully inculcated by political history. What the critics call poetic justice has been as perfectly accomplished as it could have been in any imaginary series of events.

When I think of this great conflict, and its great issues, my mind reverts to the grand imagery of the Apocalypse—to the visions in which the messengers of God came down to do his bidding among the nations, to reap the earth, ripe for the harvest, and gather the spoil of the vineyards; to tread the wine-press, till it flows

*From Godwin, *Biography*, Vol. II.

over far and wide with blood; to pour out the phials of God's judgments upon the earth, and turn its rivers into blood; and, finally, to bind the dragon, and thrust him down into the bottomless pit.

Neither you nor I, until this war began, thought that slavery would disappear from our country until more than one generation had passed away; yet a greater than man has taken the work in hand, and it is done in four years. It is a great thing to have lived long enough to see this mighty evil wrenched up from our soil by the roots and thrown into the flames. [228]

RALPH WALDO EMERSON

(1803–1882)

Essayist, lecturer, and "sage of Concord," Emerson was well established by the time of the Civil War as a foremost American man of letters. Although he resisted institutionalized reform in the 1830s and 40s (preferring to keep himself "aloof from all the moorings, and afloat"), in the 1850s he turned more and more to the abolitionist movement and also became a champion of John Brown. In a December, 1834, journal entry Emerson wrote, "Because every man has within him somewhat really divine, therefore is slavery the unpardonable outrage it is." Retaining this belief into the 1860s, Emerson was an outspoken advocate of emancipation during the early years of the war. Moreover, he had an opportunity to argue his views before the Lincoln administration when he visited Washington in February, 1862. Then on January 1, 1863, the date of the Emancipation Proclamation, Emerson formed an important part of the program at Music Hall. There he read "Boston Hymn" with its declaration, "To-day unbind the captive,/So only are ye unbound."

In a lecture entitled "War" delivered to the American Peace Society in March, 1838, Emerson sought to delineate a "true view of the nature and office of war." At that time he saw war as related to "the ignorant and childish part of mankind" and as a condition which passes away when men reach a higher stage of development. These views were modified somewhat at the beginning of the Civil War when Emerson saw the conflict as part of a revolution in humanity, and foresaw good to come from evil. The selections below are designed to give a broad view of his beliefs in this regard. Also they allow one to see changes in his ideas during the years 1861 to 1865.

from LETTER TO JAMES ELLIOT CABOT*

Concord, August 4, 1861.

My dear Cabot,
   I was very glad yesterday to hear from you, & on such high [252/ 253] matters. The war,—though from such despicable beginnings, has assumed such huge proportions that it threatens to engulf us all—no preoccupation can exclude it, & no hermitage hide us—And yet, gulf as it is, the war with its defeats & uncertainties is immensely better than what we lately called the integrity of the Republic, as amputation is better than cancer. I think we are all agreed in this, and find it out by wondering why we are so pleased, though so beaten & so poor. No matter how low down, if not in false position. If the abundance of heaven only sends us a fair share of light & conscience, we shall redeem America for all its sinful years since the century began. At first sight, it looked only as a war of manners, showing that the southerner who owes to climate & slavery his suave, cool, & picturesque manners, is so impatient of ours, that he must fight us off. And we all admired them until a long experience only varying from bad to worse has shown us, I think finally, what a noxious reptile the green & gold thing was. . . . Their perversity in still forcing us into a better position than we had taken. Their crimes force us into virtues to antagonize them and we are driven into principles by their abnegation of them. Ah if we dared think that our people would be simply good enough to take & hold this advantage to the end!—But there is no end to the views the crisis suggests, & day by day. You see I have only been following my own lead, without prying into your subtle hints of ulterior political effects. But one thing I hope,—that 'scholar' & 'hermit' will no longer be exempts, neither by the country's permission nor their own, from the public duty. The functionaries, as you rightly say, have failed. The statesmen are all at fault. The good heart & mind, out of all private corners, should speak & save. [253]

*From *The Letters of Ralph Waldo Emerson,* ed. Ralph L. Rusk (New York: Columbia University Press, 1939) , V, 252–253. Reprinted by permission of Columbia University Press.

[JOURNAL OF THE WAR YEARS]*

[May 1861] The country is cheerful and jocund in the belief that it has a government at last. The men in search of a party, parties in search of a principle, interests and dispositions that could not fuse for want of some base,—all joyfully unite in this great Northern party, on the basis of Freedom. What a healthy tone exists! I suppose when we come to fighting, and many of our people are killed, it will yet be found that the bills of mortality in the country will [325/326] show a better result of this year than the last, on account of the general health; no dyspepsia, no consumption, no fevers, where there is so much electricity, and conquering heart and mind.

[August 1861] The war is a great teacher, still opening our eyes wider to some larger consideration. It is a great reconciler, too, forgetting our petty quarrels as ridiculous:—
"On such a shrine,
What are our petty griefs? Let me not number mine."
But to me the first advantage of the war is the favourable moment it has made for the cutting out of our cancerous Slavery. Better that [335/336] war and defeats continue, until we have come to that amputation.

I suppose, if the war goes on, it will be impossible to keep the combatants from the extreme ground on either side. In spite of themselves, one army will stand for Slavery pure; the other for Freedom pure.

[November 1862] There never was a nation great except through trial. A religious revolution cuts sharpest, and tests the faith and endurance. A civil war sweeps away all the false issues on which it began, and arrives presently at real and lasting questions. [459]

[November 1862] . . . The war is serving many good purposes. It is no respecter of respectable persons or of worn-out party

*From *Journals of Ralph Waldo Emerson,* ed. Edward Waldo Emerson and Waldo Emerson Forbes, 13 vols. (Boston and New York: Houghton Mifflin Company, 1909–14). Reprinted by permission of Houghton Mifflin Co. Journal entries from May, 1861, to October, 1863, are from Vol. IX (1913) and the entry of July, 1865, is from Vol. X (1914).

platforms. War is a realist, shatters everything flimsy and shifty, sets aside all false issues, and breaks through all that is not real as itself; comes to organize opinions. and parties, resting on the necessities of man; like its own cannonade, comes crushing in through party walls that have stood fifty or sixty years as if they were solid. The scream-ing of leaders, the votes by acclamation, conventions, are all idle wind. They cry for mercy, but they cry to one who never knew the word. He is the arm of the Fates, and, as has been said, "Nothing prevails against God but God." Everything must perish except that which must live.

Well, this is the task before us, to accept the benefit of the War; it has not created our false relations, they have created it. It simply demon- [461/462] strates the rottenness it found. We watch its course as we did the cholera, which goes where predisposition al-ready existed, took only the susceptible, set its seal on every putrid spot, and on none other; followed the limestone, and left the granite. So the War. Anxious statesmen try to rule it, to slacken it here and let it rage there, to not exasperate, to keep the black man out of it; to keep it well in hand, nor let it ride over old party lines, nor much molest trade, and to confine it to the frontier of the two sections. Why need Cape Cod, why need Casco Bay, why need Lake Superior, know anything of it? But the Indians have been bought, and they came down on Lake Superior; Boston and Portland are threatened by the pirate; Secession unexpectedly shows teeth in Boston; our parties have just shown you that the War is already in Massachusetts, as in Richmond.

Let it search, let it grind, let it overturn, and, like the fire when it finds no more fuel, it burns out. The War will show, as all wars do, what is wrong is intolerable, what wrong makes and breeds all this bad blood. I suppose that it shows two incompatible states of society, Freedom and Slavery. If a part of this country is civilized up to a clean insight of Freedom, [462/463] and of its necessity, and another part is not so far civilized, then I suppose that the same difficulties will continue; the War will not be extinguished; no treaties, no peace, no constitution can paper over the lips of that red crater. Only when, at last, so many parts of the country as can combine on an equal and moral contract,—not to protect each other in polygamy, or in kidnapping, or in eating men, but in humane and just activities,—only so many can combine firmly and durably. [463]

[April (?) 1863]
Uses of the War.
1. Diffusion of a taste for hardy habits.
2. Appeal to the roots of strength.

The benefit of war is that the appeal not being longer to letter and form, but now to the roots of strength in the people, the moral aspect becomes important, and is urgently presented and debated; whilst, in preceding quiet times, custom is able to stifle this discussion as sentimental, and bring in the brazen devil himself.

Certain it is that never before since I read newspapers, have the morals played so large a part in them as now.

As I have elsewhere written, when Jove has points to carry, he impresses his will on the structure of minds. Every one stands stupefied at the course of the war. None so wise as to have predicted anything that has occurred. Every one reads the ballot of the people on each new question with surprise, and the pious and once hopeless lover of freedom with trem- [492/493] bling joy. And this surprise shows that nobody did it, or thought it, but the Lord alone.

3. Besides, war is not the greatest calamity.

I see in the street about the "saloon" plenty of boys and men who are nuisances, but who only want a master to make them useful to themselves and to society. . . . "The saloons," said Edmund Hosmer, "are worse than war to their customers."

How the war teaches our youths of the *haute volée*. Do I not know how to play billiards and whist? Do I not know the violin and flute? Yet I will throw myself on those bayonets.

4. War organizes.

All decomposition is recomposition. What we call consumption is energetic growth of the fungus, or whatever new order. War disorganizes, but it also organizes; it forces individuals and states to combine and act with larger views, and sunder the best heads, and keeps the population together, producing the effect of cities; for camps are wandering cities.

My interest in my Country is not primary, but professional; I wish that war, as peace, shall bring out the genius of the men. In every company, in every town, I seek intellect and character, and so in every circumstance. War, I [493/494] know, is a potent alternative, tonic, magnetizer, reinforces manly power a hundred and a thousand times. I see it come as a frosty October, which shall restore intellectual and moral power to these languid and dissipated populations.

5. What munificence has the war disclosed! How a sentiment could unclasp the grip of avarice, and the painfullest economy!

6. It has created patriotism. We regarded our Country as we do the world. It had no enemy, and we should as soon have thought of vaunting the atmosphere or the sea; but let the comet or the moon or Mercury or Mars come down on us, we should get out our buffers and electricities and stand for the Earth with fury against all comers.

War sharpens the eyes, opens the mind of the people, so that truths we were once forbidden to speak, I hear shouted by mobs, saluted by cannon, redacted into laws.

Emancipation of Maryland, of Tennessee, of Missouri, of Louisiana.

In quiet times, the wilful man has his way; in war, the truthful man. [494]

[October (?) 1863] Washington and Cromwell, one using a moral, the other a revolutionary policy. The government of Algiers and of Turkey is, though it last for ages, revolutionary. If we continued in Boston to throw tea into the bay at pleasure, that were revolutionary. But our *revolution* was in the interest of the moral or anti-revolutionary. Slavery is Algiers, or perpetual revolution; society upside down, head over heels, and man eating his breakfast with pistols by his plate. It is man degraded to cat and dog, and society has come to an end, and all gentlemen die out.

Thus a violent conservatism is more revolutionary than abolition or freedom of speech and of press. 'T is like shutting your window when [553/554] you have lighted a pan of coals in the unchimneyed apartment.

[July 1865] It is commonly said of the War of 1812 that it made the nation honourably known; it enlarged our politics, extinguished narrow sectional parties. But the states were young and unpeopled. The present war, on a prodigiously enlarged scale, has cost us how many valuable lives; but it has made many lives valuable that were not so before, through the start and expansion it has given. It has fired selfish old men to an incredible liberality, and young men to the last devotion. The journals say it has demoralized many rebel regiments, but also it has *moralized* many of our regiments, and not only so, but *moralized* cities and states. It added [X,105/106] to every house and heart a vast enlargement. In every house and shop, an American map has been unrolled, and daily studied, and now that peace has come, every citizen finds himself a skilled student of the condition, means, and future, of this continent.

I think it a singular and marked result that the War has established a conviction in so many minds that the right will get done; has established a chronic hope for a chronic despair.

This victory the most decisive. This will stay put. It will show your enemies that what has now been so well done will be surely better and quicker done, if need be, again. [X,106]

from **AMERICAN CIVILIZATION***

In this national crisis, it is not argument that we want, but that rare courage which dares commit itself to a principle, believing that Nature is its ally, and will create the instruments it requires, and more than make good any petty and injurious profit which it may disturb. There never was such a combination as this of ours, and the rules to meet it are not set down in any history. We want men of original perception and original action, who can open their eyes wider than to a nationality, namely, to considerations of benefit to the human race, can act in the interest of civilization. Government must not be a parish clerk, a justice of the peace. It has, of necessity, in any crisis of the state, the absolute powers of a dictator. The existing administration is entitled to the utmost candor. It is to be thanked for its angelic virtue, compared with any executive experiences with which we have been familiar. But the times will not allow us to indulge in compliment. I wish I saw in the people that inspiration which, if gov- [302/303] ernment would not obey the same, would leave the government behind and create on the

*From *The Complete Works of Ralph Waldo Emerson*, ed. Edward Waldo Emerson, Centenary Edition (Boston and New York: Houghton Mifflin Company, 1903–21), Vol. XI. This is modified from a lecture Emerson gave at the Smithsonian Institution in Washington, D.C., Jan. 31, 1862. It was first published in the *Atlantic Monthly,* April, 1862.

moment the means and executors it wanted. Better the war should more dangerously threaten us,—should threaten fracture in what is still whole, and punish us with burned capitals and slaughtered regiments, and so exasperate the people to energy, exasperate our nationality. There are Scriptures written invisibly on men's hearts, whose letters do not come out until they are enraged. They can be read by war-fires, and by eyes in the last peril.

We cannot but remember that there have been days in American history, when, if the free states had done their duty, slavery had been blocked by an immovable barrier, and our recent calamities forever precluded. The free states yielded, and every compromise was surrender and invited new demands. Here again is a new occasion which heaven offers to sense and virtue. It looks as if we held the fate of the fairest possession of mankind in our hands, to be saved by our firmness or to be lost by hesitation.

The one power that has legs long enough and strong enough to wade across the Potomac offers itself at this hour; the one strong enough [303/304] to bring all the civility up to the height of that which is best, prays now at the door of Congress for leave to move. Emancipation is the demand of civilization. That is a principle; everything else is an intrigue. This is a progressive policy, puts the whole people in healthy, productive, amiable position, puts every man in the South in just and natural relations with every man in the North, laborer with laborer. [304]

from THE PRESIDENT'S PROCLAMATION*

In so many arid forms which States incrust themselves with, once in a century, if so often, a poetic act and record occur. These are the jets of thought into affairs, when, roused by danger or inspired by genius, the political leaders of the day break the else insurmountable routine of class and local legislation, and take a step forward in the direction of catholic and universal interests. Every step in the history of political liberty is a sally of the human mind into the untried future, and has the interest of genius, and is fruitful in

*From R. W. Emerson, "The President's Proclamation," *Atlantic Monthly*, X (Nov., 1862), 638–642.

heroic anecdotes. Liberty is a slow fruit. It comes, like religion, for short periods, and in rare [638/639] conditions, as if awaiting a culture of the race which shall make it organic and permanent. Such moments of expansion in modern history were the Confession of Augsburg, the plantation of America, the English Commonwealth of 1648, the Declaration of American Independence in 1776, the British emancipation of slaves in the West Indies, the passage of the Reform Bill, the repeal of the Corn-Laws, the Magnetic Ocean-Telegraph, though yet imperfect, the passage of the Homestead Bill in the last Congress, and now, eminently, President Lincoln's Proclamation on the twenty-second of September. These are acts of great scope, working on a long future, and on permanent interests, and honoring alike those who initiate and those who receive them. These measures provoke no noisy joy, but are received into a sympathy so deep as to apprise us that mankind are greater and better than we know. . . . [639/641] . . .

. . . It is to be noted, that, in the Southern States, the tenure of land, and the local laws, with slavery, give the social system not a democratic, but an aristocratic complexion; and those States have shown every year a more hostile and aggressive temper, until the instinct of self-preservation forced us into the war. And the aim of the war on our part is indicated by the aim of the President's Proclamation, namely, to break up the false combination of Southern society, to destroy the piratic feature in it which makes it our enemy only as it is the enemy of the human race, and so allow its reconstruction on a just and healthful basis. Then new affinities will act, the old repulsions will cease, and, [641/642] the cause of war being removed, Nature and trade may be trusted to establish a lasting peace.

We think we cannot overstate the wisdom and benefit of this act of the Government. The malignant cry of the Secession press within the Free States, and the recent action of the Confederate Congress, are decisive as to its efficiency and correctness of aim. Not less so is the silent joy which has greeted it in all generous hearts, and the new hope it has breathed into the world.

It was well to delay the steamers at the wharves, until this edict could be put on board. It will be an insurance to the ship as it goes plunging through the sea with glad tidings to all people. Happy are the young who find the pestilence cleansed out of the earth, leaving

open to them an honest career. Happy the old, who see Nature
purified before they depart. Do not let the dying die: hold them
back to this world, until you have charged their ear and heart with
this message to other spiritual societies, announcing the melioration
of our planet.

> "Incertainties now crown themselves assured,
> And Peace proclaims olives of endless age."

Meantime that ill-fated, much-injured race which the Proclamation respects will lose somewhat of the dejection sculptured for
ages in their bronzed countenance, uttered in the wailing of their
plaintive music,—a race naturally benevolent, joyous, docile, industrious, and whose very miseries sprang from their great talent for
usefulness, which, in a more moral age, will not only defend their
independence, but will give them a rank among nations. [642]

VOLUNTARIES*

I

Low and mournful be the strain,
Haughty thought be far from me;
Tones of penitence and pain,
Moanings of the tropic sea;
Low and tender in the cell
Where a captive sits in chains,
Crooning ditties treasured well
From his Afric's torrid plains.
Sole estate his sire bequeathed,
Hapless sire to hapless son,   10
Was the wailing song he breathed,
And his chain when life was done.

* From *The Complete Works of Ralph Waldo Emerson*, ed. Edward Waldo
Emerson, Centenary Edition (Boston and New York: Houghton Mifflin Co.,
1904), Vol. IX. First published in the *Atlantic Monthly*, Oct., 1863. The poem
in part eulogizes Col. Robert Gould Shaw, who died in leading his 54th Massachusetts regiment of colored troops in an attack upon Battery Wagner in
Charleston harbor, July 18, 1863.

What his fault, or what his crime?
Or what ill planet crossed his prime?
Heart too soft and will too weak
To front the fate that crouches near,
Dove beneath the vulture's beak;
Will song dissuade the thirsty spear?
Dragged from his mother's arms and breast,
Displaced, disfurnished here,   20
His wistful toil to do his best
Chilled by a ribald jeer. [205/206]
Great men in the Senate sate,
Sage and hero, side by side,
Building for their sons the State,
Which they shall rule with pride.
They forbore to break the chain
Which bound the dusky tribe,
Checked by the owners' fierce disdain,
Lured by 'Union' as the bribe.   30
Destiny sat by, and said,
'Pang for pang your seed shall pay,
Hide in false peace your coward head,
I bring round the harvest day.'

II

Freedom all winged expands,
Nor perches in a narrow place;
Her broad van seeks unplanted lands;
She loves a poor and virtuous race.
Clinging to a colder zone
Whose dark sky sheds the snowflake down,   40
The snowflake is her banner's star,
Her stripes the boreal streamers are.
Long she loved the Northman well;
Now the iron age is done,
She will not refuse to dwell
With the offspring of the Sun;
Foundling of the desert far,
Where palms plume, siroccos blaze, [206/207]
He roves unhurt the burning ways

In climates of the summer star.   50
He has avenues to God
Hid from men of Northern brain,
Far beholding, without cloud,
What these with slowest steps attain.
If once the generous chief arrive
To lead him willing to be led,
For freedom he will strike and strive,
And drain his heart till he be dead.

III

In an age of fops and toys,
Wanting wisdom, void of right,   60
Who shall nerve heroic boys
To hazard all in Freedom's fight,—
Break sharply off their jolly games,
Forsake their comrades gay
And quit proud homes and youthful dames
For famine, toil and fray?
Yet on the nimble air benign
Speed nimbler messages,
That waft the breath of grace divine
To hearts in sloth and ease.   70
So nigh is grandeur to our dust,
So near is God to man,
When Duty whispers low, *Thou must,*
The youth replies, *I can.* [207/208]

IV

O, well for the fortunate soul
Which Music's wings infold,
Stealing away the memory
Of sorrows new and old!
Yet happier he whose inward sight,
Stayed on his subtile thought,   80
Shuts his sense on toys of time,
To vacant bosoms brought.

But best befriended of the God
He who, in evil times,
Warned by an inward voice,
Heeds not the darkness and the dread,
Biding by his rule and choice,
Feeling only the fiery thread
Leading over heroic ground,
Walled with mortal terror round,   90
To the aim which him allures,
And the sweet heaven his deed secures.
Peril around, all else appalling,
Cannon in front and leaden rain
Him duty through the clarion calling
To the van called not in vain.

   Stainless soldier on the walls,
Knowing this,—and knows no more,—
Whoever fights, whoever falls,
Justice conquers evermore, [208/209]   100
Justice after as before,—
And he who battles on her side,
God, though he were ten times slain,
Crowns him victor glorified,
Victor over death and pain.

V

Blooms the laurel which belongs
To the valiant chief who fights;
I see the wreath, I hear the songs
Lauding the Eternal Rights,
Victors over daily wrongs: 110
Awful victors, they misguide
Whom they will destroy,
And their coming triumph hide
In our downfall, or our joy:
They reach no term, they never sleep,
In equal strength through space abide;
Though, feigning dwarfs, they crouch and creep,

The strong they slay, the swift outstride:
Fate's grass grows rank in valley clods,
And rankly on the castled steep,—   120
Speak it firmly, these are gods,
All are ghosts beside. [209]

from HARVARD COMMEMORATION SPEECH*

The old Greek Heraclitus said, "War is the Father of all things."
He said it, no doubt, as science, but we of this day can repeat it as
political and social truth. War passes the power of all chemical
solvents, breaking up the old adhesions, and allowing the atoms of
society to take a new order. It is not the Government, but the War,
that has appointed the good generals, sifted out the pedants, put in
the new and vigorous blood. The War has lifted many other people
besides Grant and Sherman into [341/342] their true places. Even
Divine Providence, we may say, always seems to work after a certain
military necessity. Every nation punishes the General who is not
victorious. It is a rule in games of chance that the cards beat all the
players, and revolutions disconcert and outwit all the insurgents.

The revolutions carry their own points, sometimes to the ruin
of those who set them on foot. The proof that war also is within the
highest right, is a marked benefactor in the hands of the Divine
Providence, is its *morale*. The war gave back integrity to this erring
and immoral nation. It charged with power, peaceful, amiable men,
to whose life war and discord were abhorrent. What an infusion of
character went out from this and other colleges! What an infusion
of character down to the ranks! The experience has been uniform
that it is the gentle soul that makes the firm hero after all. It is easy
to recall the mood in which our young men, snatched from every
peaceful pursuit, went to the war. Many of them had never handled
a gun. They said, "It is not in me to resist. I go because I must. It is
a duty which I shall never forgive myself if I decline. I do not know
that I can make a soldier. I may be [342/343] very clumsy. Perhaps

*From *The Complete Works of Ralph Waldo Emerson,* Centenary Edition
(1911), Vol. XI. The speech was delivered July 21, 1865.

I shall be timid; but you can rely on me. Only one thing is certain, I can well die, but I cannot afford to misbehave."

In fact the infusion of culture and tender humanity from these scholars and idealists who went to the war in their own despite—God knows they had no fury for killing their old friends and countrymen—had its signal and lasting effect. It was found that enthusiasm was a more potent ally than science and munitions of war without it. "It is a principle of war," said Napoleon, "that when you can use the thunderbolt you must prefer it to the cannon." Enthusiasm was the thunderbolt. Here in this little Massachusetts, in smaller Rhode Island, in this little nest of New England republics it flamed out when the guilty gun was aimed at Sumter. [343]

from **DEDICATION OF THE SOLDIER'S MONUMENT IN CONCORD***

April 19, 1867

. . . Every principle is a war-note. When the rights of man are recited under any old government, every one of them is a declaration of war. War civilizes, rearranges the population, distributing by ideas,—the innovators on one side, the antiquaries on the other. It opens the eyes wider. Once we were patriots up to the townbounds, or the state-line. But when you replace the love of family or clan by a principle, as freedom, instantly that fire runs over the state-line into New Hampshire, Vermont, New York and Ohio, into the prairie and beyond, leaps the mountains, bridges river and lake, burns as hotly in Kansas and California as in Boston, and no chemist can discriminate between [353/354] one soil and the other. It lifts every population to an equal power and merit.

As long as we debate in council, both sides may form their private guess what the event may be, or which is the strongest. But the moment you cry "Every man to his tent, O Israel!" the delusions of hope and fear are at an end;—the strength is now to be tested by the eternal facts. There will be no doubt more. The world is equal

*From *The Complete Works of Ralph Waldo Emerson,* Centenary Edition (1911), Vol. XI.

to itself. The secret architecture of things begins to disclose itself; the fact that all things were made on a basis of right; that justice is really desired by all intelligent beings; that opposition to it is against the nature of things; and that, whatever may happen in this hour or that, the years and the centuries are always pulling down the wrong and building up the right.

The war made the Divine Providence credible to many who did not believe the good Heaven quite honest. Every man was an abolitionist by conviction, but did not believe that his neighbor was. The opinions of masses of men, which the tactics of primary caucuses and the proverbial timidity of trade had concealed, the war discovered; and it was found, contrary to all popular belief, that the country was at [354/355] heart abolitionist, and for the Union was ready to die.

As cities of men are the first effects of civilization, and also instantly causes of more civilization, so armies, which are only wandering cities, generate a vast heat, and lift the spirit of the soldiers who compose them to the boiling point. The armies mustered in the North were as much missionaries to the mind of the country as they were carriers of material force, and had the vast advantage of carrying whither they marched a higher civilization. Of course, there are noble men everywhere, and there are such in the South; and the noble know the noble, wherever they meet; and we have all heard passages of generous and exceptional behavior exhibited by individuals there to our officers and men, during the war. But the common people, rich or poor, were the narrowest and most conceited of mankind, as arrogant as the negroes on the Gambia River; and, by the way, it looks as if the editors of the Southern press were in all times selected from this class. The invasion of Northern farmers, mechanics, engineers, tradesmen, lawyers and students did more than forty years of peace had done to educate the South. . . .
[355]

THOMAS WENTWORTH HIGGINSON

(1823–1911)

T. W. Higginson grew up in Cambridge, Massachusetts, where he participated in some of the more radical reform movements of his day—particularly woman suffrage and abolitionism. After graduating from Harvard College and then from Harvard Divinity School, he was a Unitarian minister from 1847 to 1861. A social activist, Higginson attempted to liberate Anthony Burns, a fugitive slave, in 1854; he assisted Kansas freesoilers; and he extended open sympathy to John Brown. Higginson was also a versatile writer, contributing to a number of periodicals—notably the Atlantic Monthly—*and writing a variety of books. Perhaps his best-known work other than* Army Life *is* Cheerful Yesterdays *(1898), an autobiography. He is also known for his biographies of Longfellow and Whittier, for the* Larger History of the United States *(1885), and for being Emily Dickinson's literary mentor.*

Army Life in a Black Regiment *records a high point in Higginson's life. Writing in 1862 of his new command of the first Negro regiment in the Union army, he says, "Here is . . . a position of great importance; as many persons have said, the first man who organizes and commands a successful black regiment will perform the most important service in the history of the war."* Army Life *is also a highly successful literary work. As Howard Mumford Jones remarks, Higginson's "lively humor, a fine eye for the picturesque, indignation against injustice, and real affection for his men create one of the few classics of military life in the national letters."*

from **ARMY LIFE IN A BLACK REGIMENT***

These pages record some of the adventures of the First South
Carolina Volunteers,—the first slave regiment mustered into the
service of the United States during the late civil war. . . . [1/3]
     . . . I did not seek the command of colored troops, but it
sought me. And this fact again is only important to my story for this
reason, that under these circumstances I naturally viewed the new
recruits rather as subjects for discipline than for philanthropy. I
had been expecting a war for six years, ever since the Kansas
troubles, and my mind had dwelt on military matters more or less
during all that time. The best Massachusetts regiments already exhibited a high standard of drill and discipline, and unless these
men could be brought tolerably near that standard, the fact of their
extreme blackness would afford me, even as a philanthropist, no
satisfaction. Fortunately, I felt perfect confidence that they could be
so trained,—having happily known, by experience, the qualities of
their race, and knowing also that they had home and household and
[3/4] freedom to fight for, besides that abstraction of "the Union."
Trouble might perhaps be expected from white officials, though this
turned out far less than might have been feared; but there was no
trouble to come from the men, I thought, and none ever came. On
the other hand, it was a vast experiment of indirect philanthropy,
and one on which the result of the war and the destiny of the negro
race might rest; and this was enough to tax all one's powers. I had
been an abolitionist too long, and had known and loved John
Brown too well, not to feel a thrill of joy at last on finding myself in
the position where he only wished to be.
     In view of all this, it was clear that good discipline must come
first; after that, of course, the men must be helped and elevated in
all ways as much as possible.
     Of discipline there was great need,—that is, of order and regu-
lar instruction. Some of the men had already been under fire, but
they were very ignorant of drill and camp duty. The officers, being

*From Thomas Wentworth Higginson, *Army Life in a Black Regiment*
(Boston: Fields, Osgood, & Co., 1870) .

appointed from a dozen different States, and more than as many regiments,—infantry, cavalry, artillery, and engineers,—had all that diversity of methods which so confused our army in those early days. The first need, therefore, was of an unbroken interval of training. During this period, which fortunately lasted nearly two months, I rarely left the camp, and got occasional leisure moments for a fragmentary journal, to send home, recording the many odd or novel aspects of the new experience. Camp-life was a wonderfully strange sensation to almost all volunteer officers, and mine lay among eight hundred men suddenly transformed from slaves into soldiers, and representing a race affectionate, enthusiastic, grotesque, and dramatic beyond all others. . . . [4/16]

December 3, 1862.—7 p.m.

What a life is this I lead! It is a dark, mild, drizzling evening, and as the foggy air breeds sand-flies, so it calls out melodies and strange antics from this mysterious race [16/17] of grown-up children with whom my lot is cast. All over the camp the lights glimmer in the tents, and as I sit at my desk in the open doorway, there come mingled sounds of stir and glee. Boys laugh and shout,—a feeble flute stirs somewhere in some tent, not an officer's,—a drum throbs far away in another,—wild kildeer-plover flit and wail above us, like the haunting souls of dead slave-masters,—and from a neighboring cook-fire comes the monotonous sound of that strange festival, half pow-wow, half prayer-meeting, which they know only as a "shout." These fires are usually enclosed in a little booth, made neatly of palm-leaves and covered in at top, a regular native African hut, in short, such as is pictured in books, and such as I once got up from dried palm-leaves for a fair at home. This hut is now crammed with men, singing at the top of their voices, in one of their quaint, monotonous, endless, negro-Methodist chants, with obscure syllables recurring constantly, and slight variations interwoven, all accompanied with a regular drumming of the feet and clapping of the hands, like castanets. Then the excitement spreads: inside and outside the enclosure men begin to quiver and dance, others join, a circle forms, winding monotonously round some one in the centre; some "heel and toe" tumultuously, others merely tremble and stagger on, others stoop and rise, others whirl, others caper sideways, all keep steadily circling like dervishes; spectators applaud special strokes of skill; my approach only enlivens the scene; the circle enlarges, louder grows the singing, rousing shouts of encouragement come in, half bacchanalian, half devout, "Wake 'em, brudder!" "Stan' up to 'em, brudder!"—and still the ceaseless drumming and clapping, in perfect cadence, goes steadily [17/18] on. Suddenly there comes a sort of *snap,* and the spell breaks, amid general sighing and laughter. And this not rarely and occasionally, but night after night, while in other parts of the camp the soberest prayers and exhortations are proceeding sedately.

A simple and lovable people, whose graces seem to come by nature, and whose vices by training. Some of the best superintendents confirm the first tales of innocence, and Dr. Zachos told me last night that on his plantation, a sequestered one, "they had absolutely no vices." Nor have these men of mine yet shown any worth mentioning; since I took command I have heard of no man intoxicated, and there has been but one small quarrel. I suppose that scarcely a white regiment in the army shows so little swearing. Take the "Progressive Friends" and put them in red trousers, and I verily believe they would fill a guard-house sooner than these men. If camp regulations are violated, it seems to be usually through heedlessness. They love passionately three things besides their spiritual incantations; namely, sugar, home, and tobacco. This last affection brings tears to their eyes, almost, when they speak of their urgent need of pay; they speak of their last-remembered quid as if it were some deceased relative, too early lost, and to be mourned forever. As for sugar, no white man can drink coffee after they have sweetened it to their liking.

I see that the pride which military life creates may cause the plantation trickeries to diminish. For instance, these men make the most admirable sentinels. It is far harder to pass the camp lines at night than in the camp from which I came; and I have seen none of that disposition to connive at the offences of members of one's own [18/19] company which is so troublesome among white soldiers. Nor are they lazy, either about work or drill; in all respects they seem better material for soldiers than I had dared to hope. [19/39] · · ·

January 1, 1863 (evening).

A happy New Year to civilized people,—mere white folks. Our festival has come and gone, with perfect success, and our good General has been altogether satisfied. Last night the great fires were kept smouldering in the pit, and the beeves were cooked more or less, chiefly more,—during which time they had to be carefully watched, and the great spits turned by main force. Happy were the merry fellows who were permitted to sit up all night, and watch the glimmering flames that threw a thousand fantastic shadows among the great gnarled oaks. And such a chattering as I was sure to hear whenever I awoke that night!

My first greeting to-day was from one of the most stylish sergeants, who approached me with the following little speech, evidently the result of some elaboration:—

"I tink myself happy, dis New Year's Day, for salute my own Cunnel. Dis day las' year I was servant to a Cunnel ob Secesh; but now I hab de privilege for salute my own Cunnel."

That officer, with the utmost sincerity, reciprocated the sentiment.

About ten o'clock the people began to collect by land, and also by water,—in steamers sent by General Saxton for the purpose; and from that time all the avenues of approach were thronged. The multitude were chiefly colored women, with gay handkerchiefs on their heads, and a sprinkling of men, with that peculiarly respectable look which these people always have on Sundays and holidays. There were many white visitors also,—ladies on horseback and in carriages, superintendents and teachers, officers, and cavalry-men. Our companies were marched to the neighborhood of the platform, and allowed [39/40] to sit or stand, as at the Sunday services; the platform was occupied by ladies and dignitaries, and by the band of the Eighth Maine, which kindly volunteered for the occasion; the colored people filled up all the vacant openings in the beautiful grove around, and there was a cordon of mounted visitors beyond. Above, the great live-oak branches and their trailing moss; beyond the people, a glimpse of the blue river.

The services began at half past eleven o'clock, with prayer by our chaplain, Mr. Fowler, who is always, on such occasions, simple, reverential, and impressive. Then the President's Proclamation was

read by Dr. W. H. Brisbane, a thing infinitely appropriate, a South
Carolinian addressing South Carolinians; for he was reared among
these very islands, and here long since emancipated his own slaves.
Then the colors were presented to us by the Rev. Mr. French, a
chaplain who brought them from the donors in New York. All this
was according to the programme. Then followed an incident so
simple, so touching, so utterly unexpected and startling, that I can
scarcely believe it on recalling, though it gave the key-note to the
whole day. The very moment the speaker had ceased, and just as I
took and waved the flag, which now for the first time meant anything to these poor people, there suddenly arose, close beside the
platform, a strong male voice (but rather cracked and elderly), into
which two women's voices instantly blended, singing, as if by an
impulse that could no more be repressed than the morning note of
the song-sparrow.—

> "My Country, 'tis of thee,
> Sweet land of liberty,
> Of thee I sing!"

People looked at each other, and then at us on the [40/41]
platform, to see whence came this interruption, not set down in the
bills. Firmly and irrepressibly the quavering voices sang on, verse
after verse; others of the colored people joined in; some whites on
the platform began, but I motioned them to silence. I never saw
anything so electric; it made all other words cheap; it seemed the
choked voice of a race at last unloosed. Nothing could be more
wonderfully unconscious; art could not have dreamed of a tribute
to the day of jubilee that should be so affecting; history will not
believe it; and when I came to speak of it, after it was ended, tears
were everywhere. If you could have heard how quaint and innocent
it was! Old Tiff and his children might have sung it; and close
before me was a little slave-boy, almost white, who seemed to
belong to the party, and even he must join in. Just think of it!—the
first day they had ever had a country, the first flag they had ever
seen which promised anything to their people, and here, while mere
spectators stood in silence, waiting for my stupid words, these
simple souls burst out in their lay, as if they were by their own
hearths at home! When they stopped, there was nothing to do for it

but to speak, and I went on; but the life of the whole day was in those unknown people's song. [41/266] . . .

We who served with the black troops have this peculiar satisfaction, that, whatever dignity or sacredness the memories of the war may have to others, they have more to us. In that contest all the ordinary ties of patriotism were the same, of course, to us as to the rest; they had no motives which we had not, as they have now no memories which are not also ours. But the peculiar privilege of associating with an outcast race, of training it to defend its rights, and to perform its duties, this was our especial need. The vacillating policy of the Government sometimes filled other officers with doubt and [266/267] shame; until the negro had justice, they were but defending liberty with one hand and crushing it with the other. From this inconsistency we were free. Whatever the Government did, we at least were working in the right direction. If this was not recognized on our side of the lines, we knew that it was admitted on the other. Fighting with ropes round our necks, denied the ordinary courtesies of war till we ourselves compelled their concession, we could at least turn this outlawry into a compliment. We had touched the pivot of the war. Whether this vast and dusky mass should prove the weakness of the nation or its strength, must depend in great measure, we knew, upon our efforts. Till the blacks were armed, there was no guaranty of their freedom. It was their demeanor under arms that shamed the nation into recognizing them as men. [267]

OLIVER WENDELL HOLMES
(1809–1894)

Oliver Wendell Holmes, essayist, poet, and teacher of anatomy, is best known in literature for his Autocrat of the Breakfast-Table, *begun in the* Atlantic Monthly *of November, 1857. He was also the author of three novels,* Elsie Venner *(1861),* The Guardian Angel *(1867), and* A Mortal Antipathy *(1885). Holmes was not as fervid in his antislavery views as were Whittier and Emerson, but nevertheless agreed with them in seeing slavery as a taint upon America and the Civil War as a divinely ordered purification of the nation.*

The July 4 oration by Holmes is similar to his "Under the Washington Elm" in its expression of the need for courage and endurance. Another writing which is more balanced in its observations on the war is Holmes's essay "My Hunt after 'The Captain,'" Atlantic Monthly, *X (December, 1862), 738–64, in which he tells of looking for his son, Oliver Wendell Holmes, Jr., who was wounded at Antietam.*

BROTHER JONATHAN'S LAMENT
FOR SISTER CAROLINE*

She has gone,—she has left us in passion and pride,—
Our stormy-browed sister, so long at our side!
She has torn her own star from our firmament's glow,
And turned on her brother the face of a foe!

*From Oliver Wendell Holmes, *The Poetical Works of Oliver Wendell Holmes* (Cambridge: Houghton Mifflin Co., 1891), Vol. I. Written March 25, 1861.

Oh, Caroline, Caroline, child of the sun,
We can never forget that our hearts have been one,—
Our foreheads both sprinkled in Liberty's name,
From the fountain of blood with the finger of flame!

You were always too ready to fire at a touch;
But we said, "She is hasty,—she does not mean much."   10
We have scowled, when you uttered some turbulent threat;
But Friendship still whispered, "Forgive and forget!"

Has our love all died out? Have its altars grown cold?
Has the curse come at last which the fathers foretold?
Then Nature must teach us the strength of the chain
That her petulant children would sever in vain. [284/285]

They may fight till the buzzards are gorged with their spoil,
Till the harvest grows black as it rots in the soil,
Till the wolves and the catamounts troop from their caves,
And the shark tracks the pirate, the lord of the waves: 20

In vain is the strife! When its fury is past,
Their fortunes must flow in one channel at last,
As the torrents that rush from the mountains of snow
Roll mingled in peace through the valleys below.

Our Union is river, lake, ocean, and sky:
Man breaks not the medal, when God cuts the die!
Though darkened with sulphur, though cloven with steel,
The blue arch will brighten, the waters will heal!

Oh, Caroline, Caroline, child of the sun,
There are battles with Fate that can never be won!   30
The star-flowering banner must never be furled,
For its blossoms of light are the hope of the world!

Go, then, our rash sister! afar and aloof,
Run wild in the sunshine away from our roof;
But when your heart aches and your feet have grown sore,
Remember the pathway that leads to our door! [285]

UNDER THE WASHINGTON ELM, CAMBRIDGE*

Eighty years have passed, and more,
    Since under the brave old tree
Our fathers gathered in arms, and swore
They would follow the sign their banners bore,
    And fight till the land was free.

Half of their work was done,
    Half is left to do,—
Cambridge, and Concord, and Lexington!
When the battle is fought and won,
    What shall be told of you?   10

Hark!—'t is the south-wind moans,—
    Who are the martyrs down?
Ah, the marrow was true in your children's bones
That sprinkled with blood the cursèd stones
    Of the murder-haunted town!

What if the storm-clouds blow?
    What if the green leaves fall?
Better the crashing tempest's throe
Than the army of worms that gnawed below;
    Trample them one and all!   20

Then, when the battle is won,
    And the land from traitors free, [230/231]
Our children shall tell of the strife begun
When Liberty's second April sun
    Was bright on our brave old tree!

---

*From *The Poetical Works of Oliver Wendell Holmes,* Vol. II. Written
April 27, 1861.

from **THE INEVITABLE TRIAL***

**An Oration Delivered Before the City Authorities
of Boston, on the 4th of July, 1863**

As we look at the condition in which we find ourselves on this
fourth day of July, 1863, at the beginning of the Eighty-eighth Year
of American Independence, we may well ask ourselves what right
we have to indulge in public rejoicings. If the war in which we are
engaged is an accidental one, which might have been avoided but
for our fault; if it is for any ambitious or unworthy purpose on our
part; if it is hopeless, and we are madly persisting in it; if it is our
duty and in our power to make a safe and honorable peace, and we
refuse to do it; if our free institutions are in danger of becoming
subverted, and giving place to an irresponsible tyranny; if we are
moving in the narrow circles which are to ingulf us in national
ruin,—then we had better sing a dirge, and leave this idle as-
semblage, and hush the noisy cannon which are reverberating
through the air, and tear down the scaf- [81/82] folds which are
soon to blaze with fiery symbols; for it is mourning and not joy that
should cover the land; there should be silence, and not the echo of
noisy gladness, in our streets; and the emblems with which we tell
our nation's story and prefigure its future should be traced, not in
fire, but in ashes.

If, on the other hand, this war is no accident, but an inevitable
result of long-incubating causes; inevitable as the cataclysms that
swept away the monstrous births of primeval nature; if it is for no
mean, unworthy end, but for national life, for liberty everywhere,
for humanity, for the kingdom of God on earth; if it is not hopeless,
but only growing to such dimensions that the world shall remember
the final triumph of right throughout all time; if there is no safe
and honorable peace for us but a peace proclaimed from the capital
of every revolted province in the name of the sacred, inviolable
Union; if the fear of tyranny is a phantasm, conjured up by the
imagination of the weak, acted on by the craft of the cunning; if so

*From Oliver Wendell Holmes, *The Writings of Oliver Wendell Holmes*
(Cambridge: Houghton Mifflin Company, 1891) , Vol. VIII.

far from circling inward to the gulf of our perdition, the movement of past years is reversed, and every revolution carries us farther and farther from the centre of the vortex, until, by God's blessing, we shall soon find ourselves freed from the outermost coil of the accursed spiral; if all these things are true; if we may hope to make them seem true, or even probable, to the doubting soul, in an hour's discourse,—then we may join without madness in the day's exultant festivities; the bells may ring, the cannon may roar, the incense of our harmless saltpetre fill the air, and the children who are to inherit the fruit of these toiling, agonizing years, go about unblamed, making day and night vocal with their jubilant patriotism. [82/83]

The struggle in which we are engaged was inevitable; it might have come a little sooner, or a little later, but it must have come. The disease of the nation was organic, and not functional, and the rough chirurgery of war was its only remedy. [83/85] . . .

The antagonism of the two sections of the Union was not the work of this or that enthusiast or fanatic. It was the consequence of a movement in mass of two different forms of civilization in different directions, and the men to whom it was attributed were only those who represented it most completely, or who talked longest and loudest about it. Long before the accents of those famous statesmen referred to ever resounded in the halls of the Capitol, long before the "Liberator" opened its batteries, the controversy now working itself out by trial of battle was foreseen and predicted. Washington warned his countrymen of the danger of sectional divisions, well knowing the line of cleavage that ran through the seemingly solid fabric. Jefferson foreshadowed the judgment to fall upon the land for its sins against a just God. Andrew Jackson announced a quarter of a century beforehand that the next pretext of revolution would be slavery. De Tocqueville recognized with that penetrating insight which analyzed our institutions and conditions so keenly, that the Union was to be endangered by slavery, not through its interests, but through the change of character it was bringing about in the people of the two sections, the same fatal change which George Mason, more than half a century before, had declared to be the most pernicious effect of the system, adding the solemn warning, now fearfully justifying itself in the [85/86] sight of his descendants, that "by an inevitable chain of causes and effects, Providence punishes national sins by national calamities." The Virginian romancer pictured the far-off scenes of the conflict which he saw approaching as the prophets of Israel painted the coming woes of Jerusalem, and the strong iconoclast of Boston announced the very year when the curtain should rise on the yet unopened drama.

The wise men of the past, and the shrewd men of our own time, who warned us of the calamities in store for our nation, never doubted what was the cause which was to produce first alienation and finally rupture. The descendants of the men "daily exercised in tyranny," the "petty tyrants," as their own leading statesmen called them long ago, came at length to love the institution which their fathers had condemned while they tolerated. It is the fearful realization of that vision of the poet where the lost angels snuff up with eager nostrils the sulphurous emanations of the bottomless abyss,— so have their natures become changed by long breathing the atmosphere of the realm of darkness.

At last, in the fulness of time, the fruits of sin ripened in a sudden harvest of crime. Violence stalked into the senate-chamber, theft and perjury wound their way into the cabinet, and, finally, openly organized conspiracy, with force and arms, made burglarious entrance into a chief stronghold of the Union. That the principle which underlay these acts of fraud and violence should be irrevocably recorded with every needed sanction, it pleased God to select a chief ruler of the false government to be its Messiah to the listening world. As with Pharaoh, the Lord hardened his heart, while he opened his mouth, as of old he opened [86/87] that of the unwise animal ridden by cursing Balaam. Then spake Mr. "Vice-President" Stephens those memorable words which fixed forever the theory of the new social order. He first lifted a degraded barbarism to the dignity of a philosophic system. He first proclaimed the gospel of eternal tyranny as the new revelation which Providence had reserved for the western Palestine. Hear, O heavens! and give ear, O earth! The corner-stone of the new-born dispensation is the recognized inequality of races; not that the strong may protect the weak, as men protect women and children, but that the strong may claim the authority of Nature and of God to buy, to sell, to scourge, to hunt, to cheat out of the reward of his labor, to keep in perpetual ignorance, to blast with hereditary curses throughout all time, the bronzed foundling of the New World, upon whose darkness has dawned the star of the occidental Bethlehem! [87/94] . . .

The war in which we are engaged is for no meanly ambitious or unworthy purpose. It was primarily, and is to this moment, for the preservation of our national existence. The first direct movement towards it was a civil request on the part of certain Southern persons, that the Nation would commit suicide, without making any unnecessary trouble about it. It was answered, with sentiments of the highest consideration, that there were constitutional and other objections to the Nation's laying violent hands upon itself. It was then requested, in a somewhat peremptory tone, that the Nation would be so obliging as to abstain from food until the natural consequences of that proceeding should manifest themselves. All this was done as between a single State and an isolated fortress; but it was not South Carolina and Fort Sumter that were talking; it was a vast conspiracy uttering its menace to a mighty nation; the whole menagerie of treason was pacing its cages, ready to spring as soon as the doors were opened; and all that the tigers of rebellion wanted to kindle their wild natures to frenzy, was the sight of flowing blood.

As if to show how coldly and calmly all this had been calculated beforehand by the conspirators, to make sure that no absence of malice aforethought should degrade the grand malignity of settled purpose into the trivial effervescence of transient passion, the torch which was literally to launch the first missile, figuratively, to "fire the southern heart" and light the flame of civil war, was given into the trembling [94/95] hand of an old white-headed man, the wretched incendiary whom history will handcuff in eternal infamy with the temple-burner of ancient Ephesus. The first gun that spat its iron insult at Fort Sumter, smote every loyal American full in the face. As when the foul witch used to torture her miniature image, the person it represented suffered all that she inflicted on his waxen counterpart, so every buffet that fell on the smoking fortress was felt by the sovereign nation of which that was the representative. Robbery could go no farther, for every loyal man of the North was despoiled in that single act as much as if a footpad had laid hands upon him to take from him his father's staff and his mother's Bible. Insult could go no farther, for over those battered walls waved the precious symbol of all we most value in the past and most hope for in the future,—the banner under which we became a nation, and which, next to the cross of the Redeemer, is the dearest object of love and honor to all who toil or march or sail beneath its waving folds of glory. [95/116] . . .

War is a grim business. Two years ago our women's fingers were busy making "Havelocks." It seemed to us then as if the Havelock made half the soldier; and now we smile to think of those days of inexperience and illusion. We know now what War means, and we cannot look its dull, dead ghastliness in the face unless we feel that there is some great and noble principle behind it. It makes little difference what we thought we were fighting for at first; we know what we are fighting for now, and what we are fighting against.

We are fighting for our existence. We say to those who would take back their several contributions to that undivided unity which we call the Nation; the bronze is cast; the statue is on its pedestal; you cannot reclaim the brass you flung into the crucible! There are rights, possessions, privileges, policies, relations, duties, acquired, retained, called into existence in virtue of the principle of absolute solidarity,—belonging to the United States as an organic whole,— which cannot be divided, which none of its constitutent parties can claim as its own, which perish out of its living frame when the wild forces of rebellion tear it limb from limb, and which it must defend, or confess self-government itself a failure.

We are fighting for that Constitution upon which our national existence reposes, now subjected by those who fired the scroll on which it was written from the cannon at Fort Sumter, to all those chances which the necessities of war entail upon every human arrangement, but still the venerable charter of our wide Republic. [116/117]

We cannot fight for these objects without attacking the one mother cause of all the progeny of lesser antagonisms. Whether we know it or not, whether we mean it or not, we cannot help fighting against the system that has proved the source of all those miseries which the author of the Declaration of Independence trembled to anticipate. And this ought to make us willing to do and to suffer cheerfully. There were Holy Wars of old, in which it was glory enough to die, wars in which the one aim was to rescue the sepulchre of Christ from the hands of infidels. The sepulchre of Christ is not in Palestine! He rose from that burial-place more than eighteen hundred years ago. He is crucified wherever his brothers are slain without cause; he lies buried wherever man, made in his Maker's image, is entombed in ignorance lest he should learn the rights which his Divine Master gave him! This is our Holy War, and we must fight it against that great General who will bring to it all the powers with which he fought against the Almighty before he was cast down from heaven. . . . [117]

ABRAHAM LINCOLN
(1809–1865)

Abraham Lincoln was more inextricably connected with the Civil War than was any other American. His election set off the secessions of Southern states, he was commander-in-chief of the Northern armies, and his death seemed to many the tragic climax to four years of civil bloodshed. As political documents, the selections included here clarify the issues of extension of slavery, preserving the union, and abolition of slavery as a war aim. As literature, they are examples of the rhetoric Lincoln used to stir the nation. Furthermore, they justify James Russell Lowell's assertion that Lincoln was "a master of a truly masculine English." In a similar vein of praise, the contributors to the Literary History of the United States *call him the "spokesman for the clearest thoughts and wisest judgments in the North," "one of the masters of prose style in the English language," and "the one American orator who survives as a literary artist."*

from **FIRST INAUGURAL ADDRESS***

March 4, 1861

Fellow-citizens of the United States: In compliance with a custom as old as the government itself, I appear before you to address you briefly, and to take in your presence the oath prescribed by the Constitution of the United States to be taken by the President "before he enters on the execution of his office."

I do not consider it necessary at present for me to discuss those

*From *Complete Works of Abraham Lincoln,* ed. John G. Nicolay and John Hay (New York: The Tandy-Thomas Company, 1905), Vol. VI.

matters of administration about which there is no special anxiety or excitement.

Apprehension seems to exist among the people [169/170] of the Southern States that by the accession of a Republican administration their property and their peace and personal security are to be endangered. There has never been any reasonable cause for such apprehension. Indeed, the most ample evidence to the contrary has all the while existed and been open to their inspection. It is found in nearly all the published speeches of him who now addresses you. I do but quote from one of those speeches when I declare that "I have no purpose, directly or indirectly, to interfere with the institution of slavery in the States where it exists. I believe I have no lawful right to do so, and I have no inclination to do so." Those who nominated and elected me did so with full knowledge that I had made this and many similar declarations, and had never recanted them. [170/173] . . .

It is seventy-two years since the first inauguration of a President under our National Constitution. During that period fifteen different and greatly distinguished citizens have, in succession, administered the executive branch of the government. They have conducted it through many perils, and generally with great success. Yet, with all this scope of precedent, I now enter upon the same task for the brief constitutional term of four years under great and peculiar difficulty. A disruption of the Federal Union, heretofore only menaced, is now formidably attempted.

I hold that, in contemplation of universal law and of the Constitution, the Union of these States is perpetual. Perpetuity is implied, if not expressed, in the fundamental law of all national governments. It is safe to assert that no government proper ever had a provision in its organic law for its own termination. [173/174]

Continue to execute all the express provisions of our National Constitution, and the Union will endure forever—it being impossible to destroy it except by some action not provided for in the instrument itself.

Again, if the United States be not a government proper, but an association of States in the nature of contract merely, can it, as a contract, be peaceably unmade by less than all the parties who made it? One party to a contract may violate it—break it, so to speak; but does it not require all to lawfully rescind it?

Descending from these general principles, we find the proposition that, in legal contemplation the Union is perpetual confirmed by the history of the Union itself. The Union is much older than the Constitution. It was formed, in fact, by the Articles of Association in 1774. It was matured and continued by the Declaration of Independence in 1776. It was further matured, and the faith of all the then thirteen States expressly plighted and engaged that it should be perpetual, by the Articles of Confederation in 1778. And, finally, in 1787 one of the declared objects for ordaining and establishing the Constitution was "to form a more perfect Union."

But if the destruction of the Union by one or by a part only of the States be lawfully possible, the Union is less perfect than before the Con- [174/175] stitution, having lost the vital element of perpetuity.

It follows from these views that no State upon its own mere motion can lawfully get out of the Union; that resolves and ordinances to that effect are legally void; and that acts of violence, within any State or States, against the authority of the United States, are insurrectionary or revolutionary, according to circumstances.

I therefore consider that, in view of the Constitution and the laws, the Union is unbroken; and to the extent of my ability I shall take care, as the Constitution itself expressly enjoins upon me, that the laws of the Union be faithfully executed in all the States. Doing this I deem to be only a simple duty on my part; and I shall perform it so far as practicable, unless my rightful masters, the American people, shall withhold the requisite means, or in some authoritative manner direct the contrary. I trust this will not be regarded as a menace, but only as the declared purpose of the Union that it will constitutionally defend and maintain itself.

In doing this there needs to be no bloodshed or violence; and there shall be none, unless it be forced upon the national authority. The power confided to me will be used to hold, occupy, and possess the property and places belonging to the government, and to collect the duties and im- [175/176] posts; but beyond what may be necessary for these objects, there will be no invasion, no using of force against or among the people anywhere. . . . [176/179] . . .

The central idea of secession is the essence of anarchy. A majority held in restraint by constitutional checks and limitations, and always changing easily with deliberate changes of popular opinions and sentiments, is the only true sovereign of a free people. Whoever rejects it does, of necessity, fly to anarchy or to despotism. Unanimity is impossible; the rule of a minority, as a permanent arrangement, is wholly inadmissible; so that, rejecting the majority principle, anarchy or despotism in some form is all that is left. [179/180] . . .

One section of our country believes slavery is right, and ought to be extended, while the other believes it is wrong, and ought not to be extended. This is the only substantial dispute. The fugitive-slave clause of the Constitution, and the law for the suppression of the foreign slave-trade, are each as well enforced, perhaps, [180/181] as any law can ever be in a community where the moral sense of the people imperfectly supports the law itself. The great body of the people abide by the dry legal obligation in both cases, and a few break over in each. This, I think, cannot be perfectly cured; and it would be worse in both cases after the separation of the sections than before. The foreign slave-trade, now imperfectly suppressed, would be ultimately revived, without restriction, in one section, while fugitive slaves, now only partially surrendered, would not be surrendered at all by the other.

Physically speaking, we cannot separate. We cannot remove our respective sections from each other, nor build an impassable wall between them. A husband and wife may be divorced, and go out of the presence and beyond the reach of each other; but the different parts of our country cannot do this. They cannot but remain face to face, and intercourse, either amicable or hostile, must continue between them. Is it possible, then, to make that intercourse more advantageous or more satisfactory after separation than before? Can aliens make treaties easier than friends can make laws? Can treaties be more faithfully enforced between aliens than laws can among friends? Suppose you go to war, you cannot fight always; and when, after much loss on both sides, and no gain on either, [181/182] you cease fighting, the identical old questions as to terms of intercourse are again upon you.

This country, with its institutions, belongs to the people who inhabit it. Whenever they shall grow weary of the existing government, they can exercise their constitutional right of amending it, or their revolutionary right to dismember or overthrow it. I cannot be ignorant of the fact that many worthy and patriotic citizens are desirous of having the National Constitution amended. While I make no recommendation of amendments, I fully recognize the rightful authority of the people over the whole subject, to be exercised in either of the modes prescribed in the instrument itself; and I should, under existing circumstances, favor rather than oppose a fair opportunity being afforded the people to act upon it. I will venture to add that to me the convention mode seems preferable, in that it allows amendments to originate with the people themselves, instead of only permitting them to take or reject propositions originated by others not specially chosen for the purpose, and which might not be precisely such as they would wish to either accept or refuse. I understand a proposed amendment to the Constitution—which amendment, however, I have not seen—has passed Congress, to the effect that the Federal Government shall never interfere with the domestic in- [182/183] stitutions of the States, including that of persons held to service. To avoid misconstruction of what I have said, I depart from my purpose not to speak of particular amendments so far as to say that, holding such a provision to now be implied constitutional law, I have no objection to its being made express and irrevocable.

The chief magistrate derives all his authority from the people, and they have conferred none upon him to fix terms for the separation of the States. The people themselves can do this also if they choose; but the executive, as such, has nothing to do with it. His duty is to administer the present government, as it came to his hands, and to transmit it, unimpaired by him, to his successor.

Why should there not be a patient confidence in the ultimate justice of the people? Is there any better or equal hope in the world? In our present differences is either party without faith of being in the right? If the Almighty Ruler of Nations, with his eternal truth and justice, be on your side of the North, or on yours of the South, that truth and that justice will surely prevail by the judgment of this great tribunal of the American people.

By the frame of the government under which we live, this same people have wisely given their public servants but little power for mischief; [183/184] and have, with equal wisdom, provided for the return of that little to their own hands at very short intervals. While the people retain their virtue and vigilance, no administration, by any extreme of wickedness or folly, can very seriously injure the government in the short space of four years.

My countrymen, one and all, think calmly and well upon this

whole subject. Nothing valuable can be lost by taking time. If there be an object to hurry any of you in hot haste to a step which you would never take deliberately, that object will be frustrated by taking time; but no good object can be frustrated by it. Such of you as are now dissatisfied, still have the old Constitution unimpaired, and, on the sensitive point, the laws of your own framing under it; while the new administration will have no immediate power, if it would, to change either. If it were admitted that you who are dissatisfied hold the right side in the dispute, there still is no single good reason for precipitate action. Intelligence, patriotism, Christianity, and a firm reliance on Him who has never yet forsaken this favored land, are still competent to adjust in the best way all our present difficulty.

In your hands, my dissatisfied fellow-countrymen, and not in mine, is the momentous issue of civil war. The government will not assail you. [184/185] You can have no conflict without being yourselves the aggressors. You have no oath registered in heaven to destroy the government, while I shall have the most solemn one to "preserve, protect, and defend it."

I am loath to close. We are not enemies, but friends. We must not be enemies. Though passion may have strained, it must not break our bonds of affection. The mystic chords of memory, stretching from every battle-field and patriot grave to every living heart and hearthstone all over this broad land, will yet swell the chorus of the Union when again touched, as surely they will be, by the better angels of our nature. [185]

LETTER TO HORACE GREELEY*

EXECUTIVE MANSION,

WASHINGTON, AUGUST 22, 1862.

Dear Sir: I have just read yours of the 19th, addressed to myself through the New York "Tribune." If there be in it any statements or assumptions of fact which I may know to be erroneous, I do not now and here, controvert them. If there be in it any inferences which I may believe to be falsely drawn, I do not, now and here, argue

*From *Complete Works of Abraham Lincoln,* Vol. VIII.

against them. If there be perceptible in it an impatient and dictatorial tone, I waive it in deference to an old friend whose heart I have always supposed to be right.

As to the policy I "seem to be pursuing," as you say, I have not meant to leave any one in doubt.

I would save the Union. I would save it the shortest way under the Constitution. The [15/16] sooner the national authority can be restored, the nearer the Union will be "the Union as it was." If there be those who would not save the Union unless they could at the same time save slavery, I do not agree with them. If there be those who would not save the Union unless they could at the same time destroy slavery, I do not agree with them. My paramount object in this struggle is to save the Union, and is not either to save or to destroy slavery. If I could save the Union without freeing any slave, I would do it; and if I could save it by freeing all the slaves, I would do it; and if I could save it by freeing some and leaving others alone, I would also do that. What I do about slavery and the colored race, I do because I believe it helps to save the Union; and what I forbear, I forbear because I do not believe it would help to save the Union. I shall do less whenever I shall believe what I am doing hurts the cause, and I shall do more whenever I shall believe doing more will help the cause. I shall try to correct errors when shown to be errors, and I shall adopt new views so fast as they shall appear to be true views.

I have here stated my purpose according to my view of official duty; and I intend no modification of my oft-expressed personal wish that all men everywhere could be free. Yours,

A. LINCOLN [16]

MEDITATION ON THE DIVINE WILL*

September [2?], 1862

The will of God prevails. In great contests each party claims to act in accordance with the will of God. Both may be, and one must be,

*From *Complete Works of Abraham Lincoln*, Vol. VIII. Roy P. Basler in *The Collected Works of Abraham Lincoln* (1953) theorizes that this private notation was written following the Second Battle of Bull Run and before the Preliminary Emancipation Proclamation, the issuing of which Nicolay and Hay call "the weightiest question of his life."

wrong. God cannot be for and against the same thing at the same time. In the present civil war it is quite possible that God's purpose is something different from the purpose of either party; and yet the human instrumentalities, working just as they do, are of the best adaptation to effect his purpose. I am almost ready to say that this is probably true; that God wills this contest, and wills that it shall not end yet. By his mere great power on the minds of the now contestants, he could have either saved or destroyed the Union without a human contest. Yet the contest began. And, having begun, he [52/ 53] could give the final victory to either side any day. Yet the contest proceeds.

from **PRELIMINARY EMANCIPATION PROCLAMATION***

September 22, 1862

By the President of the United States of America:

A Proclamation.

I, Abraham Lincoln, President of the United States of America, and commander-in-chief of the army and navy thereof, do hereby proclaim and declare that hereafter, as heretofore, the war will be prosecuted for the object of practically restoring the constitutional relation between the United States and each of the States, [36/37] and the people thereof, in which States that relation is or may be suspended or disturbed.

That it is my purpose, upon the next meeting of Congress, to again recommend the adoption of a practical measure tendering pecuniary aid to the free acceptance or rejection of all slave States, so called, the people whereof may not then be in rebellion against the United States, and which States may then have voluntarily adopted, or thereafter may voluntarily adopt, immediate or gradual abolishment of slavery within their respective limits; and that the effort to colonize persons of African descent with their consent upon this continent or elsewhere, with the previously obtained consent of the governments existing there, will be continued.

*From *Complete Works of Abraham Lincoln,* Vol. VIII.

That on the first day of January, in the year of our Lord one thousand eight hundred and sixty-three, all persons held as slaves within any State or designated part of a State the people whereof shall then be in rebellion against the United States, shall be then, thenceforward, and forever free; and the Executive Government of the United States, including the military and naval authority thereof, will recognize and maintain the freedom of such persons, and will do no act or acts to repress such persons, or any of them, in any efforts they may make for their actual freedom. [37/38]

That the Executive will, on the first day of January aforesaid, by proclamation designate the States and parts of States, if any, in which the people thereof, respectively shall then be in rebellion against the United States; and the fact that any State or the people thereof, shall on that day be in good faith represented in the Congress of the United States by members chosen thereto at elections wherein a majority of the qualified voters of such State shall have participated, shall, in the absence of strong countervailing testimony, be deemed conclusive evidence that such State, and the people thereof, are not then in rebellion against the United States. [38]

ADDRESS AT THE DEDICATION OF
THE GETTYSBURG NATIONAL CEMETERY*

November 19, 1863

Fourscore and seven years ago our fathers brought forth on this continent a new nation, conceived in liberty, and dedicated to the proposition that all men are created equal.

Now we are engaged in a great civil war, testing whether that nation, or any nation so conceived and so dedicated, can long endure. We are met on a great battle-field of that war. We have come to dedicate a portion of that field as a final resting-place for those who here gave [209/210] their lives that that nation might live. It is altogether fitting and proper that we should do this.

But, in a larger sense, we cannot dedicate—we cannot conse-

*From *Complete Works of Abraham Lincoln,* Vol. IX.

crate—we cannot hallow—this ground. The brave men, living and
dead, who struggled here, have consecrated it far above our poor
power to add or detract. The world will little note nor long remember what we say here, but it can never forget what they did
here. It is for us, the living, rather, to be dedicated here to the
unfinished work which they who fought here have thus far so nobly
advanced. It is rather for us to be here dedicated to the great task
remaining before us—that from these honored dead we take increased devotion to that cause for which they gave the last full
measure of devotion; that we here highly resolve that these dead
shall not have died in vain; that this nation, under God, shall have
a new birth of freedom; and that government of the people, by the
people, for the people, shall not perish from the earth. [210]

SECOND INAUGURAL ADDRESS*

March 4, 1865

Fellow-countrymen: At this second appearing to take the oath of
the presidential office, there is less occasion for an extended address
than there was at the first. Then a statement, somewhat in detail, of
a course to be pursued, seemed fitting and proper. Now, at the
expiration of four years, during which public declarations have
been constantly called forth on every point and phase of the great
contest which still absorbs the attention and engrosses the energies
of the nation, little that is new could be presented. The progress of
our arms, upon which all else chiefly depends, is as well known to
the public as to myself; and it is, I trust, reasonably satisfactory and
encouraging to all. With high hope for the future, no prediction in
regard to it is ventured.

On the occasion corresponding to this four years ago, all
thoughts were anxiously directed to an impending civil war. All
dreaded it—all sought to avert it. While the inaugural address was
being delivered from this place, devoted altogether to saving the
Union without [44/45] war, insurgent agents were in the city seeking to destroy it without war—seeking to dissolve the Union, and

*From *Complete Works of Abraham Lincoln,* Vol. XI.

divide effects, by negotiation. Both parties deprecated war; but one of them would make war rather than let the nation survive; and the other would accept war rather than let it perish. And the war came.

One-eighth of the whole population were colored slaves, not distributed generally over the Union, but localized in the Southern part of it. These slaves constituted a peculiar and powerful interest. All knew that this interest was, somehow, the cause of the war. To strengthen, perpetuate, and extend this interest was the object for which the insurgents would rend the Union, even by war; while the government claimed no right to do more than to restrict the territorial enlargement of it.

Neither party expected for the war the magnitude or the duration which it has already attained. Neither anticipated that the cause of the conflict might cease with, or even before, the conflict itself should cease. Each looked for an easier triumph, and a result less fundamental and astounding. Both read the same Bible, and pray to the same God; and each invokes his aid against the other. It may seem strange that any men should dare to ask a just God's assistance in wringing their bread from the sweat of other [45/46] men's faces; but let us judge not, that we be not judged. The prayers of both could not be answered—that of neither has been answered fully.

The Almighty has his own purposes. "Woe unto the world because of offenses! for it must needs be that offenses come; but woe to that man by whom the offense cometh." If we shall suppose that American slavery is one of those offenses which, in the providence of God, must needs come, but which, having continued through his appointed time, he now wills to remove, and that he gives to both North and South this terrible war, as the woe due to those by whom the offense came, shall we discern therein any departure from those divine attributes which the believers in a living God always ascribe to him? Fondly do we hope—fervently do we pray—that this mighty scourge of war may speedily pass away. Yet, if God wills that it continue until all the wealth piled by the bondsman's two hundred and fifty years of unrequited toil shall be sunk, and until every drop of blood drawn with the lash shall be paid by another drawn with the sword, as was said three thousand years ago, so still it must be said, "The judgments of the Lord are true and righteous altogether."

With malice toward none; with charity for all; with firmness in the right, as God gives us [46/47] to see the right, let us strive on to finish the work we are in; to bind up the nation's wounds; to care for him who shall have borne the battle, and for his widow, and his orphan—to do all which may achieve and cherish a just and lasting peace among ourselves, and with all nations.

JAMES RUSSELL LOWELL

(1819–1891)

Lowell was part of a coterie of New England literati which included Emerson, Hawthorne, Longfellow, Thoreau, and Holmes. He was Smith professor of modern languages at Harvard from 1855 to 1886 and was editor of the Atlantic Monthly *from 1857 to 1861. Under the influence of his wife, Maria White Lowell, he engaged in humanitarian activities in the 1840s and 1850s. An example of this is his attack on the slavery interests in his first series of* The Biglow Papers, *written during the Mexican War. His pacifism in that work, epitomized in Hosea Biglow's "Ez fer war, I call it murder," was changed to patriotism during the Civil War. During that period he wrote the second series of* The Biglow Papers, *in which he supported unionism and opposed the Southern slave power. He was also active in writing essays on war issues, exemplified in "The Rebellion: Its Causes and Consequences," and in writing some nondialect poems such as "The Washers of the Shroud."*

from SUNTHIN' IN THE PASTORAL LINE*

I ollus feel the sap start in my veins
In Spring, with curus heats an' prickly pains,
Thet drive me, when I git a chance, to walk   110

*From James Russell Lowell, *The Biglow Papers*, Second Series (Boston: Ticknor and Fields, 1867). The persona writing the poem is Hosea Biglow, a New England countryman with "homely common-sense vivified and heated by conscience." The grandfather in the dream had fought in the Commonwealth War with Oliver Cromwell ("Crommle") before coming to America. "Sunthin' . . ." was first published in the *Atlantic Monthly*, June, 1862.

Off by myself to hev a privit talk
With a queer critter thet can't seem to 'gree
Along o' me like most folks,—Mister Me. [158/159]

Ther' 's times when I'm unsoshle ez a stone,
An' sort o' suffocate to be alone,—
I'm crowded jes' to think thet folks are nigh,
An' can't bear nothin' closer than the sky;
Now the wind's full ez shifty in the mind
Ez wut it is ou'-doors, ef I ain't blind,
An' sometimes, in the fairest sou'west weather,   120
My innard vane pints cast for weeks together,
My natur' gits all goose-flesh, an' my sins
Come drizzlin' on my conscience sharp ez pins:
Wal, et sech times I jes' slip out o' sight
An' take it out in a fair stan'-up fight
With the one cuss I can't lay on the shelf,
The crook'dest stick in all the heap,—Myself.

'T wuz so las' Sabbath arter meetin'-time:
Findin' my feelin's would n't noways rhyme
With nobody's, but off the hendle flew   130
An' took things from an east-wind pint o' view,
I started off to lose me in the hills
Where the pines be, up back o' 'Siah's Mills. [159/161]
.   .   .   .

Now, 'fore I knowed, thet Sabbath arternoon
Thet I sot out to tramp myself in tune,
I found me in the school'us' on my seat,
Drummin' the march to No-wheres with my feet
Thinkin' o' nothin,' I've heard ole folks say,   170
Is a hard kind o'dooty in its way:
It's thinkin' everythin' you ever knew,
Or ever hearn, to make your feelin's blue.
I sot there tryin' thet on for a spell:
I thought o' the Rebellion, then o' Hell,
Which some folks tell ye now is jest a metterfor [161/162]
(A the'ry, p'raps, it wun't *feel* none the better for) ;

I thought o' Reconstruction, wut we 'd win
Patchin' our patent self-blow-up agin:
I thought ef this 'ere milkin' o' the wits,   180
So much a month, warn't givin' Natur' fits,—
Ef folks warn't druv, findin' their own milk fail,
To work the cow that hez an iron tail,
An' ef idees 'thout ripenin' in the pan
Would send up cream to humor ary man:
From this to thet I let my worryin' creep,
Till finally I must ha' fell asleep. [162/163]
.   .   .   .

Now I wuz settin' where I'd ben, it seemed,
An' ain't sure yit whether I r'ally dreamed,
Nor, ef I did, how long I might ha' slep',
When I hearn some un stompin' up the step,
An' lookin' round, ef two an' two make four,
I see a Pilgrim Father in the door.
He wore a steeple-hat, tall boots, an' spurs   210
With rowels to 'em big ez ches'nut-burrs,
An' his gret sword behind him sloped away
Long 'z a man's speech thet dunno wut to say.—
"Ef your name's Biglow, an' your given-name
Hosee," sez he, "it's arter you I came;
I'm your gret-gran'ther multiplied by three."—
"My *wut?*" sez I.—"Your gret-gret-gret," sez he:
"You would n't ha' never ben here but for me. [163/164]
Two hundred an' three years ago this May
The ship I come in sailed up Boston Bay;   220
I'd been a cunnle in our Civil War,—
But wut on airth hev *you* gut up one for?
Coz we du things in England, 'tain't for you
To git a notion you can du 'em tu:
I'm told you write in public prints: ef true,
It's nateral you should know a thing or two."—
"Thet air 's an argymunt I can't endorse,—
'T would prove, coz you wear spurs, you kep' a horse:
For brains," sez I, "wutever you may think,
Ain't boun' to cash the drafs o' pen-an'-ink,—   230

Though mos' folks write ez ef they hoped jes' quickenin'
The churn would argoo skim-milk into thickenin';
But skim-milk ain't a thing to change its view
O' wut it 's meant for more 'n a smoky flue.
But du pray tell me, 'fore we furder go,
How in all Natur' did you come to know
'Bout our affairs," sez I, "in Kingdom-Come?"—
"Wal, I worked round at sperrit-rappin' some,
An' danced the tables till their legs wuz gone,
In hopes o' larnin' wut wuz goin' on," [164/165]   240
Sez he, "but mejums lie so like all-split
Thet I concluded it wuz best to quit.
But, come now, ef you wun't confess to knowin',
You've some conjectures how the thing 's a-goin'."—
"Gran'ther," sez I, "a vane warn't never known
Nor asked to hev a jedgment of its own;
An' yit, ef 't ain't gut rusty in the jints,
It's safe to trust its say on certin pints:
It knows the wind's opinions to a T,
An' the wind settles wut the weather 'll be."   250
"I never thought a scion of our stock
Could grow the wood to make a weathercock;
When I wuz younger 'n you, skurce more 'n a shaver,
No airthly wind," sez he, "could make me waver!"
(Ez he said this, he clinched his jaw an' forehead,
Hitchin' his belt to bring his sword-hilt forrard.) —
"Jes' so it wuz with me," sez I, "I swow,
When *I* wuz younger 'n wut you see me now,—
Nothin' from Adam's fall to Huldy's bonnet,
Thet I warn't full-cocked with my jedgment on it;   260
But now I'm gittin' on in life, I find
It's a sight harder to make up my mind,— [165/166]
Nor I don't often try tu, when events
Will du it for me free of all expense.
The moral question 's ollus plain enough,—
It 's jes' the human-natur' side thet 's tough;
Wut 's best to think may n't puzzle me nor you,—
The pinch comes in decidin' wut to *du;*
Ef you *read* History, all runs smooth ez grease,

Coz there the men ain't nothin' more 'n idees,—   270
But come to *make* it, ez we must to-day,
Th' idees hev arms an' legs an' stop the way:
It 's easy fixin' things in fact an' figgers,—
They can't resist, nor warn't brought up with niggers;
But come to try your the'ry on,—why, then
Your facts an' figgers change to ign'ant men
Actin' ez ugly—" —"Smite 'em hip an' thigh!"
Sez gran'ther, "and let every man-child die!
Oh for three weeks o' Crommle an' the Lord!
Up, Isr'el, to your tents an' grind the sword!"—   280
"That kind o' thing worked wal in ole Judee,
But you forgit how long it 's ben A.D.;
You think thet 's ellerkence,—I call it shoddy,
A thing," sez I, "wun't cover soul nor body; [166/167]
I like the plain all-wool o' common-sense,
Thet warms ye now, an' will a twelvemonth hence.
You took to follerin' where the Prophets beckoned,
An', fust you knowed on, back come Charles the Second;
Now wut I want 's to hev all *we* gain stick,
An' not to start Millennium too quick;   290
We hain't to punish only, but to keep,
An' the cure 's gut to go a cent'ry deep."
"Wal, milk-an' water ain't the best o' glue,"
Sez he, "an' so you 'll find before you 're thru;
Ef reshness venters sunthin', shilly-shally
Loses ez often wut's ten times the vally.
Thet exe of ourn, when Charles's neck gut split,
Opened a gap thet ain't bridged over yit:
Slav'ry 's your Charles, the Lord hez gin the exe—"—
"Our Charles," sez I, "hez gut eight million necks.   300
The hardest question ain't the black man's right,
The trouble is to 'mancipate the white;
One 's chained in body an' can be sot free,
But t'other 's chained in soul to an idee:
It 's a long job, but we shall worry thru it;
Ef bag'nets fail, the spellin'-book must du it." [167/168]
"Hosee," sez he, "I think you 're goin' to fail:
The rettlesnake ain't dangerous in the tail;

This 'ere rebellion 's nothin' but the rettle,—
You 'll stomp on thet an' think you 've won the bettle;   310
It 's Slavery that 's the fangs an' thinkin' head,
An' ef you want selvation, cresh it dead,—
An' cresh it suddin, or you 'll larn by waitin'
Thet Chance wun't stop to listen to debatin'!—
"God's truth!" sez I,—"an ef *I* held the club,
An' knowed jes' where to strike,—but there's the rub!"—
"Strike soon," sez he, "or you 'll be deadly ailin',—
Folks thet's afeared to fail are sure o' failin';
God hates your sneakin' cretures thet believe
He'll settle things they run away an' leave!"   320
He brought his foot down fercely, ez he spoke,
An' give me sech a startle thet I woke. [168]

from **THE REBELLION: ITS CAUSES
AND CONSEQUENCES***

The fact that no adequate reasons for Secession have ever been
brought forward, either by the Seceding States at the time, or by
their apologists since, can only be explained on the theory that
nothing more than a *coup d'état* was intended, which should put
the South in possession of the government. Owing to the wretched
policy (if supineness deserve the name) largely prevalent in the
North, of sending to the lower house of Congress the men who
needed rather than those who ought to go there,—men without the
responsibility or the independence which only established reputation, social position, long converse with great questions, or native
strength of character can give,—and to the habit of looking on a
seat in the national legislature more as a reward for partisan activity than as imposing a service of the highest nature, so that
representatives were changed as often as there were new political
debts to pay or cliques to be conciliated,—owing to these things, the
South maintained an easy superiority at Washington, and learned
to measure the Free States by men who represented [257/258] their

*From James Russell Lowell, "The Rebellion: Its Causes and Consequences,"
The North American Review, XCIX (July, 1864) , 246–268.

weakest, and sometimes their least honorable characteristics. We doubt if the Slave States have sent many men to the Capitol who could be bought, while it is notorious that from the north of Mason and Dixon's line many an M. C. has cleared, like a ship, for Washington and a market. Southern politicians judge the North by men without courage and without principle, who would consent to any measure if it could be becomingly draped in generalities, or if they could evade the pillory of the yeas and nays. The increasing drain of forensic ability toward the large cities, with the mistaken theory that residence in the district was a necessary qualification in candidates, tended still more to bring down the average of Northern representation. The "claims" of a section of the State, or even part of a district, have been allowed to have weight, as if square miles or acres were to be weighed against capacity and experience. We attached too little importance to the social prestige which the South acquired and maintained at the seat of government, forgetting the necessary influence it would exert upon the independence of many of our own members. These in turn brought home the new impressions they had acquired, till the fallacy gradually became conviction of a general superiority in the South, though it had only so much truth in it as this, that the people of that section sent their men of character and position to Washington, and kept them there till every year of experience added an efficiency which more than made up for their numerical inferiority. Meanwhile, our thinking men allowed, whether from timidity or contempt, certain demagogic fallacies to become axioms by dint of repetition, chief among which was the notion that a man was a better representative of the democratic principle who had contrived to push himself forward to popularity by whatever means, and who represented the average instead of the highest culture of the community, thus establishing an aristocracy of mediocrity, nay, even of vulgarity, in some less intelligent constituencies. The one great strength of democracy is, that it opens all the highways of power and station to the better man, that it gives every man the chance of rising to his natural level, and its great weakness is in its tendency to urge this principle to a vicious excess, by pushing men forward into positions for which they [258/259] are unfit, not so much because they deserve to rise, or because they have risen by great qualities, as because they began low. Our quadriennial change of offices, which turns public service into a matter of bargain and sale instead of the reward of merit and capacity, which sends men to Congress to represent private interests in the sharing of plunder, without regard to any claims of statesmanship or questions of national policy, as if the ship of state were periodically captured by privateers, has hastened our downward progress in the evil way. By making the administration prominent at the cost of the government, and by its constant lesson of scramble and vicissitude, almost obliterating the idea of orderly permanence, it has tended in no small measure to make disruption possible, for Mr. Lincoln's election threw the weight of every office-holder in the South into the scale of Secession. The war, however, has proved that the core of Democracy was sound, that the people, if they had been neglectful of their duties, or had misapprehended them, had not become corrupt. [259/260] . . .

. . . A consecutive statement of such of the events in our history as bear directly on the question of Slavery, separated from all secondary circumstances, shows two things clearly;—first, that the doctrine that there was any national obligation to consider slaves as merely property, or to hold our tongues about slavery, is of comparatively recent origin; and, second, that there was a pretty uniform ebb of antislavery sentiment for nearly sixty years after the adoption of the Constitution, the young flood beginning to set strongly in again after the full meaning of the annexation of Texas began to be understood at the North, but not fairly filling up again even its own deserted channels till the Southern party succeeded in cutting the embankment of the Missouri Compromise. Then at last it became evident that the real danger to be guarded against was the abolition of Freedom, and the reaction was as violent as it was sudden. [260/262] . . .

The influence of the Southern States in the national politics was due manly to the fact of their having a single interest on which they were all united, and, though fond of contrasting their more chivalric character with the commercial spirit of the North, it will be found that profit has been the motive to all the encroachments of Slavery. These encroachments first assumed the offensive with the annexation of Texas. In the admission of Missouri, though the Free States might justly claim a right to fix the political destiny of half the territory, bought with the common money of the nation, and though events have since proved that the compromise of 1820 was a fatal mistake, yet, as slavery was already established there, the South might, with some show of reason, claim to be on the defensive. In one sense, it is true, every enlargement of the boundaries of slavery has been an aggression. For it cannot with any fairness be assumed that the framers of the Constitution intended to foreordain a perpetual balance of power between the Free and the Slave States. If they had, it is morally certain that they would not so have arranged the basis of representation as to secure to the South an unfair preponderance, to be increased with every addition of territory. It is much more probable that they expected the Southern States to fall more and more into a minority of population and wealth, and were willing to strengthen this minority by yielding it somewhat more than its just share of power in Congress. Indeed, it was mainly on the ground of the undue advantage which the South would gain, politically, that the admission of Missouri was distasteful to the North.

It was not till after the Southern politicians had firmly established their system of governing the country by an alliance with the Democratic party of the Free States, on the basis of a [262/263] division of offices, that they dreamed of making their "institution" the chief concern of the nation. . . . We see them first pleading for the existence of slavery, then for its equality, and at last claiming for it an absolute dominion. Such had been the result of uniform concession on the part of the North for the sake of Union, such the decline of public spirit, that, within sixty years of the time when slaveholders like George Mason of Virginia could denounce slavery for its inconsistency with the principles on which our Revolution had triumphed, the leaders of a party at the North claiming a kind of patent in the rights of man as an expedient for catching votes were decrying the doctrines of the Declaration of Independence as visionary and impracticable. Was it the Slave or the Free States that had just cause to be alarmed for their peculiar institutions? . . . [263/266] . . .

But in seeking for the cause of the rebellion, with any fairness toward the Southern people, and any wish to understand their motives and character, it would be unwise to leave out of view the fact that they have been carefully educated in the faith that secession is not only their right, but the only safe-guard of their freedom. While it is perfectly true that the great struggle now going on is intrinsically between right and privilege, between law and license, and while on the part of its leaders the Southern revolt was a conspiracy against popular government, and an attempt to make a great Republic into a mere convenient drudge for Slavery, yet we should despair of our kind did we believe that the rank and file of the Confederate armies were consciously spending so much courage and endurance in behalf of barbarism. It is more consoling, [266/267] as it is nearer the truth, to think that they are fighting for what they have been taught to believe their rights, and their inheritance as a free people. The high qualities they have undoubtedly shown in the course of the war, their tenacity, patience, and discipline, show that, under better influences, they may become worthy to take their part in advancing the true destinies of America.

It is yet too early to speculate with much confidence on the remote consequences of the war. One of its more immediate results has already been to disabuse the Southern mind of some of its most fatal misconceptions as to Northern character. They thought us a trading people, incapable of lofty sentiment, ready to sacrifice everything for commercial advantage,—a heterogeneous rabble, fit only to be ruled by a superior race. They are not likely to make that mistake again, and must have learned by this time that the best blood is that which has in it most of the iron of purpose and constancy. War, the sternest and dearest of teachers, has already made us a soberer and older people on both sides. It has brought questions of government and policy home to us as never before, and has made us feel that citizenship is a duty to whose level we must rise, and not a privilege to which we are born. The great principles of humanity and politics, which had faded into the distance of abstraction and history, have been for four years the theme of earnest thought and discussion at every fireside and wherever two men met together. They have again become living and operative in the heart and mind of the nation. What was before a mighty population, is grown a great country united in one hope, inspired by one thought, and welded into one power. But have not the same influences produced the same result at the South, and created there also a nation hopelessly alien and hostile? To a certain extent this is true, but not in the unlimited way in which it is stated by enemies in England, or politicians at home, who would gladly put the people out of heart, because they themselves are out of office. With the destruction of slavery, the one object of the war will have been lost by the Rebels, and its one great advantage gained by the government. . . . [267/268] If the war be waged manfully, as becomes a thoughtful people, without insult or childish triumph in success, if we meet opinion with wiser opinion, waste no time in badgering prejudice till it become hostility, and attack slavery as a crime against the nation, and not as individual sin, it will end, we believe, in making us the most powerful and prosperous community the world ever saw. Our example and our ideas will react more powerfully than ever on the Old World, and the consequence of a rebellion, aimed at the natural equality of all men, will be to hasten incalculably the progress of equalization over the whole earth. Above all, Freedom will become the one absorbing interest of the whole people, making us a nation alive from sea to sea with the consciousness of a great purpose and a noble destiny, and uniting us as slavery has hitherto combined and made powerful the most hateful aristocracy known to man. [268]

from ODE RECITED AT THE

HARVARD COMMEMORATION*

July 21, 1865

I

Weak-winged is song,
Nor aims at that clear-ethered height
Whither the brave deed climbs for light:
        We seem to do them wrong,
Bringing our robin's-leaf to deck their hearse
Who in warm life-blood wrote their nobler verse,
Our trivial song to honor those who come
With ears attuned to strenuous trump and drum,
And shaped in squadron-strophes their desire,
Live battle-odes whose lines were steel and fire: 10

*From James Russell Lowell, *The Writings of James Russell Lowell* (Boston and New York: Houghton Mifflin Co., 1890), Vol. XI. The undertone of sorrow felt in this poem is undoubtedly an extension of the personal sorrow Lowell felt at the deaths of three favorite nephews, all former Harvard students.

Yet sometimes feathered words are strong,
A gracious memory to buoy up and save
From Lethe's dreamless ooze, the common grave
   Of the unventurous throng.

II

To-day our Reverend Mother welcomes back
   Her wisest Scholars, those who understood
The deeper teaching of her mystic tome,
   And offered their fresh lives to make it good:
         No lore of Greece or Rome,
No science peddling with the names of things,   20
Or reading stars to find inglorious fates,
         Can lift our life with wings
Far from Death's idle gulf that for the many waits,
         And lengthen out our dates [17/18]
With that clear fame whose memory sings
In manly hearts to come, and nerves them and dilates:
Nor such thy teaching, Mother of us all!
         Not such the trumpet-call
         Of thy diviner mood,
         That could thy sons entice   30
From happy homes and toils, the fruitful nest
Of those half-virtues which the world calls best,
         Into War's tumult rude;
         But rather far that stern device
The sponsors chose that round thy cradle stood
         In the dim, unventured wood,
         The VERITAS that lurks beneath
         The letter's unprolific sheath,
   Life of whate'er makes life worth living,
Seed-grain of high emprise, immortal food,   40
   One heavenly thing whereof earth hath the giving. [18/25]

.   .   .   .

VIII

We sit here in the Promised Land
That flows with Freedom's honey and milk:
But 't was they won it, sword in hand,
Making the nettle danger soft for us as silk.

We welcome back our bravest and our best;—
Ah me! not all! some come not with the rest,
Who went forth brave and bright as any here!
I strive to mix some gladness with my strain,
    But the sad strings complain,   240
    And will not please the ear:
I sweep them for a pæan, but they wane
    Again and yet again
Into a dirge, and die away, in pain.
In these brave ranks I only see the gaps,
Thinking of dear ones whom the dumb turf wraps,
Dark to the triumph which they died to gain:
    Fitlier may others greet the living,
    For me the past is unforgiving;
    I with uncovered head   250
    Salute the sacred dead,
Who went, and who return not.—Say not so!
'T is not the grapes of Canaan that repay,
But the high faith that failed not by the way;
Virtue treads paths that end not in the grave;
No ban of endless night exiles the brave;
    And to the saner mind
We rather seem the dead that stayed behind.
Blow, trumpets, all your exultations blow! [25/28]

.   .   .   .

             X
    Who now shall sneer?
    Who dare again to say we trace   330
    Our lines to a plebeian race?
    Roundhead and Cavalier!
Dumb are those names erewhile in battle loud;
Dream-footed as the shadow of a cloud,
    They flit across the ear:
That is best blood that hath most iron in 't.
To edge resolve with, pouring without stint
    For what makes manhood dear.
    Tell us not of Plantagenets,
Hapsburgs, and Guelfs, whose thin bloods crawl   340
Down from some victor in a border-brawl!

How poor their outworn coronets,
Matched with one leaf of that plain civic wreath
Our brave for honor's blazon shall bequeath,
   Through whose desert a rescued Nation sets
Her heel on treason, and the trumpet hears
Shout victory, tingling Europe's sullen ears
   With vain resentments and more vain regrets! [28/29]

                         XI
         Not in anger, not in pride,
         Pure from passion's mixture rude   350
         Ever to base earth allied,
         But with far-heard gratitude,
         Still with heart and voice renewed,
      To heroes living and dear martyrs dead,
The strain should close that consecrates our brave.
      Lift the heart and lift the head!
         Lofty be its mood and grave,
         Not without a martial ring,
         Not without a prouder tread
         And a peal of exultation: 360
         Little right has he to sing
         Through whose heart in such an hour
         Beats no march of conscious power,
         Sweeps no tumult of elation!
         'T is no Man we celebrate,
         By his country's victories great,
      A hero half, and half the whim of Fate,
         But the pith and marrow of a Nation
         Drawing force from all her men,
         Highest, humblest, weakest, all,   370
         For her time of need, and then
         Pulsing it again through them,
Till the basest can no longer cower,
Feeling his soul spring up divinely tall,
Touched but in passing by her mantle-hem.
Come back, then, noble pride, for 't is her dower!
         How could poet ever tower,
         If his passions, hopes, and fears, [29/30]

If his triumphs and his tears,
Kept not measure with his people? 380
Boom, cannon, boom to all the winds and waves!
Clash out, glad bells, from every rocking steeple!
Banners, adance with triumph, bend your staves!
    And from every mountain-peak
    Let beacon-fire to answering beacon speak,
    Katahdin tell Monadnock, Whiteface he,
And so leap on in light from sea to sea,
    Till the glad news be sent
    Across a kindling continent,
Making earth feel more firm and air breathe braver: 390
"Be proud! for she is saved, and all have helped to save her!
    She that lifts up the manhood of the poor,
    She of the open soul and open door,
    With room about her hearth for all mankind!
    The fire is dreadful in her eyes no more;
    From her bold front the helm she doth unbind,
    Sends all her handmaid armies back to spin,
    And bids her navies, that so lately hurled
    Their crashing battle, hold their thunders in,
    Swimming like birds of calm along the unharmful shore. 400
    No challenge sends she to the elder world,
    That looked askance and hated; a light scorn
    Plays o'er her mouth, as round her mighty knees
    She calls her children back, and waits the morn
Of nobler day, enthroned between her subject seas." [30/31]

XII

Bow down, dear Land, for thou hast found release!
    Thy God, in these distempered days,
    Hath taught thee the sure wisdom of His ways,
And through thine enemies hath wrought thy peace!
    Bow down in prayer and praise! 410
No poorest in thy borders but may now
Lift to the juster skies a man's enfranchised brow.
O Beautiful! my Country! ours once more!
Smoothing thy gold of war-dishevelled hair
O'er such sweet brows as never other wore,

And letting thy set lips,
Freed from wrath's pale eclipse,
The rosy edges of their smile lay bare,
What words divine of lover or of poet
Could tell our love and make thee know it,   420
Among the Nations bright beyond compare?
What were our lives without thee?
What all our lives to save thee?
We reck not what we gave thee;
We will not dare to doubt thee,
But ask whatever else, and we will dare! [31]

FRANCIS PARKMAN

(1823–1893)

Francis Parkman established himself as a man of letters with his artistically attractive The Oregon Trail *(1849). He followed this with* History of the Conspiracy of Pontiac *(1851), the first volume of his recounting the struggle of the French and British for the continent.*

When the Civil War came, Parkman was unable to join his friends in active duty because of weakness of sight and affliction of the nervous system. With effort he could write, though, and he composed numerous letters to the editors of the Boston Daily Advertiser *in which he vigorously supported the war effort and encouraged the patrician class to assume its rightful role.*

THE NATION'S ORDEAL*

[September 4, 1861]

To the Editors of the *Boston Daily Advertiser:*

Every day the gravity of the nation's position seems more and more impressed on the minds of the people. Enthusiasm is giving place—at least it is to be hoped so—to a deeper and intenser purpose. All is at stake; the die is cast; we must do or perish. The peril, the solemnity of the hour cannot be too earnestly pondered. It is well to survey our stormy horizon, not in despondency and trembling, but in the firmer spirit of one who observes his ground, takes account of his dangers, and forearms himself against the worst. Our

*The three Parkman selections are from the *Boston Daily Advertiser,* Sept. 4, 1861, Oct. 17, 1862, and July 14, 1863.

house is divided against itself. Our own blood has risen in arms against us, and we grapple for life or death with a fraternal foe, the most restless and war-like of mankind; ambitious, aggressive, and now maddened with an insane hate. With such an adversary there is no safety but in conquest. He or we must be humbled. If we but act the part of men, the conflict is one of no doubtful issue; but it is one which may tax our strength and constancy more than the less momentous struggle of the Revolution taxed those of our fathers. Nor is Southern treason our only danger; for if those among ourselves who have neither conscience to feel the course of right, nor manhood to feel the course of honor, nor wit to feel the course of safety,—if the counsels of such should prevail, then indeed would all be lost. The nation might hide her dishonored head and wait in ignominy the sure steps of her dissolution.

This might seem enough, but this is not all. Other storms are threatening in the outer darkness. There are contingencies, not probable, perhaps, but only possible, which it behoves us to consider and confront. The commercial interest, with its profits cut off, and the aristocratic interest eager for the ruin of republicanism, might, in case of a new reverse to our arms, or a protracted war, bring foreign interference into the contest. If we listen to the dictates of a foreign power, or of all foreign powers combined, and suffer ourselves to be turned from our great enterprise, there is but one result,—disintegration, decay, contempt, ruin. But if we stand to our work, doing that which truth and human liberty demand of us, then the whirlwind and the storm will be our portion. Yet let us not hesitate, nor shrink for an instant from the stern alternative. Marathon would grow dim before the splendor and the majesty of such a conflict, and the heroic tale would ring through unborn centuries, how, to vindicate the right, a nation of freemen stood against the world in arms.

Our position is a solemn and critical, but not a melancholy one. Perhaps, even, it is one not to be lamented. There is close analogy between the life of nations and of individuals. Conflict and endurance are necessary to both, and without them both become emasculate. Rome grew colossal through centuries of war. Out of the agony of civil strife came constitutional liberty to England, and vigor and unity to France. The individual is rare and the nation never yet was seen which the continuous smiles of fortune could not weaken or pervert. Our own unmatched prosperity has wrought its inevitable work. We are a *parvenu* nation with the faults and follies of a *parvenu*. Rising with astounding suddenness to wealth and greatness, we have not always been noted for the modesty or the dignity with which we have filled our new position. A too exclusive pursuit of material success has notoriously cramped and vitiated our growth. In the absence of a high interest or ruling idea, a superficial though widespread culture has found expression and aliment in a popular literature commonly frivolous and often corrupt. In the absence of any exigency to urge or any great reward to tempt it, the best character and culture of the nation has remained for the most part in privacy, while a scum of reckless politicians has choked all the avenues of power. Already, like a keen fresh breeze, the war has stirred our clogged and humid atmosphere. The time may be at hand when, upheaved from its depths, fermenting and purging itself, the nation will stand at length clarified and pure in a renewed and strengthened life. It behoves us, then, less in fear than in hope, to bide the tempest; for among its blackest clouds shines a star of promise.

It was said of Washington, that in the Revolution, he was slow to draw the sword, but, having drawn it, he threw away the scabbard. The North has been slow to draw the sword, but the steel is bare at last, and now let her, too, throw away the scabbard.

F. P. [2]

CONSERVATISM

[October 17, 1862]

To the Editors of the *Boston Daily Advertiser:*

Well is it said that extremes meet. The Conservatism that anchors on rottenness and grapples to forms without life,—that struggles with infatuated dullness to dam back the flowing current instead of guiding it to safe and beneficent issues, is destruction in disguise. Conservatists and destroyers, timid respectability on one hand, and Woods, Vallandighams, and copperheads on the other, circle on their convergent paths till they seem on the point of joining hands. At least, the latter, with their customary astuteness have contrived to make those in whose nostrils they are an offence, colaborers and tools in their devil's work.

Eighteen months of war have wrought ruin enough; and there is more in store; but, like thunderstorms in a thick and fever burdened air, the war has been a fearful minister of good. The weeks that preceded the final outrage at Fort Sumter, are never to be forgotten: menace upon menace, insult upon insult; demands outrageous alike to God and man, urged with an unheard of insolence and passively received, till it seemed that all manhood, all honor, all conscience had fled the nation, and that she would drain the cup of her abasement to the uttermost dregs. It was the climax towards which many years had tended. More and more, the mean and bad elements of the nation had risen in influence. Material interests and base political rivalries ruled us. There was no limit to their exactions, and seemingly no limit to concession and sacrifice in their behalf. The national mind and heart were fast subsiding into one vast platitude, over whose level monotony great thoughts and noble purposes did not rise, and would scarcely have been tolerated if they had risen. More and more, worth and character had withdrawn from public life. Rarely did a man above the stamp of mediocrity appear among those who made or administered the laws. All that was best and ablest dwindled in obscurity, and an ill-instructed zeal, often assumed to cover mean designs, was left to battle after its own fashion with unscrupulous self-interest and the passions of demagogues and adventurers. Yet there was peace, such as it was; or rather the stagnation which precedes the ebullitions of inward corruption. Treason grew audacious with long-continued triumphs, never dreaming that, though buried deep in ashes, the old fire was not dead. From threats and intrigue, it passed to open violence. The rebel cannon at Fort Sumter were the resurrection of our manhood. With that infatuated blast, the forked flame leaped up, and to its utmost bounds the renovated nation burned with heroic fire.

Who can ever forget the day when from spires and domes, windows and housetops, the stars and stripes were flung to the wind, in token that the land was roused at last from deathly torpor. They were the symbols of a new life; portentous of storm and battle, yet radiant with hope. Our flag was never so glorious. On that day, it became the emblem of truth and right and justice. Through it, a mighty people proclaimed a new faith,—that peace, wealth, ease, material progress, were not the sum and substance of all good. Loyalty to it became loyalty to humanity and to God. The shackles of generations were thrown off. We were a people disenthralled, rising from abasement abject and insupportable. An electric life thrilled to the heart of the nation, and they who had stood aloof, in despondency and scorn, from the foul arena of party strife, now with an eager and buoyant alacrity, offered their breasts to the cannon. Women, with sympathies bounded till now by the circles of private life, threw into the conflict lives more valued than their own. Shall these sacrifices be vain? Shall that bright hope be the herald of the opening day, or was it but the sinister gaping of the clouds that portends a thicker night? Must we again be the vassals of outrage and wrong, entangled in the same wretched meshwork of compromises and compliances? Shall all that is noble in our national life again be borne down and smothered, and the bats and owls of society again flock from their hiding-places, triumphant and clamorous? To buy a transient and hollow peace, a brief interval of material prosperity, shall faith, honor, conscience, loyalty, all that makes the soul of a nation, be choked and starved into annihilation, and shall this ruin be wrought in the name of Conservatism? It would be a wholesale crime, as unavailing as monstrous. It would be a suicidal folly. To the eye, the mockery of a cure.

"While rank corruption, mining all within,
Infects unseen."

It would make a desert, and call it peace. The safety of the nation lies in being true to herself. A true peace must be hewn out with the sword. We fight against incarnate wrong, and, come what may, we must crush it.

F. P. [2]

ARISTOCRATS AND DEMOCRATS

[July 14, 1863]

To the Editors of the *Boston Daily Advertiser:*
It was a strange union that linked us to the South, and one that

can never be renewed until we have thrust regeneration, total and absolute, into the innermost being of our adversary. Meanwhile, to consider for a moment, how well and boldly he has fronted us— how, with means scarcely the tithe of ours, he has stood at bay for two long years, and despite the zeal, the devotion, the courage of a mighty people, has led his warlike hordes to plunder at our thresholds. There is much to be learned from him, and, if we are as sagacious as we have been wont to think ourselves, we may draw profit from our adversity.

A head full of fire, a body ill-jointed, starved, attenuated, is matched against a muscular colossus, a Titan in energy and force— full of blood, full of courage, prompt for fight, and confident of victory. Strong head and weak body against strong body and weak head; oligarchy against democracy.

A few men—the leaven of the whole fermenting mass might almost be counted on the fingers—may be said to form the South, for they control and animate it. A truer aristocracy never existed, or a worse one when considered in its origin and foundation. But that which it most imports us to feel is the fearful efficiency of its education. We of New England are a bookish people. With us, the idea of education is inseparable from school-houses, school-masters, lyceums, public libraries, colleges, and diplomas. Yet these are but secondary agencies; pallid, nerveless, and emasculate, beside those mighty educational powers which spring out of the currents of life itself, the hopes, the fears, the responsibilities, the exigencies; the action or the idleness, the enjoyment or the suffering; the associations, the friendships, enmities, rivalries, and conflicts, which make the sum of each man's vital history. Not that the Southern aristocracy is ignorant of books. Of its number, are men high in scholarly accomplishment, valuable to those who know how to use it; futile in the mere votaries of the lamp. The culture of the South has long been the heart and focus of its political life, while that of the North has been rather an excrescence upon the vital system than a part of it. But this alone is not the education which has held back the mighty surges of democracy and dammed the Nile with bulrushes.

From his cradle the slave oligarch is taught that he holds a place of power and peril, isolated, pelted with opprobrium, beset with swarming foes,—a post to be held only by every effort of will and brain. A small class of men are linked together by a common interest and a common spirit; the pride, more than feudal, which belongs to their unbridled power over those who are less than vassals, is chafed to redoubled intensity by attacks from these whom they despise no less than they hate. With them, politics are a battleground where the issues are victory or ruin, and where passion, self-interest, self-preservation, urge to intensest action every power of their nature. Hence the vigor of their development, which can find no match either in our own best instructed classes, so weak in political influence and political training, or in that swarm of professed politicians, who, like flies in August, suck each his petty nutriment from the body of the long-suffering nation.

The Southern leaders knew the North chiefly through three classes of its population. They knew the merchants, whom they scorned as the feudal noble scorned the rich burgher, and politicians in whom they found no concession too abject, no abasement too deep. Here lay their hope. In the subserviency of self-interest and low ambition, seeking to abase the nation to their level, the slaveholder saw his triumph. But there was another class, whom, despising not less, he hated with a bitter hate, the abolition agitators, whose clamors wakened the earthquake under his feet. That he should recognize the sound and earnest basis of this agitation was not in human nature. He saw it only in its extravagance, fanaticism and obstreperous weakness; classed it indiscriminately with that morbid brood of moral and social crudities which, to his thinking, was the natural progeny of pestilent New England, and the spawn of sickly minds besotted with the little learning said to be so dangerous.

These classes the Southern leaders knew, or thought they knew, and, knowing them, vainly thought they knew the Northern people. They knew at least, that the Northern people were politically without a head. The eagle soared on our banners; the crow, the buzzard, and the owl, clamored in our council-halls. But they never dreamed how, under a surface of froth and scum, the great national heart still beat with the pulsations of patriotic manhood. The error has been their ruin.

They confront us in an antagonism as fierce and inevitable as that of steel white hot to the flood that quenches it. Oligarchy and Democracy, the strong head and the strong body, cannot live side by side. In war we can in time master them. In peace, every advantage will be with the concentrated will, the trained and subtle intellect. Our safety is in the destruction of their system and the purging of our own; in the development and use of the statesmanship latent among us, and long kept latent by the perverted action of our political machinery. An incalculable waste of wealth, time, life and honor, would have been spared to us, had the servants of the people been worthy of their trust.

F. P. [2]

EDMUND C. STEDMAN
(1833–1908)

As a staff member of the New York World when war seemed imminent, Edmund C. Stedman was sent to Washington to be a war correspondent. He continued this until January, 1862, when he joined the staff of the Attorney-General; then in September, 1863, he joined a brokerage firm on Wall Street and the next year opened a brokerage house of his own. He continued brokerage work throughout the remainder of his life but remained at heart a literary man, publishing several volumes of poetry, and editing among other things A Library of American Literature . . . (11 vols., 1889–90) and (with George E. Woodberry) The Works of Edgar Allan Poe (10 vols., 1894–95).

from LETTER TO ELIZABETH DODGE STEDMAN*

[Washington, October 16, 1861]

I have enlisted all my humble energies in this cause, then, for two reasons: First, one of selfishness—the necessity for personal shaking-up and rejuvenating—the old, healthy love of action rising in me, as described in the first part of the "Flood Tide"; the credit and reputation to be derived, and the subsistence [241/242] earned, by my present occupation—the love of adventure, etc. Second, one of principle. I am really surprised to find myself sometimes forgetting self, and feeling human love and heartthrobs and patriotism. I think the War right and noble. For the first time, the hackneyed

---

*From Laura Stedman and George M. Gould, Life and Letters of Edmund Clarence Stedman (New York: Moffat, Yard and Company, 1910), Vol. I. His mother was living in Italy at the time.

stars-and-stripes have to me a significance. With the half-million
noble and more simple-hearted men who are fighting for their
country, I think that "the individual lessens and the cause is more
and more." For eight years I have cared *nothing* for politics—have
been disgusted with American life and, doings. Now, for the first
time, I am proud of my country and my grand, heroic brethren.
The greatness of the crisis, the Homeric grandeur of the contest,
surrounds and elevates us all. See what it is:

i. *A complete revolution and renovation of all the customs and
constitution of Americans North and South. A.* One million of the
late emasculate Americans are put under magnificent hygienic
training. Strong men and noble will henceforth inherit the land. *B.*
The base passions attendant upon scheming and money-grubbing
are laid aside for simple, chivalric, national love and hate, and
henceforth the sentimental and poetic will fuse with the intellectual
to dignify and elevate our race. The pride, pomp and *circumstance*
of glorious war, and the big contests, *do* make ambition, virtue; and
all *here, on the spot, see* that even bloodshed doeth its own good
work. Men, that we once despised as small politicians, loafers,
traders and what-not, are having all the good and heroic in them
developed—are brightly transformed amid these altered scenes and
nobler motives. *C.* Thousands of men of real talent, *born soldiers,*
for whom in this country there has been no use hitherto, and who
have consequently been "black sheep," gamblers, vagabonds and
loafers, are now finding their legitimate calling—shooting back into
their natural spheres. Suppose, there was no such thing as literature—what would fellows like myself do but be vagabonds and
proletarians? Just so with your late filibusters.

ii. *The War is a duty on the part of the North.* It is not waged
by abolitionists, is *not* the result of abolitionism. We are not sure
but that slavery is a very good thing in the Cotton states. In other
latitudes I see for myself that it is good enough for the negroes, but
ruinous to the whites. There is a theory, that the Virginia and
Kentucky gentry own slaves; this is false: I have [242/243] seen for
myself that the *niggers own the gentry.* Now I wish to make you
and Mary understand that, although we see that this War will
probably settle the slavery question, and possibly forever limit
slavery to the Cotton states, *yet we are not fighting the negro's
cause.* Slavery has been the cause of the War in no sense other than

that it has added another distinctness to the line betwixt North and South which climate and race had already drawn. The real cause of the War is a bitter and criminal hatred, entertained by the South against the North, and based on other than slave interests. For fifty years the *character* of Southerners has become daily more domineering, insolent, irrational, haughty, scornful of justice. They have so long cracked their whips over negroes that they now assume a certain inherent right to crack them over *white men;* assume the positive rights of a superior race; and have taken advantage of the North's desire for quiet and peace to impose upon us without stint. For years the tone of their actions and speeches, in Congress and society has expressed this sentiment and determination. Even Southern students at College, when I was at Yale, adopted the same tactics. One hundred of them—poor scholars, but blustering with rum and bowie-knives—lorded it over four hundred studious New Englanders, simply because the latter *were* studious and desired to attain the objects aimed at in a collegiate course. At length the thing became degrading, and we arose one day and kicked them all out. For fifty years the same plan has been practised on a larger scale in our national affairs. The South, assisted by Northern merchants whom it has governed, has been true enough to the Union, so long as every election gave *it* the power, and as foreign missions, army and navy commissions, presidencies, etc., were held in its own hands. But the census of 1850 shewed that the enterprising and industrious North was getting the balance of power. Then the South began to rebel and would have seceded had not the Clay compromise taken away *its sole pretext.* Now the census of 1860, and the Lincoln election have revived *both the desire and the pretext,* and it *has* seceded. To give you an illustration of my meaning: The South and the North have been like a large and small boy at school—the former thrashing the latter without mercy for years, and the latter constitutionally submitting to the joke; now the North has grown big enough to lick the South and has done it for the first time—whereupon the irrational South gets angry and [243/ 244] secedes. Slavery furnishes a plausible pretext. That's all. If the slaves should now rebel, as they probably will, and commit atrocities, we should probably *unite with the South* to save our white brothers and sisters—but should then insist on the cause of such horrors being forever removed, *for the sake of the white man.*

iii. *Right, power, and noble sentiments being on our side, it is our duty to carry on the War.* The South took active part in last Fall's election, thereby pledging itself to acquiesce in the result, and now *breaks* its pledge. The South has attacked the North; the South commenced the War; the South proceeded from domineering in Congress to actual hostilities, and I say that the North ignored the necessity of fighting for a period that became almost degrading. You would perhaps like to have Northerners turn themselves into spittoons at once. Why, I was so indignant at the *too* long-suffering of the North, that I seriously thought of disowning my country and going to Canada or England to live. Tell your husband that if the Union is to be shattered at the will of a minority, we might as well give up the idea of nationality at once, disown patriotism and let all go to pieces. That nation is noblest which is most sensitive about its own integrity, and will shed the most blood for a *principle,* and noble nations make noble individual men.

For such reasons I think the War of 1861 a benefit to both North and South, a duty on the part of the North, and please God, it shall be pushed to the true end. For one I have no objection to let the South go, and hope they will; but the dignity of right must first be sustained, and the injury to the republic avenged, and *they must ask to go in the proper way.* They might easily have effected a peaceful separation, by petition and vote, years ago. But that course would not have elevated Davis and the other ambitious men, now deluding their brave but senseless followers. And if we should now make peace, without proving our determination, power and heroism, we should forever hereafter be the world's laughing stock and the white slaves of our Southern neighbors. [244]

ARTEMUS WARD
(CHARLES F. BROWNE)
(1834–1867)

Charles F. Browne first appears as Artemus Ward in his sketches for the Cleveland Plain Dealer *(February, 1858). He kept the name in his writings for* Vanity Fair, *whose staff he joined in 1859. These writings were collected in 1862 as* Artemus Ward: His Book. *From 1863 until his death, Browne was a popular lecturer throughout the country.*

from THE SHOW IS CONFISCATED*

You hav perhaps wondered wharebouts I was for these many dase gone and past. Perchans you sposed I'd gone to the Tomb of the Cappylets, tho I don't know what those is. It's a popler noospaper frase.

Listen to my tail, and be silent that ye may here. I've been among the Seseshers, a earnin my daily peck by my legitimit perfeshun, and havn't had no time to weeld my facile quill for "the Grate Komick paper," if you'll alow me to kote from your troothful advertisement.

My success was skaly, and I likewise had a narrer scape of my life. If what I've bin threw is "suthern hosspitality," 'bout which we've hearn so much, then I feel bound to observe that they made two much of me. They was altogether too lavish with their attenshuns. [189/190]

---

*From Charles F. Browne, *Artemus Ward, His Book* (New York: Carleton, 1862). Both selections first appeared during the preceding year in the comic periodical *Vanity Fair*.

I went amung the Seseshers with no feelins of annermosity. I
went in my perfeshernal capacity. I was actooated by one of the
most Loftiest desires which can swell the human Buzzum, vis:—to
giv the peeple their money's worth, by showin them Sagashus Beests,
and Wax Statoots, which I venter to say air onsurpast by any other
statoots anywheres. I will not call that man who sez my statoots is
humbugs a lier and a hoss thief, but bring him be4 me and I'll
wither him with one of my scornful frowns.

But to proseed with my tail. In my travels threw the Sonny
South I heared a heap of talk about Seceshon and bustin up the
Union, but I didn't think it mounted to nothin. The politicians in
all the villages was swearin that Old Abe (sometimes called the
Prahayrie flower) should'nt never be noggerated. They also made
fools of theirselves in varis ways, but as they was used to that I
didn't let it worry me much, and the Stars and Stripes continued for
to wave over my little tent. Moor over, I was a Son of Malty and a
member of several other Temperance Societies, and my wife she was
a Daw- [190/191] ter of Malty, an I sposed these fax would secoor
me the infloonz and pertectiun of all the fust families. Alas! I was
dispinted. State arter State seseshed and it growed hotter and hotter
for the undersined. Things came to a climbmacks in a small town in
Alabamy, where I was premtorally ordered to haul down the Stars &
Stripes. . . . [191/195] [*Ward refuses to lower his flag, and so his
show is broken up and he is put in jail.*]

At larst I got a interview with Jefferson Davis, the President of
the Southern Conthieveracy. He was quite perlite, and axed me to
sit down and state my case. I did it, when he larfed and said his
gallunt men had been a little 2 enthoosiastic in confisticatin my
show.

"Yes," sez I, "they confisticated me too muchly. I had sum
hosses confisticated in the same way onct, but the confisticaters air
now poundin stun in the States Prison in Injinnapylus."

"Wall, wall, Mister Ward, you air at liberty to depart; you air
frendly to the South, I know. Even now we hav many frens in the
North, who sympathise with us, and won't mingle with this fight."

"J. Davis, there's your grate mistaik. Many of [195/196] us was
your sincere frends, and thought certin parties amung us was fussin
about you and meddlin with your consarns intirely too much. But
J. Davis, the minit you fire a gun at the piece of drygoods called the

Star-Spangled Banner, the North gits up and rises en massy, in defence of that banner. Not agin you as individooals,—not agin the South even—but to save the flag. We should indeed be weak in the knees, unsound in the heart, milk-white in the liver, and soft in the hed, if we stood quietly by and saw this glorus Govyment smashed to pieces, either by a furrin or a intestine foe. The gentle-harted mother hates to take her naughty child across her knee, but she knows it is her dooty to do it. So we shall hate to whip the naughty South, but we must do it if you don't make back tracks at onct, and we shall wallup you out of your boots! J. Davis, it is my decided opinion that the Sonny South is making a egrejus mutton-hed of herself!"

"Go on, sir, you're safe enuff. You're too small powder for me!" sed the President of the Southern Conthieveracy. [196/197]

"Wait till I go home and start out the Baldinsvill Mounted Hoss Cavalry! I'm Capting of that Corpse, I am, and J. Davis, beware! Jefferson D., I now leave you! Farewell my gay Saler Boy! Good bye, my bold buccaneer! Pirut of the deep blue sea, adoo! adoo!"

My tower threw the Southern Conthieveracy on my way home was thrillin enuff for yeller covers. It will form the subjeck of my next. Betsy Jane and the progeny air well.

Yours respectively,

A. WARD. [197]

from **THE WAR FEVER IN BALDINSVILLE**

As soon as I'd recooperated my physikil system, I went over into the village. The peasantry was glad to see me. The skoolmaster sed it was cheerin to see that gigantic intelleck among 'em onct more. That's what he called me. I like the skoolmaster, and allers send him tobacker when I'm off on a travelin campane. Besides, he is a very sensible man. Such men must be encouraged.

They don't git news very fast in Baldinsville, as nothin but a plank road runs in there twice a week, and that's very much out of repair. So my nabers wasn't much posted up in regard to the wars. 'Squire Baxter sed he'd voted the dimicratic ticket for goin on forty year, and the war was a dam black republican lie. Jo. Stackpole, who kills hogs for the 'Squire, and has got a powerful muscle into his [217/218] arms, sed he'd bet $5 he could lick the Crisis in a fair stand-up fight, if he wouldn't draw a knife on him. So it went—sum was for war, and sum was for peace. The skoolmaster, however, sed the Slave Oligarky must cower at the feet of the North ere a year had flowed by, or pass over his dead corpse. "Esto perpetua!" he added! "And sine qua non also!" sed I, sternly, wishing to make a impression onto the villagers. "Requiescat in pace!" sed the school-master. "Too troo, too troo!" I anserd, "it's a scanderlus fact!"

The newspapers got along at last, chock full of war, and the patriotic fever fairly bust out in Baldinsville. 'Squire Baxter sed he didn't b'lieve in Coercion, not one of 'em, and could prove by a file of *Eagles of Liberty* in his garrit, that it was all a Whig lie, got up to raise the price of whisky and destroy our other liberties. But the old 'Squire got putty riley, when he heard how the rebels was cutttin up, and he sed he reckoned he should skour up his old muskit and do a little square fitin for the Old Flag, which had allers bin on the ticket *he'd* voted, [218/219] and he was too old to Bolt now. The 'Squire is all right at heart, but it takes longer for him to fill his venerable Biler with steam than it used to when he was young and frisky. As I previously informed you, I am Captin of the Baldins-ville Company. I riz gradooally but majesticly from drummer's Secretary to my present position. But I found the ranks wasn't full by no means, and commenced for to recroot. Havin notist a gineral desire on the part of young men who are into the Crisis to wear eppylits, I determind to have my company composed excloosively of offissers, everybody to rank as Brigadeer-Ginral. The follerin was among the varis questions which I put to recroots:

Do you know a masked battery from a hunk of gingerbread?

Do you know a eppylit from a piece of chalk?

If I trust you with a real gun, how many men of your own company do you speck you can manage to kill durin the war?

Hav you ever heard of Ginral Price of Missouri, and can you avoid simler accidents in case of a battle? [219/220]

Have you ever had the measles, and if so, how many?

How air you now?

Show me your tongue, &c., &c. Sum of the questions was sarcus-stical. [220/222] . . .

We air progressin pretty well with our drill. As all air commandin offissers, there ain't no jelusy; and as we air all exceedin smart, it t'aint worth while to try to outstrip each other. The idee of a company composed excloosively of Commanders-in-Chiefs, orriggernated, I spose I skurcely need say, in these Brane. Considered *as* a idee, I flatter myself it is putty hefty. We've got all the tackticks at our tongs' ends, but what we particly excel in is restin muskits. We can rest muskits with anybody.

Our corpse will do its dooty. We go to the aid of Columby—we fight for the stars!

We'll be chopt into sassige meat before we'll exhibit our coat-tales to the foe.

We'll fight till there's nothin left of us but our little toes, and even they shall defiantly wiggle!

Ever of thee,"

A. WARD. [222]

WALT WHITMAN

(1819–1892)

Whitman's background as a schoolteacher, carpenter, and newspaper editor, combined with his inherent love of people, were contributing factors to the egalitarianism he exhibited during the Civil War. Whitman's close involvement with the war began in December, 1862, when he heard that his brother George had been wounded in the first Fredericksburg battle and went to Virginia to find him. Subsequently he began ministering to wounded soldiers in Washington hospitals, and did so for three years. In Memoranda During the War *he considers he assisted from 80,000 to 100,000 sick and wounded. During this time he also gained firsthand knowledge of the war by visiting the Virginia battlefront.*

According to Whitman, the Civil War was the "axle" on which his major work turned. His experiences increased his democratic nationalism, confirmed his faith in democracy, enlarged his brotherhood, and allowed him to see firsthand, as he said, "the virtues of the American en-masse." George M. Frederickson in The Inner Civil War *says Whitman sought "access to the deepest emotions of the war." Some of these emotions were of pessimism and despair, though, as Whitman realized while watching suffering, brutality, and death.*

Important to any study in depth of Whitman and the Civil War are Charles I. Glicksberg, ed., Walt Whitman and the Civil War: A Collection of Original Articles and Manuscripts *(1933); Walter Lowenfels, ed.,* Walt Whitman's Civil War *(1961); and the notes in the definitive* The Collected Writings of Walt Whitman, *ed. Gay Wilson Allen and Sculley Bradley, et al.*

[A GREAT LITERATURE]*

And now . . . the rapid succession of well-known events (too well known—I believe, these days, we almost hate to hear them mention'd) —the national flag fired on at Sumter—the uprising of the North, in paroxysms of astonishment and rage—the chaos of divided councils—the call for troops—the first Bull Run—the stunning cast-down, shock, and dismay of the North—and so in full flood the secession war. Four years of lurid, bleeding, murky, murderous war. Who paint those years, with all their scenes?—the hard-fought engagements—the defeats, plans, failures—the gloomy hours, days, when [244/245] our Nationality seem'd hung in pall of doubt, perhaps death—the Mephistophelean sneers of foreign lands and attachés—the dreaded Scylla of European interference, and the Charybdis of the tremendously dangerous latent strata of secession sympathizers throughout the free States (far more numerous than is supposed) —the long marches in summer—the hot sweat, and many a sunstroke, as on the rush to Gettysburg in '63— the night battles in the woods, as under Hooker at Chancellorsville—the camps in winter—the military prisons—the hospitals— (alas! alas! the hospitals) .

The secession war? Nay, let me call it the Union war. Though whatever call'd, it is even yet too near us—too vast and too closely overshadowing—its branches unform'd yet, (but certain,) shooting too far into the future—and the most indicative and mightiest of them yet ungrown. A great literature will yet arise out of the era of those four years, those scenes—era compressing centuries of native passion, first-class pictures, tempests of life and death—an inexhaustible mine for the histories, drama, romance, and even philosophy, of peoples to come—indeed the verteber of poetry and art (of personal character too) for all future America—far more grand, in my opinion, to the hands capable of it, than Homer's siege of Troy, or the French wars to Shakspere. [245]

*From "Death of Abraham Lincoln: Lecture Deliver'd in New York, April 14, 1879—in Philadelphia, '80—in Boston, '81," *The Complete Prose Works of Walt Whitman*, ed. Richard Maurice Bucke, Thomas B. Harned, and Horace L. Traubel (New York and London: G. P. Putnam's Sons, 1902) , Vol. II.

BEAT! BEAT! DRUMS!*

Beat! beat! drums!—blow! bugles! blow!
Through the windows—through doors—burst like a ruthless force,
Into the solemn church, and scatter the congregation,
Into the school where the scholar is studying;
Leave not the bridegroom quiet—no happiness must he have now
    with his bride,
Nor the peaceful farmer any peace, ploughing his field or
    gathering his grain,
So fierce you whirr and pound you drums—so shrill you bugles
    blow.

Beat! beat! drums!—blow! bugles! blow!
Over the traffic of cities—over the rumble of wheels in the streets;
Are beds prepared for sleepers at night in the houses? no sleepers
    must sleep in those beds, [44/45]   10
No bargainers' bargains by day—no brokers or speculators—
    would they continue?
Would the talkers be talking? would the singer attempt to sing?
Would the lawyer rise in the court to state his case before the
    judge?
Then rattle quicker, heavier drums—you bugles wilder blow.

Beat! beat! drums!—blow! bugles! blow!
Make no parley—stop for no expostulation,
Mind not the timid—mind not the weeper or prayer,
Mind not the old man beseeching the young man,
Let not the child's voice be heard, nor the mother's entreaties,
Make even the trestles to shake the dead where they lie awaiting
    the hearses,   20
So strong you thump O terrible drums—so loud you bugles
    blow. [45]

*This and the rest of the Whitman poems are from Walt Whitman, *Leaves
of Grass,* ed. Richard Maurice Bucke, Thomas B. Harned, and Horace L. Traubel
(New York and London: G. P. Putnam's Sons, 1902), Vol. II. These poems were
first published together in *Drum-Taps* (1865). "Beat! Beat! Drums!" was first
published in Sept., 1861. Line six was added to "Cavalry Crossing a Ford" in 1871.
For helpful notes on the *Drum-Taps* poems, see Harold W. Blodgett and Sculley
Bradley, eds., *Leaves of Grass,* Comprehensive Reader's Edition (1965).

[THE UNION AND DEMOCRACY]*

I have said somewhere that the three Presidentiads preceding 1861 show'd how the weakness and wickedness of rulers are just as eligible here in America under republican, as in Europe under dynastic influences. But what can I say of that prompt and splendid wrestling with secession slavery, the arch-enemy personified, the instant he unmistakably show'd his face? The volcanic upheaval of the nation, after that firing on the flag at Charleston, proved for certain [29/30] something which had been previously in great doubt, and at once substantially settled the question of disunion. In my judgment it will remain as the grandest and most encouraging spectacle yet vouchsafed in any age, old or new, to political progress and democracy. It was not for what came to the surface merely— though that was important—but what it indicated below, which was of eternal importance. Down in the abysms of New World humanity there had form'd and harden'd a primal hardpan of national Union will, determin'd and in the majority, refusing to be tamper'd with or argued against, confronting all emergencies, and capable at any time of bursting all surface bonds, and breaking out like an earthquake. It is, indeed, the best lesson of the century, or of America, and it is a mighty privilege to have been part of it. (Two great spectacles, immortal proofs of democracy, unequall'd in all the history of the past, are furnish'd by the secession war—one at the beginning, the other at its close. Those are, the general, voluntary, arm'd upheaval, and the peaceful and harmonious disbanding of the armies in the summer of 1865.) [30]

[CHANCELLORSVILLE]**

There was part of the late battle at Chancellorsville, (second Fredericksburg,) a little over a week ago, Saturday, Saturday night

*From *The Complete Prose Works of Walt Whitman*, Vol. I. This volume is *Specimen Days*, first published in 1882, with the material on the war being essentially a rewriting of *Memoranda During the War* (1875), which in turn was a linking together of Whitman's notebook entries made during the war.
**From *The Complete Prose Works of Walt Whitman*, Vol. I.

and Sunday, under Gen. Joe Hooker, I would like to give just a glimpse of— (a moment's look in a terrible storm at sea—of which a few suggestions are enough, and full details impossible.) The fighting had been very hot during the day, and after an intermission the latter part, was resumed at night, and kept up with furious energy till 3 o'clock in the morning. That afternoon (Saturday) an attack sudden and strong by Stonewall Jackson had gain'd a great advantage to the Southern army, and broken our lines, entering us like a wedge, and leaving things in that position at dark. But Hooker at 11 at night made a desperate push, drove the secesh forces back, restored his original lines, and resumed his plans. This night scrimmage was very exciting, and afforded countless strange and fearful pictures. The fighting had been general both at Chancellorsville and northeast at Fredericksburg. (We hear of some poor fighting, episodes, skedaddling on our part. I think not of it. [53/54] I think of the fierce bravery, the general rule.) One corps, the 6th, Sedgewick's, fights four dashing and bloody battles in thirty-six hours, retreating in great jeopardy, losing largely but maintaining itself, fighting with the sternest desperation under all circumstances, getting over the Rappahannock only by the skin of its teeth, yet getting over. It lost many, many brave men, yet it took vengeance, ample vengeance.

But it was the tug of Saturday evening, and through the night and Sunday morning, I wanted to make a special note of. It was largely in the woods, and quite a general engagement. The night was very pleasant, at times the moon shining out full and clear, all Nature so calm in itself, the early summer grass so rich, and foliage of the trees—yet there the battle raging, and many good fellows lying helpless, with new accessions to them, and every minute amid the rattle of muskets and crash of cannon, (for there was an artillery contest too,) the red life-blood oozing out from heads or trunks or limbs upon that green and dew-cool grass. Patches of the woods take fire, and several of the wounded, unable to move, are consumed—quite large spaces are swept over, burning the dead also—some of the men have their hair and beards singed—some, burns on their faces and hands—others holes burnt in their clothing. The flashes of fire from the cannon, the quick flaring flames and smoke, and the immense [54/55] roar—the musketry so general, the light nearly bright enough for each side to see the other—the crashing, tramping of men—the yelling—close quarters—we hear the secesh

yells—our men cheer loudly back, especially if Hooker is in sight—
hand to hand conflicts, each side stands up to it, brave, determin'd
as demons, they often charge upon us—a thousand deeds are done
worth to write newer greater poems on—and still the woods on fire—
still many are not only scorch'd—too many, unable to move, are
burned to death.

Then the camps of the wounded—O heavens, what scene is
this?—is this indeed *humanity*—these butchers' shambles? There
are several of them. There they lie, in the largest, in an open space
in the woods, from 200 to 300 poor fellows—the groans and
screams—the odor of blood, mixed with the fresh scent of the night,
the grass, the trees—that slaughter-house! O well is it their mothers,
their sisters cannot see them—cannot conceive, and never conceiv'd,
these things. One man is shot by a shell, both in the arm and
leg—both are amputated—there lie the rejected members. Some
have their legs blown off—some bullets through the breast—some
indescribably horrid wounds in the face or head, all mutilated,
sickening, torn, gouged out—some in the abdomen—some mere
boys—many rebels, badly hurt—they take their regular turns with
the rest, just the same as any—the surgeons [55/56] use them just
the same. Such is the camp of the wounded—such a fragment, a
reflection afar off of the bloody scene—while all over the clear, large
moon comes out at times softly, quietly shining. Amid the woods,
that scene of flitting souls—amid the crack and crash and yelling
sounds—the impalpable perfume of the woods—and yet the pun-
gent, stifling smoke—the radiance of the moon, looking from
heaven at intervals so placid—the sky so heavenly—the clear-ob-
scure up there, those buoyant upper oceans—a few large placid stars
beyond, coming silently and languidly out, and then disappearing
—the melancholy, draperied night above, around. And there, upon
the roads, the fields, and in those woods, that contest, never one
more desperate in any age or land—both parties now in force—
masses—no fancy battle, no semi-play, but fierce and savage demons
fighting there—courage and scorn of death the rule, exceptions
almost none.

What history, I say, can ever give—for who can know—the
mad, determin'd tussle of the armies, in all their separate large and
little squads—as this—each steep'd from crown to toe in desperate,
mortal purports? Who know the conflict, hand-to-hand—the many

conflicts in the dark, those shadowy-tangled, flashing moonbeam'd woods—the writhing groups and squads—the cries, the din, the cracking guns and pistols—the distant cannon—the cheers and calls and threats and awful music of the oaths—[56/57] the indescribable mix—the officers' orders, persuasions, encouragements—the devils fully rous'd in human hearts—the strong shout, *Charge, men, charge*—the flash of the naked sword, and rolling flame and smoke? And still the broken, clear and clouded heaven—and still again the moonlight pouring silvery soft its radiant patches over all. [57]

CAVALRY CROSSING A FORD

A line in long array where they wind betwixt green islands,
They take a serpentine course, their arms flash in the sun—hark
     to the musical clank, [63/64]
Behold the silvery river, in it the splashing horses loitering stop
     to drink,
Behold the brown-faced men, each group, each person a picture, the
     negligent rest on the saddles,
Some emerge on the opposite bank, others are just entering the
     ford—while,
Scarlet and blue and snowy white,
The guidon flags flutter gayly in the wind. [64]

VIGIL STRANGE I KEPT IN THE FIELD ONE NIGHT

Vigil strange I kept in the field one night;
When you my son and my comrade dropt at my side that day,
One look I but gave which your dear eyes return'd with a look
     I shall never forget, [67/68]
One touch of your hand to mine O boy, reach'd up as you lay
     on the ground,
Then onward I sped in the battle, the even-contested battle,

Till late in the night reliev'd to the place at last again I made
  my way,
Found you in death so cold dear comrade, found your body son
  of responding kisses, (never again on earth responding,)
Bared your face in the starlight, curious the scene, cool blew
  the moderate night-wind,
Long there and then in vigil I stood, dimly around me the
  battle-field spreading,
Vigil wondrous and vigil sweet there in the fragrant silent night, 10
But not a tear fell, not even a long-drawn sigh, long, long I gazed,
Then on the earth partially reclining sat by your side leaning
  my chin in my hands,
Passing sweet hours, immortal and mystic hours with you dear-
  est comrade—not a tear, not a word,
Vigil of silence, love and death, vigil for you my son and my
  soldier,
As onward silently stars aloft, eastward new ones upward stole,
Vigil final for you brave boy, (I could not save you, swift was
  your death,
I faithfully loved you and cared for you living, I think we shall
  surely meet again,)
Till at latest lingering of the night, indeed just as the dawn
  appear'd,
My comrade I wrapt in his blanket, envelop'd well his form,
  [68/69]
Folded the blanket well, tucking it carefully over head and
  carefully under feet, 20
And there and then and bathed by the rising sun, my son in
  his grave, in his rude-dug grave I deposited,
Ending my vigil strange with that, vigil of night and battle-
  field dim,
Vigil for boy of responding kisses, (never again on earth
  responding,)
Vigil for comrade swiftly slain, vigil I never forget, how as day
  brighten'd,
I rose from the chill ground and folded my soldier well in his
  blanket,
And buried him where he fell. [69]

THE WOUND-DRESSER

1

An old man bending I come among new faces,
Years looking backward resuming in answer to children,
Come tell us old man, as from young men and maidens that love
    me,
(Arous'd and angry, I'd thought to beat the alarum, and urge
    relentless war,
But soon my fingers fail'd me, my face droop'd and I resign'd
    myself,
To sit by the wounded and soothe them, or silently watch the
    dead;)
Years hence of these scenes, of these furious passions, these
    chances,
Of unsurpass'd heroes, (was one side so brave? the other was
    equally brave;)
Now be witness again, paint the mightiest armies of earth,
Of those armies so rapid so wondrous what saw you to tell us?
    [73/74]   10
What stays with you latest and deepest? of curious panics,
Of hard-fought engagements or sieges tremendous what deepest
    remains?

2

O maidens and young men I love and that love me,
What you ask of my days those the strangest and sudden your
    talking recalls,
Soldier alert I arrive after a long march cover'd with sweat and
    dust,
In the nick of time I come, plunge in the fight, loudly shout in
    the rush of successful charge,
Enter the captur'd works—yet lo, like a swift-running river they
    fade,

Pass and are gone they fade—I dwell not on soldiers' perils or
　　soldiers' joys,
(Both I remember well—many the hardships, few the joys, yet I
　　was content.)

But in silence, in dreams' projections, 20
While the world of gain and appearance and mirth goes on,
So soon what is over forgotten, and waves wash the imprints off
　　the sand,
With hinged knees returning I enter the doors, (while for you
　　up there,
Whoever you are, follow without noise and be of strong heart.)

Bearing the bandages, water and sponge,
Straight and swift to my wounded I go,
Where they lie on the ground after the battle brought in, [74/75]
Where their priceless blood reddens the grass the ground,
Or to the rows of the hospital tent, or under the roof'd hospital,
To the long rows of cots up and down each side I return, 30
To each and all one after another I draw near, not one do I miss,
An attendant follows holding a tray, he carries a refuse pail,
Soon to be fill'd with clotted rags and blood, emptied, and fill'd
　　again.

I onward go, I stop,
With hinged knees and steady hand to dress wounds,
I am firm with each, the pangs are sharp yet unavoidable,
One turns to me his appealing eyes—poor boy! I never knew you,
Yet I think I could not refuse this moment to die for you, if that
　　would save you.

3

On, on I go, (open doors of time! open hospital doors!)
The crush'd head I dress, (poor crazed hand tear not the
　　bandage away,) 40
The neck of the cavalry-man with the bullet through and
　　through I examine,

Hard the breathing rattles, quite glazed already the eye, yet life
    struggles hard,
(Come sweet death! be persuaded O beautiful death!
In mercy come quickly.)

From the stump of the arm, the amputated hand,
I undo the clotted lint, remove the slough, wash off the matter
    and blood, [75/76]
Back on his pillow the soldier bends with curv'd neck and side-
    falling head,
His eyes are closed, his face is pale, he dares not look on the
    bloody stump,
And has not yet look'd on it.

I dress a wound in the side, deep, deep,   50
But a day or two more, for see the frame all wasted and sinking,
And the yellow-blue countenance see.

I dress the perforated shoulder, the foot with the bullet-wound,
Cleanse the one with a gnawing and putrid gangrene, so sicken-
    ing, so offensive,
While the attendant stands behind aside me holding the tray
    and pail.

I am faithful, I do not give out,
The fractur'd thigh, the knee, the wound in the abdomen,
These and more I dress with impassive hand, (yet deep in my
    breast a fire, a burning flame.)

4

Thus in silence in dreams' projections,
Returning, resuming, I thread my way through the hospitals,   60
The hurt and wounded I pacify with soothing hand,
I sit by the restless all the dark night, some are so young,
Some suffer so much, I recall the experience sweet and sad,
(Many a soldier's loving arms about his neck have cross'd and
    rested,
Many a soldier's kiss dwells on these bearded lips.) [76]

LONG, TOO LONG AMERICA

Long, too long America,
Traveling roads all even and peaceful you learn'd from joys and
    prosperity only,
But now, ah now, to learn from crises of anguish, advancing,
    grappling with direct fate and recoiling not,
And now to conceive and show to the world what your children
    en-masse really are,
(For who except myself has yet conceiv'd what your children
    en-masse really are?) [77]

from LETTER TO NATHANIEL BLOOM

AND JOHN F. S. GRAY*

Washington, March 19, 1863.

Dear Nat, and Fred Gray:
    Since I left New York, I was down in the Army of the Potomac
in front with my brother a good part of the winter, commencing
time of the battle of Fredericksburgh—have seen *war-life,* the real
article—folded myself in a blanket, lying down in the mud with
composure—relished salt [80/81] pork & hard tack—have been on
the battle-field among the wounded, the faint and the bleeding, to
give them nourishment—have gone over with a flag of truce the
next day to help direct the burial of the dead—have struck up a
tremendous friendship with a young Mississippi captain (about 19)
that we took prisoner badly wounded at Fredericksburgh—(he has
followed me here, is in Emory hospital here, minus a leg—he wears
his confederate uniform, proud as the devil—I met him first at
Falmouth, in the Lacy house, middle of December last, his leg just
cut off, and cheered him up—poor boy, he has suffered a great deal,

*From *Walt Whitman, The Correspondence, Vol. I: 1842–1867,* ed. Edwin
Haviland Miller (New York: New York University Press, 1961). Reprinted by
permission of New York University Press.

and still suffers—has eyes bright as a hawk, but face pale—our affection is quite an affair, quite romantic—sometimes when I lean over to say I am going, he puts his arm round my neck, draws my face down, &c. quite a scene for the New Bowery.)

I spent the Christmas holidays on the Rappahannock—during January came up hither, took a lodging room here—did the 37th Congress, especially the night sessions the last three weeks, explored the Capitol then, meandering the gorgeous painted interminable senate corridors, getting lost in them, (a new sensation, rich & strong, that endless painted interior at night) —got very much interested in some particular cases in Hospitals here—go now steadily to more or less of said Hospitals by day or night—find always the sick and dying soldiers forthwith begin to cling to me in a way that makes a fellow feel funny enough. These Hospitals, so different from all others—these thousands, and tens and twenties of thousands of American young men, badly wounded, all sorts of wounds, operated on, pallid with diarrhea, languishing, dying with fever, pneumonia, &c. open a new world somehow to me, giving closer insights, new things, exploring deeper mines than any yet, showing our humanity, (I sometimes put my- [81/82] self in fancy in the cot, with typhoid, or under the knife,) tried by terrible, fearfulest tests, probed deepest, the living soul's, the body's tragedies, bursting the petty bonds of art. To these, what are your dramas and poems, even the oldest and the tearfulest? Not old Greek mighty ones, where man contends with fate, (and always yields) —not Virgil showing Dante on and on among the agonized & damned, approach what here I see and take a part in. For here I see, not at intervals, but quite always, how certain, man, our American man—how he holds himself cool and unquestioned master above all pains and bloody mutilations. It is immense, the best thing of all, nourishes me of all men. This then, what frightened us all so long! Why it is put to flight with ignominy, a mere stuffed scarecrow of the fields. O death where is thy sting? O grave where is thy victory? . . . [82]

from **LETTER TO LOUISA VAN VELSOR WHITMAN***

[July 7, 1863]

Mother, it seems to be certain that Meade has gained the day, &
that the battles there in Pennsylvania have been about as terrible as
any in the war—O what a sight must have been presented by the
field of action—I think the killed & wounded there on both sides
were as many as eighteen or twenty thousand—in one place, four or
five acres, there were a thousand dead, at daybreak on Saturday
morning—Mother, one's heart grows sick of war, after all, when you
see what it really is—every once in a while I feel so horrified &
disgusted—it seems to me like a great slaughter-house & the men
mutually butchering each other—then I feel how impossible it
[114/115] appears, again, to retire from this contest, until we have
carried our points— (it is cruel to be so tossed from pillar to post in
one's judgment) .

[THE PEOPLE AND THE WAR]**

The movements of the late secession war, and their results, to any
sense that studies well and comprehends them, show that popular
democracy, whatever its faults and dangers, practically justifies itself
beyond the proudest claims and wildest hopes of its enthusiasts.
Probably no future age can know, but I well know, how the gist of
this fiercest and most resolute of the world's war-like contentions
resided exclusively in the unnamed, unknown rank and file; and
how the brunt of its labor of death was, to all essential purposes,
volunteer'd. The People, of their own choice, fighting, dying for
their own idea, insolently attack'd by the secession-slave-power, and
its very existence imperil'd. Descending to detail, entering any of
the armies, and mixing with the private soldiers, we see and have

*From *Walt Whitman, The Correspondence, Vol. I.* Reprinted by permission
of New York University Press.
**From *The Complete Prose Works of Walt Whitman,* Vol. II. This material
on the war was first published in an essay, entitled "Democracy," in *The Galaxy,*
Dec., 1867.

seen august spectacles. We have seen the alacrity with which the
American-born populace, the peaceablest and most good-natured
race in the world, and the most personally independent and intelligent, and the least fitted to submit to the irksomeness and ex-
asperation of regimental discipline, sprang, at the first tap of the
drum, to arms—not for gain, nor even glory, nor to repel invasion—
but for an emblem, a mere abstraction—for the life, *the safety of
the flag.* We have seen the unequal'd docility and obedience of
these soldiers. We have seen them tried long and long by hopeless-
ness, mismanagement, and by defeat; have seen the incredible
slaughter toward or through which the [73/74] armies (as at first
Fredericksburg, and afterward at the Wilderness) still unhesitat-
ingly obey'd orders to advance. We have seen them in trench, or
crouching behind breastwork, or tramping in deep mud, or amid
pouring rain or thick-falling snow, or under forced marches in
hottest summer (as on the road to get to Gettysburg)—vast suffo-
cating swarms, divisions, corps, with every single man so grimed and
black with sweat and dust, his own mother would not have known
him—his clothes all dirty, stain'd and torn, with sour, accumulated
sweat for perfume—many a comrade, perhaps a brother, sun-struck,
staggering out, dying, by the roadside, of exhaustion—yet the great
bulk bearing steadily on, cheery enough, hollow-bellied from hunger, but sinewy with unconquerable resolution.

We have seen this race proved by wholesale, by drearier, yet
more fearful tests—the wound, the amputation, the shatter'd face or
limb, the slow hot fever, long impatient anchorage in bed, and all
the forms of maiming, operation and disease. Alas! America have
we seen, though only in her early youth, already to hospital
brought. There have we watch'd these soldiers, many of them only
boys in years—mark'd their decorum, their religious nature and
fortitude, and their sweet affection. Wholesale, truly. For at the
front, and through the camps, in countless tents, stood the regimental, brigade and division hospitals; while everywhere amid the
land, [74/75] in or near cities, rose clusters of huge, white-wash'd,
crowded, one-story wooden barracks; and there ruled agony with
bitter scourge, yet seldom brought a cry; and there stalk'd death by
day and night along the narrow aisles between the rows of cots, or
by the blankets on the ground, and touch'd lightly many a poor
sufferer, often with blessed, welcome touch.

I know not whether I shall be understood, but I realize that it is finally from what I learn'd personally mixing in such scenes that I am now penning these pages. One night in the gloomiest period of the war, in the Patent-office hospital in Washington city, as I stood by the bedside of a Pennsylvania soldier, who lay, conscious of quick approaching death, yet perfectly calm, and with noble, spiritual manner, the veteran surgeon, turning aside, said to me, that though he had witness'd many, many deaths of soldiers, and had been a worker at Bull Run, Antietam, Fredericksburg, &c., he had not seen yet the first case of man or boy that met the approach of dissolution with cowardly qualms or terror. My own observation fully bears out the remark.

What have we here, if not, towering above all talk and argument, the plentifully-supplied, last-needed proof of democracy, in its personalities? Curiously enough, too, the proof on this point comes, I should say, every bit as much from the South, as from the North. Although I have spoken only of the latter, yet I deliberately include all. [75/76] Grand, common stock! to me the accomplish'd and convincing growth, prophetic of the future; proof undeniable to sharpest sense, of perfect beauty, tenderness and pluck, that never feudal lord, nor Greek, nor Roman breed, yet rival'd. Let no tongue ever speak in disparagement of the American races, North or South, to one who has been through the war in the great army hospitals. [76]

DEATH OF PRESIDENT LINCOLN*

I find in my notes of the time, this passage on the death of Abraham Lincoln: He leaves for America's history and biography, so far, not only its most dramatic reminiscence—he leaves, in my opinion, the greatest, best, most characteristic, artistic, moral personality. Not but that he had faults, and show'd them in the Presidency; but honesty, goodness, shrewdness, conscience, and (a new virtue, unknown to other lands, and hardly yet really known here, but the foundation and tie of all, as the future will grandly develop,) UNIONISM, in its truest and amplest sense, form'd the hard-pan of his character. These he seal'd with his life. The tragic splendor of

*From *The Complete Prose Works of Walt Whitman,* Vol. I.

his death, purging, illuminating all, throws round his form, his head, an aureole that will remain and will grow brighter through time, while history lives, and love of country lasts. By many has this Union been help'd; but if one name, one man, must be pick'd out, he, most of all, is the conservator of it, to the future. He was assassinated—but the Union is not assassinated—*ça ira!* One falls and another falls. The soldier drops, sinks like a wave—but the ranks of the ocean eternally press on. Death does its work, obliterates a hundred, a thousand—President, general, captain, private,—but the Nation is immortal. [118]

THE MILLION DEAD*

The dead in this war—there they lie, strewing the fields and woods and valleys and battle-fields of the South—Virginia, the Peninsula —Malvern Hill and Fair Oaks—the banks of the Chickahominy— the terraces of Fredericksburg—Antietam bridge—the grisly ravines of Manassas—the bloody promenade of the Wilderness—the varieties of the *strayed* dead, (the estimate of the War Department is 25,000 national soldiers kill'd in battle and never buried at all, 5,000 drown'd—15,000 inhumed by strangers, or on the march in haste, in hitherto unfound localities—2,000 graves cover'd by sand and mud by Mississippi freshets, 3,000 carried away by caving-in of banks, &c.,) —Gettysburg, the West, Southwest—Vicksburg—Chattanooga—the trenches of Petersburg—the numberless battles, camps, hospitals everywhere—the crop reap'd by the mighty reapers, typhoid, dysentery, inflammations—and blackest and loathsomest of all, the dead and living burial-pits, the prison-pens of Andersonville, Salisbury, Belle Isle, &c., (not Dante's pictured hell and all its woes, its degradations, filthy torments, excell'd those prisons) —the dead, the dead, the dead—*our* dead—or [137/138] South or North, ours all, (all, all, all, finally dear to me) —or East or West—Atlantic coast or Mississippi valley—somewhere they crawl'd to die, alone, in bushes, low gullies, or on the sides of hills— (there, in secluded spots, their skeletons, bleach'd bones, tufts of hair, buttons, fragments of clothing, are occasionally found yet) —our young men

*From *The Complete Prose Works of Walt Whitman,* Vol. I.

once so handsome and so joyous, taken from us—the son from the mother, the husband from the wife, the dear friend from the dear friend—the clusters of camp graves, in Georgia, the Carolinas, and in Tennessee—the single graves left in the woods or by the roadside, (hundreds, thousands, obliterated)—the corpses floated down the rivers, and caught and lodged, (dozens, scores, floated down the upper Potomac, after the cavalry engagements, the pursuit of Lee, following Gettysburg)—some lie at the bottom of the sea—the general million, and the special cemeteries in almost all the States—the infinite dead—(the land entire saturated, perfumed with their impalpable ashes' exhalation in Nature's chemistry distill'd, and shall be so forever, in every future grain of wheat and ear of corn, and every flower that grows, and every breath we draw)—not only Northern dead leavening Southern soil—thousands, aye tens of thousands, of Southerners, crumble to-day in Northern earth.

And everywhere among these countless graves—everywhere in the many soldier Cemeteries of the [138/139] Nation, (there are now, I believe, over seventy of them)—as at the time in the vast trenches, the depositories of slain, Northern and Southern, after the great battles—not only where the scathing trail passed those years, but radiating since in all the peaceful quarters of the land—we see, and ages yet may see, on monuments and gravestones, singly or in masses, to thousands or tens of thousands, the significant word *Unknown*.

(In some of the cemeteries nearly *all* the dead are unknown. At Salisbury, N.C., for instance, the known are only 85, while the unknown are 12,027, and 11,700 of these are buried in trenches. A national monument has been put up here, by order of Congress, to mark the spot—but what visible, material monument can ever fittingly commemorate that spot?) [139]

THE REAL WAR WILL NEVER GET IN THE BOOKS*

And so good-bye to the war. I know not how it may have been, or may be, to others—to me the main interest I found, (and still, on recollection, find,) in the rank and file of the armies, both sides,

*From *The Complete Prose Works of Walt Whitman,* Vol. I.

and in those specimens amid the hospitals, and even the dead on
the field. To me the points illustrating the latent personal character
and eligibilities of these States, in the two or three millions of
American young and middle-aged men, North and South, embodied
in those armies—and especially the one third or one fourth of their
number, stricken by wounds or disease [139/140] at some time in
the course of the contest—were of more significance even than the
political interests involved. (As so much of a race depends on how
it faces death, and how it stands personal anguish and sickness. As,
in the glints of emotions under emergencies, and the indirect traits
and asides in Plutarch, we get far profounder clues to the antique
world than all its more formal history.)

Future years will never know the seething hell and the black
infernal background of countless minor scenes and interiors, (not
the official surface-courteousness of the Generals, not the few great
battles) of the Secession war; and it is best they should not—the
real war will never get in the books. In the mushy influences of
current times, too, the fervid atmosphere and typical events of those
years are in danger of being totally forgotten. I have at night
watch'd by the side of a sick man in the hospital, one who could not
live many hours. I have seen his eyes flash and burn as he raised
himself and recurr'd to the cruelties on his surrender'd brother, and
mutilations of the corpse afterward. (See in the preceding pages,
the incident at Upperville—the seventeen kill'd as in the description were left there on the ground. After they dropt dead, no one
touch'd them—all were made sure of, however. The carcasses were
left for the citizens to bury or not, as they chose.)

Such was the war. It was not a quadrille in a ball-room. Its
interior history will not only never be [140/141] written—its prac-
ticality, minutiæ of deeds and passions, will never be even suggested. The actual soldier of 1862–'65, North and South, with all his
ways, his incredible dauntlessness, habits, practices, tastes, language,
his fierce friendship, his appetite, rankness, his superb strength and
animality, lawless gait, and a hundred unnamed lights and shades
of camp, I say, will never be written—perhaps must not and should
not be.

The preceding notes may furnish a few stray glimpses into that
life, and into those lurid interiors, never to be fully convey'd to the
future. The hospital part of the drama from '61 to '65 deserves

indeed to be recorded. Of that many-threaded drama, with its
sudden and strange surprises, its confounding of prophecies, its
moments of despair, the dread of foreign interference, the interminable campaigns, the bloody battles, the mighty and cumbrous
and green armies, the drafts and bounties—the immense money
expenditure, like a heavy-pouring constant rain—with, over the
whole land, the last three years of the struggle, an unending, universal mourning-wail of women, parents, orphans—the marrow of
the tragedy concentrated in those Army Hospitals— (it seem'd
sometimes as if the whole interest of the land, North and South, was
one vast central hospital, and all the rest of the affair but flanges) —
those forming the untold and unwritten history of the war—infinitely greater (like life's) than the few scraps and distortions that
are [141/142] ever told or written. Think how much, and of importance, will be—how much, civic and military, has already been
—buried in the grave, in eternal darkness.

[TWO SIDES, BUT ONE IDENTITY]*

Of the War of Attempted Secession—the greatest National event of
the first Century of the United States, and one among the great
events of all Centuries—the main points of its origin, and the *conditions* out of which it arose, are full of lessons, full of warnings yet
to the Republic, and always will be. The underlying and principal
of those points are yet singularly ignored. The Northern States were
really just as responsible for that War, (in its precedents, founda-
tions, instigations,) as the South. . . . [63/65]
      . . . As to the inception and direct instigation of the War, in
the South itself, I shall not attempt interiors or complications. Behind all, the idea that it was from a resolute and arrogant determination on the part of the extreme Slaveholders, the Calhounites,
to carry the States Rights' portion of the Constitutional Compact to
its farthest verge, and Nationalize Slavery, or else disrupt the
Union, and found a new Empire, with Slavery for its corner-stone,
was and is undoubtedly the true theory. (If successful, this attempt

*From *Walt Whitman, Memoranda During the War* (Camden, New Jersey:
Author's Publication, 1875–76) .

would of course have destroy'd not only our American Republic, in anything like first-class proportions, in itself and its prestige, but for ages at least, the cause of Liberty and Equality everywhere, and would have been the greatest triumph of reaction, and the severest blow to political and every other freedom, possible to conceive. Its worst results would have inured to the Southern States themselves.)

That our National-Democratic experiment, principle, and machinery, could triumphantly sustain such a shock, and that the Constitution could weather it, like a ship a storm, and come out of it as sound and whole as before, is by far the most signal proof yet of the stability of that experiment, Democracy, and of those principles, and that Constitution. But the case is not fully stated at that. It is certain to me that the United States, by virtue of the Secession War and its results, and through that and them only, are now ready to enter, and must certainly enter, upon their genuine career in history, as no more torn and divided in their spinal requisites, but a great Homogeneous Nation,—Free States all—a moral and political unity in variety, such as Nature shows in her grandest physical works, and as much greater than any mere work of Nature, as the moral and political, the work of man, his mind, his soul, are, in their loftiest sense, greater than the merely physical. . . . Out of that War not only has the Nationality of The States escaped from being strangled, but more than any of the rest, and, in my opinion, more than the North itself, the vital heart and breath of the South have escaped as from the pressure of a general nightmare, and are now to enter on a life, development, and active freedom, whose realities are certain in the future, notwithstanding all the Southern vexations and humiliations of the hour—a development which could not possibly have been achiev'd on any less terms, or by any other means than that War, or something equivalent to it. And I predict that the South is yet to outstrip the North.

And now I have myself, in my thought, deliberately come to unite the whole conflict, both sides, the South and North, really into One, and to view it as a struggle going on within One Identity. Like any of Nature's great convulsions, wars going on within herself—not from separated sets of laws and influences, but the same—

really, efforts, conflicts, most violent ones, for deeper harmony, freer and larger scope, completer homogeneousness and power.

What is any Nation, after all—and what is a human being—but a struggle between conflicting, paradoxical, opposing elements —and they themselves and their most violent contests, important parts of that One Identity, and of its development? [65]

DOUBTERS
North

For them who are neither partisans, nor enthusiasts, nor theorists, nor cynics, there are some doubts not readily to be solved. And there are fears.

Herman Melville

No human effort, on a grand scale, has ever yet resulted according to the purpose of its projectors.

Nathaniel Hawthorne

YEA AND NAY—
EACH HATH HIS SAY;
BUT GOD HE KEEPS THE MIDDLE WAY.

Herman Melville

HENRY ADAMS

(1838–1918)

As he relates in The Education of Henry Adams, *Henry Adams felt it a family responsibility to succeed and yet was never able to obtain the education which would help him do it. Adams entered upon a significant phase of his "inadequate" education in May, 1861, when he accompanied his father to England, where the senior Adams served with notable success during the war years as American Minister. After the war Henry Adams was a journalist in Washington, D.C., an assistant professor of history at Harvard, and an editor of the* North American Review. *Some of his more important writings are two novels,* Democracy *(1808) and* Esther *(1884), a nine-volume* History of the United States of America During the Administrations of Thomas Jefferson and James Madison *(1889–1891), and* Mont-Saint-Michel and Chartres *(1904), a companion volume to the* Education.

Part of the interest of the letters during the early war years lies in Adams's debate whether or not he should enlist in the Union army. His brother Charles tried to dissuade him from this, but Henry had already made up his mind to stay in England before he received his brother's letter. Henry Adams's position during the war is an interesting one, since he saw the conflict from the perspective of an observer in a foreign country and also of an insider to the operations of the Union Department of State. Additional biographical information on this period of Adams's life can be found in Ernest Samuels, The Young Henry Adams *(1948).*

from **LETTERS TO CHARLES FRANCIS ADAMS, JR.***

Washington, 8 January, 1861.

I think we do not feel so confident here as usual. Seward is evidently very low-spirited, though that is owing partly to the labor of preparing his speech. But I have noticed a marked change in the tone of our excellent father, consequent on information which he has received but has not yet confided in me. Until now he has steadily believed that the border states would not go, and his measures were intended to influence them. But now I think he gives it up. His theory is that all depends on Virginia and that Virginia is lost. If this turns out to be the case, it increases our difficulties very badly. It makes war inevitable; war before the 4th of March. [76/77]

God forbid that I should croak or foresee what is not to come. You and I are young enough to be sanguine where others despair. For one, I intend to remain in this city. If there is war I intend to take such part in it as is necessary or useful. It would be a comfort if such times come, to know that the Massachusetts regiments are ready, and if one can be formed on the Cromwell type, I will enroll myself. Of course we can not doubt the result; but I must confess that I had hoped to avoid a real battle. If Virginia and Maryland secede, they will strike at this city, and we shall have to give them such an extermination that it were better we had not been born. I do not want to fight them. Is thy servant a South Carolinian that he should do this thing? They are mad, mere maniacs, and I want to lock them up till they become sane; not to kill them. I want to educate, humanize and refine them, not send fire and sword among them. Let those that will howl for war. I claim to be sufficiently philanthropic to dread it, and sufficiently Christian to wish to avoid

*Letters dated 8 January, 1861, and 20 February, 1863, are from *Letters of Henry Adams* (1858–1891), ed. Worthington Chauncey Ford (Boston and New York: Houghton Mifflin Co., 1930). Reprinted by permission of Houghton Mifflin Co.

Letters dated May 22, 1862, July 17, 1863, and October 30, 1863, are from *A Cycle of Adams Letters, 1861–1865*, ed. Worthington Chauncey Ford, 2 vols. (Boston and New York: Houghton Mifflin Co., 1920). Reprinted by permission of Houghton Mifflin Co.

it and to determine to avoid it, except in self-defence. Tell your warlike friends in Massachusetts that we want no blood-thirsty men here. If the time comes when men are wanted it will be men who fight because there is no other way; not because they are angry; men who will come with their bibles as well as their rifles and who will pray God to forgive them for every life they take.

I am confident that if an actual conflict could be kept off for a few months, there could be none. The South are too weak to sustain such a delay. There would be a reaction among themselves from mere starvation and ruin. But if Virginia goes out, I do not see how it is to be avoided.

This is solemn, but I have enough self-respect to keep me from joining with any body of men who act from mere passion and the sense of wrong. Don't trust yourself to that set, for they will desert you when you need their support. They don't know what they're after. Support any honorable means of conciliation. Our position will be immensely strengthened by it. We cannot be too much in the right. It is time for us who claim to lead this movement to become cool and to do nothing without the fear of God before our eyes. . . . [77]

London, May 22, 1862.

We are still in great anxiety to know the results of the Yorktown business, having as yet arrived only as far as Williamsburg and West Point. On McClellan's success in dispersing the Southern army and capturing all the means for carrying on a war will depend more than I like to think of. If we can disperse them, too, we can immediately reduce our army one-half, and all our expenses on the same scale. I dread the continuance of this war and its demoralizing effects more than anything else, and happy would be the day when we could see the first sign of returning peace. It's likely to be hard enough work to keep our people educated and honest anyway, and the accounts that reach us of the wholesale demoralization in the army of the west from camp-life, and of their dirt, and whiskey and general repulsiveness, are not encouraging to one who wants to see them taught to give up that blackguard habit of drinking liquor in bar-rooms, to brush their teeth and hands and wear clean clothes, and to believe that they have a duty in life besides that of getting ahead, and a responsibility for other people's acts as well as their own. The little weaknesses I speak of are faults of youth; but what will they become if America in its youth takes a permanent course towards every kind of idleness, vice and ignorance?

As for our position here, it is all that could be wished. Everyone congratulates us on the success of our arms and there is no longer any hint that even a remonstrance, [I, 151/152] though there are questions between the Governments which in our bitter state of feeling may bring difficulty. I am very anxious to avoid anything of this sort. We must have peace for many years if we are to heal our wounds and put the country on the right track. We must bring back or create a respect for law and order and the Constitution and the civil and judicial authorities. The nation has been dragged by this infernal cotton that had better have been burning in Hell, far away from its true course, and its worst passions and tastes have been developed by a forced and bloated growth. It will depend on the generation to which you and I belong, whether the country is to be brought back to its true course and the New England element is to carry the victory, or whether we are to be carried on from war to war and debt to debt and one military leader to another, till we lose all our landmarks and go ahead like France with a mere blind necessity to get on, without a reason or a principle. No more wars. Let's have peace, for the love of God. [I, 152]

London, 20 February, 1863.

I wish you were out of your "long siege in mud and rain," which is likely to be as unpleasantly famous as any in Flanders. Hilton Head, I should have thought, would have been a Paradise compared with this.

Bad as your report is about the army of the Potomac, and bad as I fully expect the news to be of the attack on Charleston and Vicksburg, still I have derived a grain of comfort from what I think looks like a gleam of improvement in the political look of things at home. Of all results, a restoration of the Union on a pro-slavery basis would be most unfortunate. Yet I dread almost equally a conquest that would leave us with a new and aggravated Poland on our hands. If we could only fight a peace that would give us Virginia, Tennessee and Mississippi river, then we might easily allow slavery to gather to a head in the cotton states, and crush it out at our leisure on the first good opportunity; but such a vision is reserved for the just made perfect.

As to your avowal of belligerent intentions for life, if you expect me to quarrel with you on that account, you will be disappointed. . . . If I know it, our country has had about as much war as she wants for the present, and if we don't have peace and long peace, our game is up. You and I look at things [94/95] from different points. My view is that peace and small armaments will be our salvation as a united and solvent nation. You prefer to speculate on the chances of war or convulsions, and throw your net in troubled waters.

[London,] July 17, 1863.

We are in receipt of all your sanguinary letters, as well as of news down to the 4th, telling of Cyclopean battles, like the struggles of Saturn and Terra and Hyperion for their empire, lasting through sunrise after sunrise, in an agony such as heralds the extinction of systems. It's a pity that we're civilized. What a grand thing Homer would have made of it; while in our day, men only conceive of a battle as of two lines of men shooting at each other till one or the other gives way. At this distance, though, even now it's very grand and inspiring. There's a magnificence about the pertinacity of the struggle, lasting so many days, and closing, so far as we know on the eve of our single national [II, 46/47] anniversary, with the whole nation bending over it, that makes even these English cubs silent. Dreadful I suppose it is, and God knows I feel anxious and miserable enough at times, but I doubt whether any of us will ever be able to live contented again in times of peace and laziness. Our generation has been stirred up from its lowest layers and there is that in its history which will stamp every member of it until we are all in our graves. We cannot be commonplace. The great burden that has fallen on us must inevitably stamp its character on us. I have hopes for us all, as we go on with the work. . . . [II, 47]

London, October 30, 1863.

If it weren't for our own anxiety about you, I think we should get on swimmingly in these times. The war has taken a chronic shape, and it seems pretty clear that it must burn itself out, or perhaps I should say, burn the rebels out. After having passed through all the intermediate phases of belief, I have come out a full-blown fatalist, and what has greatly aided this result has been the observation of the steady movement of affairs at home. The world grows just like a cabbage; or, if the simile is vulgar, we'll say, like an oak. The result will come when the time is ripe, and the only thing that disgusts me much is the consciousness [II, 96/97] that we are unable to govern it, and the condition that a man of sense can only prove his possession of a soul by remaining in mind a serene and indifferent spectator of the very events to which all his acts most eagerly contribute. This has been in one form or another the result of every philosophical system since men became conscious of the inexplicable contradiction of their existence, and though it may seem nonsense to you with bullets flying round, it does very well for a theory of existence so long as it has no occasion to regulate the relation between one man and another. But there, I confess, it rubs, and naturally enough. So I can contemplate with some philosophy the battles and the defeats, which are indeed only of the same sort of interest as the story of Marathon or Naseby, a degree intensified, but not so with your hasards. The race will go on all right or wrong; either way it's the result of causes existing, but not within our reach; but unfortunately if you were to get into trouble, you might not go on at all, which from my point of view would be disagreeable to us all, yourself inclusive, and would not admit of the application of your old though fallacious maxim that life is a system of compensations, a maxim probably just, if we speak of the race as a unit. . . . [II, 97]

[THE WAR YEARS]*

Hardly a week passed when the newspapers announced that President Lincoln had selected Charles Francis Adams as his Minister to England. Once more, silently, Henry put Blackstone back on its shelf. As Friar Bacon's head sententiously announced many centuries before: Time had passed! The Civil Law lasted a brief day; the Common Law prolonged its shadowy existence for a week. The law, altogether, as path of education, vanished in April, 1861, leaving a million young men planted in the mud of a lawless world, to begin a new life without education at all. They asked few questions, but if they had asked millions they would have got no answers. No one could help. Looking back on this moment of crisis, nearly fifty years afterwards, one could only shake one's white beard in silent horror. Mr. Adams once more intimated that he thought himself entitled to the services of one of his sons, and he indicated Henry as the only one who could be spared from more serious duties. . . . [110/111] . . .

. . . On April 13 the storm burst and rolled several hundred thousand young men like Henry Adams into the surf of a wild ocean, all helpless like himself, to be beaten about for four years by the waves of war. Adams still had time to watch the regiments form ranks before Boston State House in the April evenings and march southward, quietly enough, with the air of business they wore from their cradles, but with few signs or sounds of excitement. He had time also to go down the harbor [111/112] to see his brother Charles quartered in Fort Independence before being thrown, with a hundred thousand more, into the furnace of the Army of the Potomac to get educated in a fury of fire. Few things were for the moment so trivial in importance as the solitary private secretary crawling down to the wretched old Cunard steamer Niagara at East Boston to start again for Liverpool. This time the pitcher of education had gone to the fountain once too often; it was fairly broken;

*From Henry Adams, *The Education of Henry Adams: An Autobiography* (Boston: Houghton Mifflin Co., 1961). Reprinted by permission of Houghton Mifflin Co.; English rights granted by Constable & Company, Ltd. First published in 1918.

and the young man had got to meet a hostile world without defence —or arms. [112/128] . . .

Of the year 1862 Henry Adams could never think without a shudder. The war alone did not greatly distress him; already in his short life he was used to seeing people wade in blood, and he could plainly discern in history, that man from the beginning had found his chief amusement in bloodshed; but the ferocious joy of destruction at its best requires that one should kill what one hates, and young Adams neither hated nor wanted to kill his friends the rebels, while he wanted nothing so much as to wipe England off the earth. Never could any good come from that besotted race! He was feebly trying to save his own life. Every day the British Government deliberately crowded him one step further into the grave. . . .

The Minister, no doubt, endured it, but he had support and consideration, while his son had nothing to think about but his [128/129] friends who were mostly dying under McClellan in the swamps about Richmond, or his enemies who were exulting in Pall Mall. He bore it as well as he could till midsummer, but, when the story of the second Bull Run appeared, he could bear it no longer, and after a sleepless night, walking up and down his room without reflecting that his father was beneath him, he announced at breakfast his intention to go home into the army. His mother seemed to be less impressed by the announcement than by the walking over her head, which was so unlike her as to surprise her son. His father, too, received the announcement quietly. No doubt they expected it, and had taken their measures in advance. In those days, parents got used to all sorts of announcements from their children. Mr. Adams took his son's defection as quietly as he took Bull Run; but his son never got the chance to go. He found obstacles constantly rising in his path. The remonstrances of his brother Charles, who was himself in the Army of the Potomac, and whose opinion had always the greatest weight with Henry, had much to do with delaying action; but he felt, of his own accord, that if he deserted his post in London, and found the Capuan comforts he expected in Virginia where he would have only bullets to wound him, he would never forgive himself for leaving his father and mother alone to be devoured by the wild beasts of the British amphitheatre. This reflection might not have stopped him, but his father's suggestion was decisive. The Minister pointed out that it was too late for him to take part in the actual campaign, and that long before next spring they would all go home together. [129/168] . . .

As the spring of 1863 drew on, the vast field cleared itself for action. A campaign more beautiful—better suited for training the mind of a youth eager for training—has not often unrolled itself for study, from the beginning, before a young man perched in so commanding a position. Very slowly, indeed, after two years of solitude, one began to feel the first faint flush of new and imperial life. One was twenty-five years old, and quite ready to assert it; some of one's friends were wearing stars on [168/169] their collars; some had won stars of a more enduring kind. At moments one's breath came quick. One began to dream the sensation of wielding unmeasured power. The sense came, like vertigo, for an instant, and passed, leaving the brain a little dazed, doubtful, shy. With an intensity more painful than that of any Shakespearean drama, men's eyes were fastened on the armies in the field. Little by little, at first only as a shadowy chance of what might be, if things could be rightly done, one began to feel that, somewhere behind the chaos in Washington power was taking shape; that it was massed and guided as it had not been before. Men seemed to have learned their business—at a cost that ruined— and perhaps too late. A private secretary knew better than most people how much of the new power was to be swung in London, and almost exactly when; but the diplomatic campaign had to wait for the military campaign to lead. The student could only study.

Life never could know more than a single such climax. In that form, education reached its limits. As the first great blows began to fall, one curled up in bed in the silence of night, to listen with incredulous hope. As the huge masses struck, one after another, with the precision of machinery, the opposing mass, the world shivered. Such development of power was unknown. The magnificent resistance and the return shocks heightened the suspense. During the July days Londoners were stupid with unbelief. They were learning from the Yankees how to fight. [169/208] . . .

The campaign of 1864, and the reëlection of Mr. Lincoln in November set the American Minister on so firm a footing that he could safely regard his own anxieties as over, and the anxieties of Earl Russell and the Emperor Napoleon as begun. With a few months more his own term of four years would come to an end, and even though the question still under discussion with England should somewhat prolong his stay, he might look forward with some confidence to his return hime in 1865. His son no longer fretted. The time for going into the army had passed. If he were to be useful at all, it must be as a son, and as a son he was treated with the widest indulgence and trust. He knew that he was doing himself no good by staying in London, but thus far in life he had done himself no good anywhere, and reached his twenty-seventh birthday without having advanced a step, that he could see, beyond his twenty-first. For the most part, his friends were worse off than he. The war was about to end and they were to be set adrift in a world they would find altogether strange.

At this point, as though to cut the last thread of relation, six months were suddenly dropped out of his life in England. The London climate had told on some of the family; the physicians prescribed a winter in Italy. Of course the private secretary was detached as their escort, since this was one of his professional functions; and he passed six months, gaining an education as Italian courier, while the Civil War came to its end. . . . [208/209]

The assassination of President Lincoln fell on the party while they were at Rome, where it seemed singularly fitting to that nursery of murderers and murdered, as though America were also getting educated. Again one went to meditate on the steps of the Santa Maria in Ara Cœli, but the lesson seemed as shallow as before. Nothing happened. The travellers changed no plan or movement. The Minister did not recall them to London. The season was over before they returned; and when the private secretary sat down again at his desk in Portland Place before a mass of copy in arrears, he saw before him a world so changed as to be beyond connection with the past. His identity, if one could call a bundle of disconnected memories an identity, seemed to remain; but his life was once more broken into separate pieces; he was a spider and had to spin a new web in some new place with a new attachment. [209]

AMBROSE BIERCE

(1842–1914?)

Ambrose Bierce was born in Meigs County, Ohio, June 24, 1842. When hostilities began in 1861 he joined the 9th Indiana Infantry and served with distinction throughout the war. He was at Chickamauga, Shiloh, Murfreesboro, Kenesaw Mountain (where he was severely wounded), Franklin, and Nashville. After the war he moved to San Francisco, where he wrote for the weeklies. From 1872 to 1876 he was in England, where he published humorous articles and was on the staff of Fun. *He then returned to San Francisco and continued in journalism, publishing* Tales of Soldiers and Civilians (1891) *as his first volume of short stories. Other significant works are his tales of the supernatural,* Can Such Things Be? (1893), *and* The Devil's Dictionary (1906).

Bierce gives factual accounts of his war experiences in Bits of Autobiography (1909). *Other information on Bierce and the war is found in William McCann, ed.,* Ambrose Bierce's Civil War (1956); *Napier Wilt, "Ambrose Bierce and the Civil War,"* American Literature, I (November, 1929), 260–85; *and Richard O'Connor,* Ambrose Bierce: A Biography (1967).

An enigmatic person, even to those closest to him, Bierce sustained conflicting views on the Civil War. In his autobiography he shows some feeling for war as purgative, and before his departure for Mexico he revisited Civil War battlegrounds. Yet his fiction on the war is almost totally gloomy and pessimistic—portraying the horrors, meaninglessness, and ironic reversals of war. His best-known story of this sort is "An Occurrence at Owl Creek Bridge."

CHICKAMAUGA*

One sunny autumn afternoon a child strayed away from its rude
home in a small field and entered a forest unobserved. It was happy
in a new sense of freedom from control—happy in the opportunity
of exploration and adventure; for this child's spirit, in bodies of its
ancestors, had for many thousands of years been trained to memorable feats of discovery and conquest—victories in battles whose
critical moments were centuries, whose victors' camps were cities of
hewn stone. From the cradle of its race it had conquered its way
through two continents, and, passing a great sea, had penetrated a
third, there to be born to war and dominance as a heritage.

The child was a boy, aged about six years, the son of a poor
planter. In his younger manhood the father had been a soldier, had
fought against naked savages, and followed the flag of his country
into the capital of a civilised race to the far South. In the peaceful
life of a planter the warrior-fire survived; once kindled it is never
extinguished. The man loved military books and pictures, and the
boy had understood enough to make himself a wooden sword, [41/
42] though even the eye of his father would hardly have known it
for what it was. This weapon he now bore bravely, as became the
son of an heroic race, and, pausing now and again in the sunny
spaces of the forest, assumed, with some exaggeration, the postures
of aggression and defence that he had been taught by the engraver's
art. Made reckless by the ease with which he overcame invisible foes
attempting to stay his advance, he committed the common enough
military error of pushing the pursuit to a dangerous extreme, until
he found himself upon the margin of a wide but shallow brook,
whose rapid waters barred his direct advance against the flying foe
who had crossed with illogical ease. But the intrepid victor was not
to be baffled; the spirit of the race which had passed the great sea
burned unconquerable in that small breast and would not be
denied. Finding a place where some boulders in the bed of the
stream lay but a step or a leap apart, he made his way across and

---

*From Ambrose Bierce, *In the Midst of Life: Tales of Soldiers and Civilians*
(London: Chatto and Windus, 1892) .

fell again upon the rear guard of his imaginary foe, putting all to the sword.

Now that the battle had been won, prudence required that he withdraw to his base of operations. Alas! like many a mightier conqueror, and like one, the mightiest, he could not

> curb the lust for war,
> Nor learn that tempted Fate will leave the loftiest star.

Advancing from the bank of the creek, he suddenly found himself confronted with a new and more formidable enemy; in the path that he was following, [42/43] bolt upright, with ears erect and paws suspended before it, sat a rabbit. With a startled cry the child turned and fled, he knew not in what direction, calling with inarticulate cries for his mother, weeping, stumbling, his tender skin cruelly torn by brambles, his little heart beating hard with terror—breathless, blind with tears—lost in the forest! Then, for more than an hour, he wandered with erring feet through the tangled undergrowth, till at last, overcome with fatigue, he lay down in a narrow space between two rocks, within a few yards of the stream, and, still grasping his toy sword, no longer a weapon but a companion, sobbed himself to sleep. The wood birds sang merrily above his head; the squirrels, whisking their bravery of tail, ran barking from tree to tree, unconscious of the pity of it, and somewhere far away was a strange, muffled thunder, as if the partridges were drumming in celebration of nature's victory over the son of her immemorial enslavers. And back at the little plantation, where white men and black were hastily searching the fields and hedgerows in alarm, a mother's heart was breaking for her missing child.

Hours passed, and then the little sleeper rose to his feet. The chill of the evening was in his limbs, the fear of the gloom in his heart. But he had rested, and he no longer wept. With some blind instinct which impelled to action, he struggled through the undergrowth about him and came to a more open ground—on his right the brook, to the [43/44] left a gentle acclivity studded with infrequent trees; over all the gathering gloom of twilight. A thin ghostly mist rose along the water. It frightened and repelled him; instead of recrossing, in the direction whence he had come, he turned his back upon it and went forward toward the dark inclosing wood. Sud-

denly he saw before him a strange moving object which he took to
be some large animal—a dog, a pig—he could not name it; perhaps
it was a bear. He had seen pictures of bears, but knew of nothing to
their discredit, and had vaguely wished to meet one. But something
in form or movement of this object—something in the awkwardness
of its approach—told him that it was not a bear, and curiosity
was stayed by fear. He stood still, and as it came slowly on, gained
courage every moment, for he saw that at least it had not the
long, menacing ears of the rabbit. Possibly his impressionable mind
was half conscious of something familiar in its shambling, awkward
gait. Before it had approached near enough to resolve his doubts,
he saw that it was followed by another and another. To right and to
left were many more; the whole open space about him was alive
with them—all moving forward toward the brook.

They were men. They crept upon their hands and knees. They
used their hands only, dragging their legs. They used their knees
only, their arms hanging useless at their sides. They strove to rise to
their feet, but fell prone in the attempt. They [44/45] did nothing
naturally, and nothing alike, save only to advance foot by foot in
the same direction. Singly, in pairs, and in little groups, they came
on through the gloom, some halting now and again while others
crept slowly past them, then resuming their movement. They came
by dozens and by hundreds; as far on either hand as one could see
in the deepening gloom they extended, and the black wood behind
them appeared to be inexhaustible. The very ground seemed in
motion toward the creek. Occasionally one who had paused did not
again go on, but lay motionless. He was dead. Some, pausing, made
strange gestures with their hands, erected their arms and lowered
them again, clasped their heads; spread their palms upward, as men
are sometimes seen to do in public prayer.

Not all of this did the child note; it is what would have been
noted by an older observer; he saw little but that these were men,
yet crept like babes. Being men, they were not terrible, though some
of them were unfamiliarly clad. He moved among them freely,
going from one to another and peering into their faces with childish
curiosity. All their faces were singularly white and many were
streaked and gouted with red. Something in this—something too,
perhaps, in their grotesque attitudes and movements—reminded
him of the painted clown whom he had seen last summer in the

circus, and he laughed as he watched them. But on and ever on they crept, these maimed and bleeding men, as heedless as he of [45/46] the dramatic contrast between his laughter and their own ghastly gravity. To him it was a merry spectacle. He had seen his father's negroes creep upon their hands and knees for his amusement—had ridden them so, 'making believe' they were his horses. He now approached one of these crawling figures from behind and with an agile movement mounted it astride. The man sank upon his breast, recovered, flung the small boy fiercely to the ground as an unbroken colt might have done, then turned upon him a face that lacked a lower jaw—from the upper teeth to the throat was a great red gap fringed with hanging shreds of flesh and splinters of bone. The unnatural prominence of nose, the absence of chin, the fierce eyes, gave this man the appearance of a great bird of prey crimsoned in throat and breast by the blood of its quarry. The man rose to his knees, the child to his feet. The man shook his fist at the child; the child, terrified at last, ran to a tree near by, got upon the farther side of it, and took a more serious view of the situation. And so the uncanny multitude dragged itself slowly and painfully along in hideous pantomime—moved forward down the slope like a swarm of great black beetles, with never a sound of going—in silence profound, absolute.

Instead of darkening, the haunted landscape began to brighten. Through the belt of trees beyond the brook shone a strange red light, the trunks and branches of the trees making a black lacework against it. It struck the creeping figures and gave [46/47] them monstrous shadows, which caricatured their movements on the lit grass. It fell upon their faces, touching their whiteness with a ruddy tinge, accentuating the stains with which so many of them were freaked and maculated. It sparkled on buttons and bits of metal in their clothing. Instinctively the child turned toward the growing splendour and moved down the slope with his horrible companions; in a few moments had passed the foremost of the throng—not much of a feat, considering his advantages. He placed himself in the lead, his wooden sword still in hand, and solemnly directed the march, conforming his pace to theirs and occasionally turning as if to see that his forces did not straggle. Surely such a leader never before had such a following.

Scattered about upon the ground now slowly narrowing by the

encroachment of this awful march to water, were certain articles to
which, in the leader's mind, were coupled no significant associations; an occasional blanket, tightly rolled lengthwise, doubled, and
the ends bound together with a string; a heavy knapsack here, and
there a broken musket—such things, in short, as are found in the
rear of retreating troops, the 'spoor' of men flying from their
hunters. Everywhere near the creek, which here had a margin of
lowland, the earth was trodden into mud by the feet of men and
horses. An observer of better experience in the use of his eyes would
have noticed that these footprints pointed in both directions; the
ground had been twice passed [47/48] over—in advance and in
retreat. A few hours before, these desperate, stricken men, with
their more fortunate and now distant comrades, had penetrated the
forest in thousands. Their successive battalions, breaking into
swarms and reforming in lines, had passed the child on every side—
had almost trodden on him as he slept. The rustle and murmur of
their march had not awakened him. Almost within a stone's throw
of where he lay they had fought a battle; but all unheard by him
were the roar of the musketry, the shock of the cannon, 'the thunder
of the captains and the shouting.' He had slept through it all,
grasping his little wooden sword with perhaps a tighter clutch in
unconscious sympathy with his martial environment, but as heedless
of the grandeur of the struggle as the dead who died to make the
glory.

The fire beyond the belt of woods on the farther side of the
creek, reflected to earth from the canopy of its own smoke, was now
suffusing the whole landscape. It transformed the sinuous line of
mist to the vapour of gold. The water gleamed with dashes of red,
and red, too, were many of the stones protruding above the surface.
But that was blood; the less desperately wounded had stained them
in crossing. On them, too, the child now crossed with eager steps; he
was going to the fire. As he stood upon the farther bank, he turned
about to look at the companions of his march. The advance was
arriving at the creek. The stronger had already [48/49] drawn
themselves to the brink and plunged their faces in the flood. Three
or four who lay without motion appeared to have no heads. At this
the child's eyes expanded with wonder; even his hospitable under-
standing could not accept a phenomenon implying such vitality as
that. After slaking their thirst these men had not the strength to
back away from the water, nor to keep their heads above it. They

were drowned. In rear of these the open spaces of the forest showed the leader as many formless figures of his grim command as at first; but not nearly so many were in motion. He waved his cap for their encouragement and smilingly pointed with his weapon in the direction of the guiding light—a pillar of fire to this strange exodus.

Confident of the fidelity of his forces, he now entered the belt of woods, passed through it easily in the red illumination, climbed a fence, ran across a field, turning now and again to coquette with his responsive shadow, and so approached the blazing ruin of a dwelling. Desolation everywhere. In all the wide glare not a living thing was visible. He cared nothing for that; the spectacle pleased, and he danced with glee in imitation of the wavering flames. He ran about collecting fuel, but every object that he found was too heavy for him to cast in from the distance to which the heat limited his approach. In despair he flung in his sword—a surrender to the superior forces of nature. His military career was at an end. [49/50]

Shifting his position, his eyes fell upon some outbuildings which had an oddly familiar appearance, as if he had dreamed of them. He stood considering them with wonder, when suddenly the entire plantation, with its inclosing forest, seemed to turn as if upon a pivot. His little world swung half around; the points of the compass were reversed. He recognised the blazing building as his own home!

For a moment he stood stupefied by the power of the revelation, then ran with stumbling feet, making a half circuit of the ruin. There, conspicuous in the light of the conflagration, lay the dead body of a woman—the white face turned upward, the hands thrown out and clutched full of grass, the clothing deranged, the long dark hair in tangles and full of clotted blood. The greater part of the forehead was torn away, and from the jagged hole the brain protruded, overflowing the temple, a frothy mass of grey, crowned with clusters of crimson bubbles—the work of a shell!

The child moved his little hands, making wild, uncertain gestures. He uttered a series of inarticulate and indescribable cries—something between the chattering of an ape and the gobbling of a turkey—a startling, soulless, unholy sound, the language of a devil. The child was a deaf mute.

Then he stood motionless, with quivering lips, looking down upon the wreck. [50]

JOHN WILLIAM DE FOREST
(1826–1906)

Born in Humphreysville (now Seymour), Connecticut, John William De Forest traveled widely in his early life, and wrote about his experiences in Oriental Acquaintance (1856) and European Acquaintance (1858). After the outbreak of the war, he recruited a company of New Haven volunteers. He and his men fought first in the Southwestern states and later in the Shenandoah valley. The factual account of these experiences is recorded in De Forest's A Volunteer's Adventures, ed. James H. Croushore (1946). His fictional account is Miss Ravenel's Conversion from Secession to Loyalty, finished in 1865, in which Captain Colburne often stands for De Forest.

Writing about Miss Ravenel's Conversion in Literary History of the United States, George F. Whicher calls it "the best of the Civil War novels and one of the most notable achievements in American fiction." He commends De Forest for "lifelike portrayal of scenes of action, firm grasp of character values, and penetrating interpretation of the issues of the time." Edmund Wilson's comment in Patriotic Gore is that "the war scenes in Miss Ravenel's Conversion were the first of their kind in fiction in English, and it would be more than a decade . . . before any other writer of talent who had taken an active part in the war would describe it with equal realism."

[THE SIEGE OF PORT HUDSON]*

It is too early to tell, it is even too early to know, the whole truth concerning the siege of Port Hudson. To an honest man, anxious

*From John W. De Forest, Miss Ravenel's Conversion from Secession to Loyalty (New York: Harper & Brothers, 1867). Rinehart & Co. has a paperback edition of Miss Ravenel's Conversion (1955) with an excellent introduction by Gordon H. Haight.

that the world shall not be humbugged, it is a mournful reflection that perhaps the whole truth never will be known to any one who will dare or care to tell it. We gained a victory there; we took an important step towards the end of the Rebellion; but at what cost, through what means, and by whose merit? It was a capital idea, whosesoever it was, to clean out Taylor's Texans and Louisianians from the Teche country before we undertook the siege of Gardner's Arkansans, Alabamians, and Mississippians at Port Hudson. But for somebody's blunder at that well-named locality, Irish Bend, the plan would have succeeded better than it did, and Taylor would not have been able to reorganize, take Brashear City, threaten New Orleans, and come near driving Banks from his main enterprise. As it was we opened the siege with fair prospects of success, and no disturbing force in the rear. The garrison, lately fifteen or twenty thousand strong, had been reduced to six thousand, in order to reinforce Vicksburg; and Joe Johnston had already directed Gardner to destroy his fortifications and transfer all his [278/279] men to the great scene of contest on the central Mississippi. Banks arrived from Simmsport just in time to prevent the execution of this order. A smart skirmish was fought, in which we lost more men than the enemy, but forced Gardner to retire within his works, and accept the eventualities of an investment.

At five o'clock on the morning of the 27th of May, Colburne was awakened by an order to fall in. Whether it signified an advance on our part, or a sally by the enemy, he did not know nor ask, but with a soldier's indifference proceeded to form his company, and, that done, ate his breakfast of raw pork and hard biscuit. He would have been glad to have Henry boil him a cup of coffee; but that idle freedman was "having a good time," probably sleeping, in some unknown refuge. For two hours the ranks sat on the ground, musket in hand; then Colburne saw the foremost line, a quarter of a mile in front, advance into the forest. One of Weitzel's aids now dashed up to Carter, and immediately his staff-officers galloped away to the different commanders of regiments. An admonishing murmur of "Fall in, men!"—"Attention, men!" from the captains ran along the line of the Tenth, and the soldiers rose in their places to meet the grand, the awful possibility of battle. It was a long row of stern faces, bronzed with sunburn, sallow in many cases with malaria, grave with the serious emotions of the hour, but hardened by the habit of danger, and set as firm as flints toward the enemy. The old innocence of the peaceable New England farmer and mechanic had disappeared from these war-seared visages, and had been succeeded by an expression of hardened combativeness, not a little brutal, much like the look of a lazy bull-dog. Colburne smiled with pleasure and pride as he glanced along the line of his company, and noted this change in its physiognomy. For the purpose for which they were drawn up there they were better men than when he first knew them, and as good men as the sun ever shone upon. [279/280]

At last the Lieutenant-Colonel's voice rang out, "Battalion, forward. Guide right. March!"

To keep the ranks closed and aligned in any tolerable fighting shape while struggling through that mile of tangled forest and broken ground, was a task of terrible difficulty. Plunging through thickets, leaping over fallen trees, a continuous foliage overhead, and the fallen leaves of many seasons under foot, the air full of the damp, mouldering smell of virgin forest, the brigade moved forward with no sound but that of its own tramplings. It is peculiar of the American attack that it is almost always made in line, and always without music. The men expected to meet the enemy at every hillock, but they advanced rapidly, and laughed at each other's slippings and tumbles. Every body was breathless with climbing over obstacles or running around them. The officers were beginning to swear at the broken ranks and unsteady pace. The Lieutenant-Colonel, perceiving that the regiment was diverging from its comrades, and fearing the consequences of a gap in case the enemy should suddenly open fire, rode repeatedly up and down the line, yelling, "Guide right! Close up to the right!" Suddenly, to the amazement of every one, the brigade came upon bivouacs of Union regiments quietly engaged in distributing rations and preparing breakfast.

"What are you doing up here?" asked a Major of Colburne.

"We are going to attack. Don't you take part in it?"

"I suppose so. I don't know. We have received no orders."

Through this scene of tardiness, the result perhaps of one of those blunders which are known in military as well as in all other human operations, Weitzel's division steadily advanced, much wondering if it was to storm Port Hudson alone. The ground soon proved so difficult that the Tenth, unable to move in line of battle,

filed into a faintly marked forest road and pushed forward by the
flank in the ordin- [280/281] ary column of march. The battle had
already commenced, although Colburne could see nothing of it, and
could hear nothing but a dull *pum-pum-pum* of cannon. He passed
rude rifle-pits made of earth and large branches, which had been
carried only a few minutes previous by the confused rush of the
leading brigade. Away to the right, but not near enough to be
heard above the roar of artillery, there was a wild, scattering
musketry of broken lines, fighting and scrambling along as they best
could over thicketed knolls, and through rugged gullies, on the
track of the retiring Alabamians and Arkansans. It was the blindest
and most perplexing forest labyrinth conceivable; it was impossible
to tell whither you were going, or whether you would stumble on
friends or enemies; the regiments were split into little squads from
which all order had disappeared, but which nevertheless advanced.

The Tenth was still marching through the woods by the flank,
unable to see either fortifications or enemy, when it came under the
fire of artillery, and encountered the retiring stream of wounded. At
this moment, and for two hours afterward, the uproar of heavy
guns, bursting shells, falling trees and flying splinters was astonish-
ing, stunning, horrible, doubled as it was by the sonorous echoes of
the forest. Magnolias, oaks and beeches eighteen inches or two feet
in diameter, were cut asunder with a deafening scream of shot and
of splitting fibres, the tops falling after a pause of majestic delibera-
tion, not sidewise, but stem downwards, like a descending para-
chute, and striking the earth with a dull shuddering thunder. They
seemed to give up their life with a roar of animate anguish, as if
they were savage beasts, or as if they were inhabited by Afreets and
Demons.

The unusually horrible clamor and the many-sided nature of
the danger had an evident effect on the soldiers, hardened as they
were to scenes of ordinary battle. Grim faces turned in every direction with hasty stares of alarm, looking aloft and on every side, as
well as to the front, for [281/282] destruction. Pallid stragglers who
had dropped out of the leading brigade drifted by the Tenth,
dodging from trunk to trunk in an instinctive search for cover,
although it was visible that the forest was no protection, but rather
an additional peril. Every regiment has its two or three cowards, or
perhaps its half-dozen, weakly-nerved creatures, whom nothing can

make fight, and who never do fight. One abject hound, a corporal with his disgraced stripes upon his arm, came by with a ghastly backward glare of horror, his face colorless, his eyes projecting, and his chin shaking. Colburne cursed him for a poltroon, struck him with the flat of his sabre, and dragged him into the ranks of his own regiment; but the miserable creature was too thoroughly unmanned by the great horror of death to be moved to any show of resentment or even of courage by the indignity; he only gave an idiotic stare with outstretched neck toward the front, then turned with a nervous jerk, like that of a scared beast, and rushed rearward. Further on, six men were standing in single file behind a large beech, holding each other by the shoulders, when with a stunning crash the entire top of the tree flew off and came down among them butt foremost, sending out a cloud of dust and splinters. Colburne smiled grimly to see the paralyzed terror of their upward stare, and the frantic flight which barely saved them from being crushed jelly. A man who keeps the ranks hates a skulker, and wishes that he may be killed, the same as any other enemy.

"But in truth," says the Captain, in one of his letters, "the sights and sounds of this battle-reaped forest were enough to shake the firmest nerves. Never before had I been so tried as I was during that hour in this wilderness of death. It was not the slaughter which unmanned me, for our regiment did not lose very heavily; it was the stupendous clamor of the cannonade and of the crashing trees which seemed to overwhelm me by its mere physical power; and it made me unable to bear spectacles which I [282/283] had witnessed in other engagements with perfect composure. When one of our men was borne by me with half his foot torn off by a round shot, the splintered bones projecting clean and white from the ragged raw flesh, I grew so sick that perhaps I might have fainted if a brother officer had not given me a sip of whiskey from his canteen. It was the only occasion in my fighting experience when I have had to resort to that support. I had scarcely recovered myself when I saw a broad flow of blood stream down the face of a color-corporal who stood within arm's length of me. I thought he was surely a dead man; but it was only one of the wonderful escapes of battle. The bullet had skirted his cap where the fore-piece joins the cloth, forcing the edge of the leather through the skin, and making a clean cut to the bone from temple to temple. He went to the rear blinded and with a smart headache, but not seriously injured. That we were not slaughtered by the wholesale is wonderful, for we were closed up in a compact mass, and the shot came with stunning rapidity. A shell burst in the centre of my company, tearing one man's heel to the bone, but doing no other damage. The wounded man, a good soldier though as quiet and gentle as a bashful girl, touched his hat to me, showed his bleeding foot, and asked leave to go to the rear, which I of course granted. While he was speaking, another shell burst about six feet from the first, doing no harm at all, although so near to Van Zandt as to dazzle and deafen him."

Presently a section of Bainbridge's regular battery came up, winding slowly through the forest, the guns thumping over roots and fallen limbs, the men sitting superbly erect on their horses, and the color-sergeant holding his battle-flag as proudly as a knight-errant ever bore his pennon. In a minute the two brass Napoleons opened with a sonorous *spang,* which drew a spontaneous cheer from the delighted infantry. The edge of the wood was now reached, and Colburne could see the enemy's position. In [283/ 284] front of him lay a broad and curving valley, irregular in surface, and seamed in some places by rugged gorges, the whole made more difficult of passage by a multitude of felled trees, the leafless trunks and branches of which were tangled into an inextricable *chevaux de frise.* On the other side of this valley rose a bluff or table-land, partially covered with forest, but showing on its cleared spaces the tents and cabins of the Rebel encampments. Along the edge of the bluff, following its sinuosities, and at this distance looking like mere natural banks of yellow earth, ran the fortifications of Port Hudson. Colburne could see Paine's brigade of Weitzel's division descending into the valley, forcing its bloody way through a roaring cannonade and a continuous screech of musketry.

An order came to the commander of the Tenth to deploy two companies as skirmishers in the hollow in front of Bainbridge, and push to the left with the remainder of the regiment, throwing out other skirmishers and silencing the Rebel artillery. One of the two detached companies was Colburne's, and he took command of both as senior officer. At the moment that he filed his men out of the line a murmur ran through the regiment that the Lieutenant-Colonel was killed or badly wounded. Then came an inquiry as to the whereabouts of the Major.

"By Jove! it wouldn't be a dangerous job to hunt for him," chuckled Van Zandt.

"Why? Where is he?" asked Colburne.

"I don't believe, by Jove! that I could say within a mile or two. I only know, by Jove! that he is *non est inventus*. I saw him a quarter of an hour ago charging for the rear with his usual impetuosity. I'll bet my everlasting salvation that he's in the safest spot within ten miles of this d——d unhealthy neighborhood."

The senior captain took command of the regiment, and led it to the left on a line parallel with the fortifications. Colburne descended with his little detachment, numbering about eighty muskets, into that Valley of the Shadow of [284/285] Death, climbing over or creeping under the fallen trunks of the tangled labyrinth, and making straight for the bluff on which thundered and smoked the rebel stronghold. As his men advanced they deployed, spreading outwards like the diverging blades of a fan until they covered a front of nearly a quarter of a mile. Every stump, every prostrate trunk, every knoll and gully was a temporary breastwork, from behind which they poured a slow but fatal fire upon the rebel gunners, who could be plainly seen upon the hostile parapet working their pieces. The officers and sergeants moved up and down the line, each behind his own platoon or section, steadily urging it forward.

"Move on, men. Move on, men," Colburne repeated. "Don't expose yourselves. Use the covers; use the stumps. But keep moving on. Don't take root. Don't stop till we reach the ditch."

In spite of their intelligent prudence the men were falling under the incessant flight of bullets. A loud scream from a thicket a little to Colburne's right attracted his attention.

"Who is that?" he called.

"It is Allen!" replied a sergeant. "He is shot through the body. Shall I send him to the rear?"

"Not now, wait till we are relieved. Prop him up and leave him in the shade."

He had in his mind this passage of the Army Regulations: "Soldiers must not be permitted to leave the ranks to strip or rob the dead, nor even to assist the wounded, unless by express permission, which is only to be given after the action is decided. The highest interest and most pressing duty is to win the victory, by which only can a proper care of the wounded be ensured."

Turning to a soldier who had mounted a log and stood up at the full height of his six feet to survey the fortifications, Colburne shouted, "Jump down, you fool. You will get yourself hit for nothing." [285/286]

"Captain, I can't see a chance for a shot," replied the fellow deliberately.

"Get down!" reiterated Colburne; but the man had waited too long already. Throwing up both hands he fell backward with an incoherent gurgle, pierced through the lungs by a rifle-ball. Then a little Irish soldier burst out swearing, and hastily pulled his trousers to glare at a bullet-hole through the calf of his leg, with a comical expression of mingled surprise, alarm and wrath. And so it went on: every few minutes there was an oath of rage or a shriek of pain; and each outcry marked the loss of a man. But all the while the line of skirmishers advanced.

The sickishness which troubled Colburne in the cannon-smitten forest had gone, and was succeeded by the fierce excitement of close battle, where the combatants grow angry and savage at sight of each other's faces. He was throbbing with elation and confidence, for he had cleaned off the gunners from the two pieces in his front. He felt as if he could take Port Hudson with his detachment alone. The contest was raging in a clamorous rattle of musketry on the right, where Paine's brigade, and four regiments of the Reserve Brigade, all broken into detachments by gullies, hillocks, thickets and fallen trees, were struggling to turn and force the fortifications. On his left other companies of the Tenth were slowly moving forward, deployed and firing as skirmishers. In his front the Rebel musketry gradually slackened, and only now and then could he see a broad-brimmed hat show above the earthworks and hear the hoarse whistle of a Minie-ball as it passed him. The garrison on this side was clearly both few in number and disheartened. It seemed to him likely, yes even certain, that Port Hudson would be carried by storm that morning. At the same time, half mad as he was with the glorious intoxication of successful battle, he knew that it would be utter folly to push his unsupported detachment into the works, and that such a movement would probably end in slaughter or capture.

Fifteen or twenty, [286/287] he did not know precisely how many, of his soldiers had been hit, and the survivors were getting short of cartridges.

"Steady, men!" he shouted. "Halt! Take cover and hold your position. Don't waste your powder. Fire slow and aim sure."

The orders were echoed from man to man along the extended, straggling line, and each one disappeared behind the nearest thicket, stump or fallen tree. Colburne had already sent three corporals to the regiment to recount his success and beg for more men; but neither had the messengers reappeared nor reinforcements arrived to support his proposed assault.

"Those fellows must have got themselves shot," he said to Van Zandt. "I'll go myself. Keep the line where it is, and save the cartridges."

Taking a single soldier with him, he hurried rearward by the clearest course that he could find through the prostrate forest, without minding the few bullets that whizzed by him. Suddenly he halted, powerless, as if struck by paralysis, conscious of a general nervous shock, and a sharp pain in his left arm. His first impulse,— a very hurried impulse,—was to take the arm with his right hand and twist it to see if the bone was broken. Next he looked about him for some shelter from the scorching and crazing sunshine. He espied a green bush, and almost immediately lost sight of it, for the shock made him faint although the pain was but momentary.

"Are you hurt, Captain?" asked the soldier.

"Take me to that bush," said Colburne, pointing—for he knew where the cover was, although he could not see it.

The soldier put an arm round his waist, led him to the bush, and laid him down.

"Shall I go for help, Captain?"

"No. Don't weaken the company. All right. No bones broken. Go on in a minute."

The man tied his handkerchief about the ragged and [287/ 288] bloody hole in the coat-sleeve; then sat down and reloaded his musket, occasionally casting a glance at the pale face of the Captain. In two or three minutes Colburne's color came back, and he felt as well as ever. He rose carefully to his feet, looked about him as if to see where he was, and again set off for the regiment, followed by his silent companion. The bullets still whizzed about them, but did no harm. After a slow walk of ten minutes, during which Colburne once stopped to sling his arm in a handkerchief, he emerged from a winding gully to find himself within a few yards of Bainbridge's battery. Behind the guns was a colonel calmly sitting his horse and watching the battle.

"What is the matter?" asked the Colonel.

"A flesh wound," said Colburne. "Colonel, there is a noble chance ahead of you. Do you see that angle? My men are at the base of it, and some of them in the ditch. They have driven the artillery-men from the guns, and forced the infantry to lie low. For God's sake send in your regiment. We can certainly carry the place."

"The entire brigade that I command is engaged," replied the Colonel. "Don't you see them on the right of your position?"

"Is there no other force about here?" asked Colburne, sitting down as he felt the dizziness coming over him again.

"None that I know of. This is such an infernal country for movements that we are all dislocated. Nobody knows where any-thing is.—But you had better go to the rear, Captain. You look used up."

Colburne was so tired, so weak with the loss of blood, so worn out by the heat of the sun, and the excitement of fighting that he could not help feeling discouraged at the thought of struggling back to the position of his company. He stretched himself under a tree to rest, and in ten minutes was fast asleep. When he awoke—he never knew how long afterwards—he could not at first tell what he remembered from what he had dreamed, and only satisfied himself that he had been hit by looking at his bloody and [288/289] band-aged arm. An artilleryman brought him to his full consciousness by shouting excitedly, "There, by God! they are trying a charge. The infantry are trying a charge."

Colburne rose up, saw a regiment struggling across the valley, and heard its long-drawn charging yell.

"I must go back," he exclaimed. "My men ought to go in and support those fellows." Turning to the soldier who attended him he added, "Run! Tell Van Zandt to forward."

The soldier ran, and Colburne after him. But he had not gone twenty paces before he fell straight forward on his face, without a word, and lay perfectly still.

When Colburne came to himself he was lying on the ground in rear of the pieces. Beside him, in the shadow of the same tuft of withering bushes, lay a wounded lieutenant of the battery and four wounded artillerists. A dozen steps away, rapidly blackening in the scorching sun and sweltering air, were two more artillerists, stark dead, one with his brains bulging from a bullet-hole in his forehead, while a dark claret-colored streak crossed his face, the other's light-blue trousers soaked with a dirty carnation stain of life-blood drawn from the femoral artery. None of the wounded men writhed, or groaned, or pleaded for succor, although a sweat of suffering stood in great drops on their faces. Each had cried out when he was hit, uttering either an oath, or the simple exclamation "Oh!" in a tone of dolorous surprise; one had shrieked spasmodically, physically crazed by the shock administered to some important nervous centre; but all, sooner or later, [289/290] had settled into the calm, sublime patience of the wounded of the battlefield.

The brass Napoleons were still spanging sonorously, and there was a ceaseless spitting of irregular musketry in the distance.

"Didn't the assault succeed?" asked Colburne as soon as he had got his wits about him.

"No sir—it was beat off," said one of the wounded artillerists.
[290]

EMILY DICKINSON
(1830–1886)

Emily Dickinson, the poet-recluse of Amherst, Massachusetts, was most intensely productive during the period from 1861 to 1865. Yet her poetry and letters contain very few references to the war. Thomas W. Ford, "Emily Dickinson and the Civil War," University of Kansas City Review, XXXI (March, 1965), 199–203, finds, out of the hundreds of poems she wrote, only four which were directly inspired by the Civil War. He argues, however, that the war brought Dickinson a heightened awareness of death. Believing even more strongly in its influence on Dickinson, Genevieve Taggard in The Life and Mind of Emily Dickinson *says that "the war, which first broke up years of self-sufficiency, which appalled Emily by its chaos, its accidental and therefore immoral processes, which turned her to poetry and then to that representative of the world she professed to renounce, finally ended by walling Emily back into an even completer isolation."*

from LETTERS TO LOUISE AND FRANCES NORCROSS*

[April, 1862.]

Dear Children,—You have done more for me—'t is least that I can do, to tell you of brave Frazer—'killed at Newbern,' darlings. His big heart shot away by a 'Minie ball.'

I had read of those—I didn't think that Frazer would carry one to Eden with him. Just as he fell, in his soldier's cap, with his sword

*From *Letters of Emily Dickinson*, ed. Mabel Loomis Todd (Boston: Roberts Brothers, 1894), Vol. I. Thomas H. Johnson in his edition of *The Letters of Emily Dickinson* (1958) considers the postscript as part of a second letter possibly written in 1864.

145

at his side, Frazer rode through Amherst. Classmates to the right of him, and classmates to the left of him, to guard his narrow face! He fell by the side of Professor Clark, his superior officer—lived ten minutes in a soldier's arms, asked twice for water—murmured just, 'My God!' and passed! Sanderson, his classmate, made a box of boards in the night, put the brave boy in, covered with a [242/243] blanket, rowed six miles to reach the boat,—so poor Frazer came. They tell that Colonel Clark cried like a little child when he missed his pet, and could hardly resume his post. They loved each other very much. Nobody here could look on Frazer—not even his father. The doctors would not allow it.

The bed on which he came was enclosed in a large casket shut entirely, and covered from head to foot with the sweetest flowers. He went to sleep from the village church. Crowds came to tell him goodnight, choirs sang to him, pastors told how brave he was—early-soldier heart. And the family bowed their heads, as the reeds the wind shakes.

So our part in Frazer is done, but you must come next summer, and we will mind ourselves of this young crusader—too brave that he could fear to die. We will play his tunes—maybe he can hear them; we will try to comfort his broken-hearted Ella, who, as the clergyman said, 'gave him peculiar confidence.' . . . Austin is stunned completely. Let us love better, children, it's most that's left to do.

                    Love from   EMILY.

. . . Sorrow seems more general than it did, and not the estate of a few persons, since the war began; and if the anguish of others helped one with one's own, now would be many medicines. [243]

"THEY DROPPED LIKE FLAKES"*

They dropped like Flakes—
They dropped like Stars—
Like Petals from a Rose—

*Both poems are from *The Complete Poems of Emily Dickinson*, ed. Thomas H. Johnson (Boston and Toronto: Little, Brown & Co., 1960), by permission of Little, Brown and Co. "It feels a shame to be Alive," poem no. 444 in the Johnson

When suddenly across the June
A wind with fingers—goes—

They perished in the Seamless Grass—
No eye could find the place—[194/195]
But God can summon every face
On his Repealless—List.

"IT FEELS A SHAME TO BE ALIVE"

It feels a shame to be Alive—
When Men so brave—are dead—
One envies the Distinguished Dust—
Permitted—such a Head—

The Stone—that tells defending Whom
This Spartan put away
What little of Him we—possessed
In Pawn for Liberty—

The price is great—Sublimely paid—
Do we deserve—a Thing—
That lives—like Dollars—must be piled
Before we may obtain?

Are we that wait—sufficient worth—
That such Enormous Pearl
As life—dissolved be—for Us—
In Battle's—horrid Bowl?

It may be—a Renown to live—
I think the Men who die—
Those unsustained—Saviors—
Present Divinity—[213]

NATHANIEL HAWTHORNE

(1804–1864)

Nathaniel Hawthorne, who from 1850 to 1860 had published four novels treating the ambiguity of good and evil in man, pessimistically saw the Civil War as a manifestation of man's darker impulses. Hawthorne's response to the war is thoroughly discussed by his son, Julian Hawthorne, in Nathaniel Hawthorne and His Wife *(Boston and New York, 1884), Vol. II. There he tells us his father was so depressed by the war that his writing was seriously impaired. He further relates that Hawthorne "did not hope for the preservation of the Union; because, if it came peacefully, it would sooner or later involve the extension of slavery over the Northern States, and if by war, it seemed to him it would be only superficial and temporary. . . . At the same time the prospect of the dissolution of that mighty nation which had embodied the best hopes of mankind was a deep pain to him; it seemed likely to be the death of that old spirit of patriotism which had come down to us from the Revolution."*

from LETTER TO HORATIO BRIDGE*

Concord, May 26, 1861.

The war, strange to say, has had a beneficial effect upon my spirits, which were flagging wofully before it broke out. But it was delightful to share in the heroic sentiment of the time, and to feel that I had a country—a consciousness which seemed to make me young again. One thing, as regards this matter, I regret, and one I am glad of. The regrettable thing is that I am too old to shoulder a musket

*From Horatio Bridge, *Personal Recollections of Nathaniel Hawthorne* (London: James R. Osgood, McIlvaine & Co., 1893).

myself, and the joyful thing is that Julian is too young. He drills constantly with a company of lads, and he means to enlist as soon as he reaches the minimum age, but I trust that we shall either be victorious or vanquished before that time. Meantime (though I approve of the war as much as any man), I don't quite understand what we are fighting for, or what definite result can be expected. If we pummel the South ever so hard, they will love us none the better for it; and even if we subjugate them, our next step should be to cut them adrift. If we are fighting for the annihilation of slavery, to be sure, it may be a wise object, and offers a [188/189] tangible result, and the only one which is consistent with a future reunion between North and South. A continuance of the war would soon make this plain to us, and we should see the expediency of preparing our black brethren for future citizenship by allowing them to fight for their own liberties and educating them through heroic influences.

Whatever happens next, I must say that I rejoice that the old Union is smashed. We never were one people, and never really had a country since the Constitution was formed. [189]

from **LETTER TO FRANCIS BENNOCH***

[August (?), 1861]

. . . At present I have little heart for anything. We are, as you know, at the beginning of a great war—a war the issue of which no man can predicate, and I for one have no inclination to attempt prophesy. It is not long since the acute ruler of France—the epigrammatic speech-maker—announced to a startled Europe and a delighted country that he had gone to war for an idea,—a very nice, if not an absolutely true idea. But we Yankees have cast him entirely into the shade. We also have gone to war, and we seem to have little, or at least a very misty idea of what we are fighting for. It depends upon the speaker, and that again depends upon the section of the country in which his sympathies are enlisted. The

*From Moncure Daniel Conway, *Emerson at Home and Abroad* (Boston: James R. Osgood and Company, 1882). Bennoch was an English friend with whom Hawthorne became acquainted while serving as American consul at Liverpool.

Southern man will say: We fight for State rights, liberty, and independence. The Middle Western man will avow that he fights for the Union; whilst our Northern and Eastern man will swear that from the beginning his only idea was liberty to the Blacks and the annihilation of slavery. All are thoroughly in earnest, and all pray for the blessing of Heaven to rest upon the enterprise. The appeals are so numerous, fervent, and yet so contradictory, that the Great Arbiter to whom they so piously and solemnly appeal must be sorely puzzled how to decide. One thing is indisputable,—the spirit of our young men is thor- [273/274] oughly aroused. Their enthusiasm is boundless, and the smiles of our fragile and delicate women cheer them on. When I hear their drums beating, and see their banners flying, and witness their steady marching, I declare were it not for certain silvery monitors hanging by my temples suggesting prudence, I feel as if I could catch the infection, shoulder a musket, and be off to the way myself!

Meditating on these matters, I begin to think our custom as to war is a mistake. Why draw from our young men, in the bloom and heyday of their youth, the soldiers who are to fight our battles? Had I my way, no man should go to war under fifty years of age, such men having already had their natural share of worldly pleasures, and life's enjoyments. And I don't see how they could make a more creditable or more honourable exit from the world's stage than by becoming food for powder and gloriously dying in defence of their home and country. Then I would add a premium in favour of recruits of three-score years and upwards, as, virtually with one foot in the grave, they would not be likely to run away. I apprehend that no people ever built up the skeleton of a warlike history so rapidly as we are doing. What a fine theme for the poet! If you were not born a Britisher, from whose country we expect no help and little sympathy, I would ask you for a martial strain—a song to be sung by our campfires to soothe the feelings and rouse the energies of our troops, inspiring them to meet like men the great conflict that awaits them, resolved to conquer or to die—if dying, still to conquer. Ten thousand poetasters have tried, and tried in vain, to give us a rousing [274/275]

'Scots wha hae wi' Wallace bled.'

If we fight no better than we sing, may the Lord have mercy upon us, and upon the nation!

from CHIEFLY ABOUT WAR-MATTERS*

There is no remoteness of life and thought, no hermetically sealed seclusion, except, possibly, that of the grave, into which the disturbing influences of this war do not penetrate. Of course, the general heart-quake of the country long ago knocked at my cottage-door, and compelled me, reluctantly, to suspend the contemplation of certain fantasies, to which, according to my harmless custom, I was endeavoring to give a sufficiently life-like aspect to admit of their figuring in a romance. As I make no pretensions to state-craft or soldiership, and could promote the common weal neither by valor nor counsel, it seemed, at first, a pity that I should be debarred from such unsubstantial business as I had contrived for myself, since nothing more genuine was to be substituted for it. But I magnanimously considered that there is a kind of treason in insulating one's self from the universal fear and sorrow, and thinking one's idle thoughts in the dread time of civil war; and could a man be so cold and hard-hearted, he would better deserve to be sent to Fort Warren than many who have found their way thither on the score of violent, but misdirected sympathies. I remembered the touching rebuke administered by King Charles to that rural squire the echo of whose hunting-horn came to the poor monarch's ear on the morning before a battle, where the sovereignty and constitution of England were to be set at stake. So I gave myself up to reading newspapers and listening to the click of the telegraph, like other people; until, after a great many months of such pastime, it grew so abominably irksome that I determined to look a little more closely at matters with my own eyes.

Accordingly we set out—a friend and myself—towards Washington, while it was still the long, dreary January of our Northern year, though March in name: nor were we unwilling to clip a little margin off the five months' winter, during which there is nothing genial in New England save the fireside. . . . [43/45] . . .

*From [Nathaniel Hawthorne], "Chiefly About War-Matters," *Atlantic Monthly*, X (July, 1862) , 43–61. The article was signed "By a Peaceable Man." James T. Fields, editor of the *Atlantic*, excised certain sections he considered too skeptical or cool in tone—notably Hawthorne's evaluation of Lincoln. Hawthorne then wrote ironic footnotes for the published version of the article, under the pretense that they were from the editor.

We were not in time to see Washington as a camp. On the very day of our arrival sixty thousand men had crossed the Potomac on their march towards Manassas; and almost with their first step into the Virginia mud, the phantasmagory of a countless host and impregnable ramparts, before which they had so long remained quiescent, dissolved quite away. It was as if General McClellan had thrust his word into a gigantic enemy, and, beholding him suddenly collapse, had discovered to himself and the world that he had merely punctured an enormously swollen bladder. There are instances of a similar character in old romances, where great armies are long kept at bay by the arts of necromancers, who build airy towers and battlements, and muster warriors of terrible aspect, and thus feign a defence of seeming impregnability, until some bolder champion of the besiegers dashes forward to try an encounter with the foremost foeman, and finds him melt away in the death-grapple. With such heroic adventures let the march upon Manassas be hereafter reckoned. The whole business, though connected with the destinies of a nation, takes inevitably a tinge of the ludicrous. The vast preparation of men and warlike material,—the majestic patience and docility with which the people waited through those weary and dreary months,—the martial skill, courage, and caution, with which our movement was ultimately made,—and, at last, the tremendous shock with which we were brought suddenly up against nothing at all! The Southerners show little sense of humor nowadays, but I think they must have meant to provoke a laugh at our expense, when they planted those Quaker guns. At all events, no other Rebel artillery has played upon us with such overwhelming effect. [45/48] . . .

Among other excursions to camps and places of interest in the neighborhood of Washington, we went, one day, to Alexandria. It is a little port on the Potomac, with one or two shabby wharves and docks, resembling those of a fishing-village in New England, and the respectable old brick town rising gently behind. In peaceful times it no doubt bore an aspect of decorous quietude and dulness; but it was now thronged with the Northern soldiery, whose stir and bustle contrasted strikingly with the many closed warehouses, the absence of citizens from their customary haunts, and the lack of any symptom of healthy activity, while army-wagons trundled heavily over the pavements, and sentinels paced the sidewalks, and mounted dragoons dashed to and fro on military errands. I tried to imagine how very disagreeable the presence of a Southern army would be in a sober town of Massachusetts; and the thought considerably lessened my wonder at the cold and shy regards that are cast upon our troops, the gloom, the sullen demeanor, the declared or scarcely hidden sympathy with rebellion, which are so frequent here. It is a strange thing in human life, that the greatest errors both of men and women often spring from their sweetest and most generous qualities; and so, undoubtedly, thousands of warm-hearted, sympathetic, and impulsive persons have joined the Rebels, not from any real zeal for the cause, but because, between two conflicting loyalties, they chose that which necessarily lay nearest the heart. There never existed any other Government against which treason was so easy, and could defend itself by such plausible arguments as against that of the United States. The anomaly of two allegiances (of which that of the State comes nearest home to a man's feelings, and includes the altar and the hearth, while the General Government claims his devotion only to an airy mode of law, and has no symbol but a flag) is exceedingly mischievous in this point of view; for it has converted crowds of honest people into traitors, who seem to themselves not merely innocent, but patriotic, and who die for a bad cause with as quiet a conscience as if it were the best. In the vast extent of our country,—too vast by far to be taken into one small human heart,—we inevitably limit to our own State, or, at farthest, to our own section, that sentiment of physical love for the soil which renders an Englishman, for example, so intensely sensitive to the dignity and well-being of his little island, that one hostile foot, treading anywhere upon it, would make a bruise on each individual breast. If a man loves his own State, therefore, and is content to be ruined with her, let us shoot him, if we can, but [48/49] allow him an honorable burial in the soil he fights for.* [49/50] . . .

There is an historical circumstance, known to few, that connects the children of the Puritans with these Africans of Virginia, in a very singular way. They are our brethren, as being lineal descendants from the Mayflower, the fated womb of which, in her first

*We do not thoroughly comprehend the author's drift in the foregoing paragraph, but are inclined to think its tone reprehensible, and its tendency impolitic in the present stage of our national difficulties.

voyage, sent forth a brood of Pilgrims upon Plymouth Rock, and, in a subsequent one, spawned slaves upon the Southern soil,—a monstrous birth, but with which we have an instinctive sense of kindred, and so are stirred by an irresistible impulse to attempt their rescue, even at the cost of blood and ruin. The character of our sacred ship, I fear, may suffer a little by this revelation; but we must let her white progeny offset her dark one,—and two such portents never sprang from an identical source before.

While we drove onward, a young officer on horseback looked earnestly into the carriage, and recognized some faces that he had seen before; so he rode along by our side, and we pestered him with queries and observations, to which he responded more civilly than they deserved. He was on General McClellan's staff, and a gallant cavalier, high-booted, with a revolver in his belt, and mounted on a noble horse, which trotted hard and high [50/51] without disturbing the rider in his accustomed seat. His face had a healthy hue of exposure and an expression of careless hardihood; and, as I looked at him, it seemed to me that the war had brought good fortune to the youth of this epoch, if to none beside; since they now make it their daily business to ride a horse and handle a sword, instead of lounging listlessly through the duties, occupations, pleasures—all tedious alike—to which the artificial state of society limits a peaceful generation. The atmosphere of the camp and the smoke of the battle-field are morally invigorating; the hardy virtues flourish in them, the nonsense dies like a wilted weed. The enervating effects of centuries of civilization vanish at once, and leave these young men to enjoy a life of hardship, and the exhilarating sense of danger,— to kill men blamelessly, or to be killed gloriously,—and to be happy in following out their native instincts of destruction, precisely in the spirit of Homer's heroes, only with some considerable change of mode. One touch of Nature makes not only the whole world, but all time, akin. Set men face to face, with weapons in their hands, and they are as ready to slaughter one another now, after playing at peace and good-will for so many years, as in the rudest ages, that never heard of peace-societies, and thought no wine so delicious as what they quaffed from an enemy's skull. Indeed, if the report of a Congressional committee may be trusted, that old-fashioned kind of goblet has again come into use, at the expense of our Northern headpieces,—a costly drinking-cup to him that furnishes it! Heaven

forgive me for seeming to jest upon such a subject!—only, it is so
odd, when we measure our advances from barbarism, and find
ourselves just here!* [51/55] . . .

Looking round at these poor [Confederate] prisoners [at
Harper's Ferry], it struck me as an immense absurdity that they
should fancy us their enemies; since, whether we intend it so [55/56]
or no, they have a far greater stake on our success than we can
possibly have. For ourselves, the balance of advantages between
defeat and triumph may admit of question. For them, all truly
valuable things are dependent on our complete success; for thence
would come the regeneration of a people,—the removal of a foul
scurf that has overgrown their life, and keeps them in a state of
disease and decrepitude, one of the chief symptoms of which is, that,
the more they suffer and are debased, the more they imagine
themselves strong and beautiful. No human effort, on a grand scale,
has ever yet resulted according to the purpose of its projectors. The
advantages are always incidental. Man's accidents are God's purposes. We miss the good we sought, and do the good we little cared
for.** [56/60] . . .

The question often occurred to me,— [60/61] and, to say the
truth, it added an indefinable piquancy to the scene,—what proportion of all these people [in Washington, D.C.], whether soldiers or
civilians, were true at heart to the Union, and what part were
tainted, more or less, with treasonable sympathies and wishes, even
if such had never blossomed into purpose. Traitors there were
among them,—no doubt of that,—civil servants of the public, very
reputable persons, who yet deserved to dangle from a cord; or men
who buttoned military coats over their breasts, hiding perilous
secrets there, which might bring the gallant officer to stand pale-
faced before a file of musketeers, with his open grave behind him.
But, without insisting upon such picturesque criminality and pun-

---

*We hardly expected this outbreak in favor of war from the Peaceable Man:
but the justice of our cause makes us all soldiers at heart, however quiet in our
outward life. We have heard of twenty Quakers in a single company of a Pennsylvania regiment.

**The author seems to imagine that he has compressed a great deal of mean-
ing into these little, hard, dry pellets of aphoristic wisdom. We disagree with him.
The counsels of wise and good men are often coincident with the purposes of
Providence; and the present war promises to illustrate our remark.

ishment as this, an observer, who kept both his eyes and heart open, would find it by no means difficult to discern that many residents and visitors of Washington so far sided with the South as to desire nothing more nor better than to see everything reëstablished on a little worse than its former basis. If the cabinet of Richmond were transferred to the Federal city, and the North awfully snubbed, at least, and driven back within its old political limits, they would deem it a happy day. It is no wonder, and, if we look at the matter generously, no unpardonable crime. Very excellent people hereabouts remember the many dynasties in which the Southern character has been predominant, and contrast the genial courtesy, the warm and graceful freedom of that region, with what they call (though I utterly disagree with them) the frigidity of our Northern manners, and the Western plainness of the President. They have a conscientious, though mistaken belief, that the South was driven out of the Union by intolerable wrong on our part, and that we are responsible for having compelled true patriots to love only half their country instead of the whole, and brave soldiers to draw their swords against the Constitution which they would once have died for,—to draw them, too, with a bitterness of animosity which is the only symptom of brotherhood (since brothers hate each other best) that any longer exists. They whisper these things with tears in their eyes, and shake their heads, and stoop their poor old shoulders, at the tidings of another and another Northern victory, which, in their opinion, puts farther off the remote, the already impossible chance of a reunion.

I am sorry for them, though it is by no means a sorrow without hope. Since the matter has gone so far, there seems to be no way but to go on winning victories, and establishing peace and a truer union in another generation, at the expense, probably, of greater trouble, in the present one, than any other people ever voluntarily suffered. We woo the South "as the Lion wooes his bride"; it is a rough courtship, but perhaps love and a quiet household may come of it at last. Or, if we stop short of that blessed consummation, heaven was heaven still, as Milton sings, after Lucifer and a third part of the angels had seceded from its golden palaces,—and perhaps all the more heavenly, because so many gloomy brows, and soured, vindictive hearts, had gone to plot ineffectual schemes of mischief elsewhere.* [61]

*We regret the innuendo in the concluding sentence. The war can never be allowed to terminate, except in the complete triumph of Northern principles. We hold the event in our own hands, and may choose whether to terminate it by the methods already so successfully used, or by other means equally within our control, and calculated to be still more speedily efficacious. In truth, the work is already done.

We should be sorry to cast a doubt on the Peaceable Man's loyalty, but he will allow us to say that we consider him premature in his kindly feelings towards traitors and sympathizers with treason. As the author himself says of John Brown, (and, so applied, we thought it an atrociously cold-blooded *dictum*,) "any common-sensible man would feel an intellectual satisfaction in seeing them hanged, were it only for their preposterous miscalculation of possibilities." There are some degrees of absurdity that put Reason herself into a rage, and affect us like an intolerable crime,—which this Rebellion is, into the bargain.

HENRY JAMES
(1843–1916)

Although he was eighteen when Sumter was fired on, Henry James did not participate in the war as did his brothers Wilkinson and Robertson. This was because of a back injury he received while helping fight a fire in Newport and more importantly because, as Leon Edel puts it, "temperamentally unsuited for soldiering, unable to endure violence, he had long ago substituted acute and close observation of life for active participation in it." Thus there is a kind of ambivalence in Notes of a Son and Brother *(1914), James's main account of these years, when he looks back with some regret that he missed experiencing firsthand the most important event of the century.*

The most complete account of James's life during the war years is Edel's Henry James: 1843–1870, The Untried Years *(1953). In subsequent volumes Edel traces James's rise to success as a novelist and short-story writer in the years following the war. A few of James's best-known works are* The American *(1877),* The Portrait of a Lady *(1881),* The Wings of the Dove *(1902),* The Ambassadors *(1903), and* The Golden Bowl *(1904).*

[THE INTENSIFIED TIME]*

[It was] impossible moreover not in some degree to yield on the spot to *any* brush of the huge procession of those particular months

*The following selections are reprinted with the permission of Charles Scribner's Sons from pages 243–46, 304–5, 308–9, 310–12, 313–15, 378–80 of NOTES OF A SON AND BROTHER by Henry James. Copyright 1914 Charles Scribner's Sons; renewal copyright 1942 Henry James.

and years [of the war], even though I shall presently take occasion
to speak as I may of my own so inevitably contracted consciousness
of what the brush, with its tremendous possibilities of violence,
could consist of in the given case. I had, under stress, to content
myself with knowing it in a more indirect and muffled fashion than
might easily have been—even should one speak of it but as a matter
of mere vision of the eyes or quickened wonder of the mind or
heaviness of the heart, as a matter in fine of the closer and more
inquiring, to say nothing of the more agitated, approach. All of
which, none the less, was not to prevent the whole quite indescribably intensified time—intensified through all lapses of occasion and
frustrations of contact—from remaining with me as a more constituted and sustained act of living, in proportion to my powers and
opportunities, than any other homogeneous stretch of experience
that my memory now recovers. The case had to be in a peculiar
degree, alas, that of living inwardly—like so many of my other
cases; in a peculiar degree compared, that is, to the immense and
prolonged outwardness, outwardness naturally at the very [243/
244] highest pitch, that was the general sign of the situation. To
which I may add that my "alas" just uttered is in the key altogether
of my then current consciousness, and not in the least in that of my
present appreciation of the same—so that I leave it, even while I
thus put my mark against it, as I should restore tenderly to the shelf
any odd rococo object that might have slipped from a reliquary. My
appreciation of what I presume at the risk of any apparent fatuity
to call my "relation to" the War is at present a thing exquisite to
me, a thing of the last refinement of romance, whereas it had to be
at the time a sore and troubled, a mixed and oppressive thing—
though I promptly see, on reflection, how it must frequently have
flushed with emotions, with small scraps of direct perception even,
with particular sharpnesses in the generalised pang of participation,
that were all but touched in themselves as with the full experience.
Clear as some object presented in high relief against the evening sky
of the west, at all events, is the presence for me beside the stretcher
on which my young brother was to lie for so many days before he
could be moved, and on which he had lain during his boat-journey
from the South to New York and thence again to Newport, of lost
Cabot Russell's stricken father, who, failing, up and down the
searched field, in respect of his own [244/245] irrecoverable boy—

then dying, or dead, as afterwards appeared, well within the enemy's works—had with an admirable charity brought Wilky back to a waiting home instead, and merged the parental ache in the next nearest devotion he could find. Vivid to me still is one's almost ashamed sense of this at the hurried disordered time, and of how it was impossible not to impute to his grave steady gentleness and judgment a full awareness of the difference it would have made for him, all the same, to be doing such things with a still more intimate pity. Unobliterated for me, in spite of vaguenesses, this quasi-twilight vision of the good bereft man, bereft, if I rightly recall, of his only son, as he sat erect and dry-eyed at the guarded feast of *our* relief; and so much doubtless partly because of the image that hovers to me across the years of Cabot Russell himself, my brother's so close comrade—dark-eyed, youthfully brown, heartily bright, actively handsome, and with the arrested expression, the indefinable shining stigma, worn, to the regard that travels back to them, by those of the young figures of the fallen that memory and fancy, wanting, never ceasing to want, to "do" something for them, set as upright and clear-faced as may be, each in his sacred niche. They have each to such a degree, so ranged, the strange property or privilege—one scarce knows [245/246] what to call it—of exquisitely, for all *our* time, facing us out, quite blandly ignoring us, looking through us or straight over us at something they partake of together but that we mayn't pretend to know. We walk thus, I think, rather ruefully before them—those of us at least who didn't at the time share more happily their risk. . . . [246]

[PORTSMOUTH GROVE]

. . . The War had by itself of course, on the ground I speak of, communicated something of the quality, or rather of the quantity, otherwise deficient; only this was for my case, of which alone I speak, an apprehension without a language [304/305] or a channel—a revelation as sublime as one would like to feel it, but spreading abroad as a whole and not, alas, by any practice of mine, reducible to parts. What I promptly made out at Cambridge was that "America" would be given, as I have called it, to a tune altogether fresh, so that to hear this tune wholly played out might well become on the spot an inspiring privilege. . . . [305/308]

. . . My poor stream would have trickled, truly, had it been able to trickle at all, from the [308/309] most effective of my few occasions of "realising," up to that time, as to field and camp; literally as to camp in fact, since the occasion had consisted of a visit paid, or a pilgrimage, rather, ever so piously, so tenderly made, one August afternoon of the summer just ended, to a vast gathering of invalid and convalescent troops, under canvas and in roughly improvised shanties, at some point of the Rhode Island shore that figures to my memory, though with a certain vagueness, as Portsmouth Grove. . . . [309/310]

. . . Discriminations of the prosaic order had little to do with my first and all but sole vision of the American soldier in his multitude, and above all—for that was markedly the colour of the whole thing—in his depression, his wasted melancholy almost; an effect that somehow corresponds for memory, I bethink myself, with [310/311] the tender elegiac tone in which Walt Whitman was later on so admirably to commemorate him. The restrictions I confess to are abject, but both my sense and my aftersense of the exhibition I here allude to had, thanks to my situation, to do all the work they could in the way of representation to me of what was most publicly, most heroically, most wastefully, tragically, terribly going on. It had so to serve for my particular nearest approach to a "contact" with the active drama—I mean of course the collectively and scenically active, since the brush of interest against the soldier single and salient was an affair of every day—that were it not for just one other strange spasm of awareness, scarce relaxed to this hour, I should have been left all but pitifully void of any scrap of a substitute for the concrete experience. The long hot July 1st of '63, on which the huge battle of Gettysburg had begun, could really be—or rather couldn't possibly not be—a scrap of concrete experience for any group of united persons, New York cousins and all, who, in a Newport garden, restlessly strolling, sitting, neither daring quite to move nor quite to rest, quite to go in nor quite to stay out, actually *listened* together, in their almost ignobly safe stillness, as to the boom of far-away guns. This *was*, as it were, the War—the War palpably in Pennsylvania; not less than my [311/312] hour of a felt rage of repining at my doomed absence from the sight of that march of the 54th Massachusetts out of Boston, "Bob" Shaw at its head and our exalted Wilky among its officers, of which a great sculptor was, on the spot of their vividest passing, to set the image aloft forever. . . . [312/313] We recognise such occasions more and more as we go on, and are surely, as a general thing, glad when, for the interest of memory—which it's such a business to *keep* interesting—they constitute something of a cluster. In my queer cluster, at any rate, that flower of the connection which answers to the name of Portsmouth Grove still overtops other members of its class, so that to finger it again for a moment is to make it perceptibly exhale its very principle of life. This was, for me, at the time, neither more nor less than that the American soldier in his multitude was the most attaching and affecting and withal the most amusing figure of romance conceivable; the great sense of my vision being thus that, as the afternoon light of the place and time lingered upon him, both to the seeming enhancement of his quality and of its own, romance of a more confused kind than I shall now attempt words for attended his every movement. It was the charmingest, touchingest, dreadfullest thing in the world that my impression of him should have to be somehow of his abandonment to a rueful humour, to a stoic reserve which [313/314] could yet melt, a relation with him once established, into a rich communicative confidence; and, in particular, all over the place, of his own scanted and more or less baffled, though constantly and, as I couldn't not have it, pathetically, "knowing" devices.

The great point remained for me at all events that I could afterwards appear to myself to have done nothing but establish with him a relation, that I established it, to my imagination, in several cases—and all in the three or four hours—even to the pitch of the last tenderness of friendship. I recover that, strolling about with honest and so superior fellow-citizens, or sitting with them by the improvised couches of their languid rest, I drew from each his troubled tale, listened to his plaint on his special hard case—taking form, this, in what seemed to me the very poetry of the esoteric vernacular—and sealed the beautiful tie, the responsive sympathy, by an earnest offer, in no instance waved away, of such pecuniary solace as I might at brief notice draw on my poor pocket for. Yet again, as I indulge this memory, do I feel that I might if pushed a little rejoice in having to such an extent coincided with, not to say perhaps positively anticipated, dear old Walt—even if I hadn't come armed like him with oranges and peppermints. I ministered much more summarily, though pos-[314/315] sibly in proportion to the time and thanks to my better luck more pecuniarily; but I like to treat myself to making out that I can scarce have brought to the occasion (in proportion to the time again and to other elements of the case) less of the consecrating sentiment than he. I like further to put it in a light that, ever so curiously, if the good Walt was most inwardly stirred to his later commemorative accents by his partici- pating in the common Americanism of his hospital friends, the familiar note and shared sound of which formed its ground of appeal, I found myself victim to a like moving force through quite another logic. It was literally, I fear, because our common Ameri- canism carried with it, to my imagination, such a disclosed freshness and strangeness, working, as I might say, over such gulfs of dissocia- tion, that I reached across to *their,* these hospital friends', side of the matter, even at the risk of an imperilled consistency. It had for me, the state in question, colour and form, accent and quality, with scarce less "authority" than if instead of the rough tracks or worn paths of my casual labyrinth I had trod the glazed halls of some school of natural history. . . . [315]

[MY MISSED OPPORTUNITY OF VISION]

. . . Faded and touching pages, these letters [from Wilky and Bob] are in some abundance before me now, breathing confidence and extraordinary cheer—though surviving principally but in Wilky's admirable [378/379] hand, of all those I knew at the time the most humiliating to a feebler yet elder fist; and with their liveliest present action to recompose for me not by any means so much the scenes and circumstances, the passages of history con- cerned, as to make me know again and reinhabit the places, the hours, the stilled or stirred conditions through which I took them in. The conditions seem indeed mostly to have settled for me into the single sense of what I missed, compared to what the authors of our bulletins gained, in wondrous opportunity of vision, that is *appreciation of the thing seen*—there being clearly such a lot of this, and all of it, by my conviction, portentous and prodigious. The key to which assurance was that I longed to live by my eyes, in the midst of such far-spreading chances, in greater measure than I then had help to, and that the measure in which *they* had it gloriously overflowed. This capacity in them to deal with such an affluence of life stood out from every line, and images sprung up about them at every turn of the story. The story, the general one, of the great surge of action on which they were so early carried, was to take still other turns during the years I now speak of, some of these not of the happiest; but with the same relation to it on my part too depressingly prolonged—that of seeing, sharing, envying, applauding, [379/ 380] pitying, all from too far-off, and with the queer sense that, whether or no they would prove to have had the time of their lives, it seemed that the only time I should have had would stand or fall by theirs. . . .

HENRY WADSWORTH LONGFELLOW

(1807–1882)

The year 1861 brought two traumatic events for Longfellow, America's unofficial poet laureate at the time. The first was the dissolution of the Union and the outbreak of war. The second was the death of his wife by fire. He refers to both as "the tumult of the time disconsolate" in a sonnet he wrote while translating Dante's Divine Comedy—*a labor which helped assuage his grief over his wife's death. At the same time, like other Northern literati, he followed the war closely. Moreover, his son Charles was in the Army of the Potomac—which made the war an even more personal matter for Longfellow.*

"The Cumberland" is a poem referring to the attack of the Confederate ironclad Virginia *upon the Federal wooden ships at Hampton Roads in March, 1862. In the one-sided battle, the* Cumberland *and the* Congress *were destroyed.*

[JOURNAL AND LETTERS, 1861–65]*

[Feb. 15, 1861] The dissolution of the Union goes slowly on. Behind it all I hear the low murmur of the slaves, like the chorus in a Greek tragedy, prophesying Woe, woe! [361]

[Apr. 30, 1861] When the times have such a gunpowder flavor, all literature loses its taste. Newspapers are the only reading. They are at once the record and the romance of the day. . . . [365]

[May 2, 1861] The civil war grumbles and growls and gathers; but the storm-clouds do not yet break. Sumner comes out to tea. He

*From *Life of Henry Wadsworth Longfellow; with Extracts from His Journals and Correspondence*, ed. Samuel Longfellow (Boston: Ticknor and Company, 1886), Vol. II.

seems rather depressed. It is indeed a heavy atmosphere to breathe, —the impending doom of a nation! [365]

[May 14, 1861] If South Carolina had not been so self-conceited and precipitate, this war might have been avoided. But the North could not stand the firing on the flag at Sumter. [366]

[May 8, 1862. From letter to Fanny Farrar.] Of the civil war I say only this. It is not a revolution, but a Catalinian conspiracy. It is Slavery against Freedom; the north wind against the southern pestilence. I saw lately, at a jeweller's, a slave's collar of iron, with an iron tongue as large as a spoon, to go into the mouth. Every drop of blood in me quivered! The world forgets what Slavery really is! [382]

[Sept. 1, 1862] Yesterday we had report of a great battle at Manassas, ending in defeat of the Rebels. The moon set red and lowering; and I thought in the night of the pale, upturned faces of young men on the battlefield, and the agonies of the wounded; and my wretchedness was very great. Every shell from the cannon's mouth bursts not only on the battle-field, but in faraway homes, North or South, carrying dismay and death. What an infernal thing war is! Woe to him by whom it cometh! . . . [387]

[Jan. 1, 1863] A great day. The President's Proclamation for Emancipation of Slaves in the rebel States, goes into effect. A beautiful day, full of sunshine, ending in a tranquil moonlight night. May it be symbolical of the Emancipation. There was a grand meeting in Boston, at which Emerson recited a poem. I was not there. [390]

[May 28, 1863] In town saw the first regiment of blacks march through Beacon Street. An imposing sight, with something wild and strange about it, like a dream. At last the North consents to let the negro fight for freedom. [393]

[Nov. 10, 1864] Lincoln re-elected beyond a doubt. We breathe freer. The country will be saved. [417]

[Feb. 10, 1865. From letter to Charles Sumner.] The grand event of the century—the Anti-Slavery Enactment—has been as silent as the daybreak, or the coming of a new year. And yet this year will always be the Year of Jubilee in our history. [421]

[Apr. 7, 1865] In the afternoon comes news that Lee has surrendered. So ends the Rebellion of the slave-owners! [424]

THE CUMBERLAND*

At anchor in Hampton Roads we lay,
    On board of the Cumberland sloop-of-war;
And at times from the fortress across the bay
        The alarum of drums swept past,
        Or a bugle-blast
    From the camp on the shore.

Then far away to the South uprose
    A little feather of snow-white smoke,
And we knew that the iron ship of our foes
        Was steadily steering its course   10
        To try the force
    Of our ribs of oak.

Down upon us heavily runs,
    Silent and sullen, the floating fort;
Then comes a puff of smoke from her guns,
        And leaps the terrible death,
        With fiery breath,
    From each open port.

We are not idle, but send her straight
    Defiance back in a full broadside!   20
As hail rebounds from a roof of slate,
        Rebounds our heavier hail
        From each iron scale
    Of the monster's side. [669/670]

"Strike your flag!" the rebel cries,
    In his arrogant old plantation strain.
"Never!" our gallant Morris replies;
        "It is better to sink than to yield!"
        And the whole air pealed
    With the cheers of our men.   30

*Henry Wadsworth Longfellow, "The Cumberland," *Atlantic Monthly*, X
(Dec., 1862) , 669–670.

Then, like a kraken huge and black,
  She crushed our ribs in her iron grasp!
Down went the Cumberland all a wrack,
    With a sudden shudder of death,
    And the cannon's breath
  For her dying gasp.

Next morn, as the sun rose over the bay,
  Still floated our flag at the mainmast-head.
Lord, how beautiful was thy day!
    Every waft of the air   40
  Was a whisper of prayer,
  Or a dirge for the dead.

Ho! brave hearts that went down in the seas!
  Ye are at peace in the troubled stream.
Ho! brave land! with hearts like these,
    Thy flag, that is rent in twain,
    Shall be one again,
  And without a seam! [670]

KILLED AT THE FORD*

He is dead, the beautiful youth,
The heart of honor, the tongue of truth,
He, the life and light of us all,
Whose voice was blithe as a bugle-call,
Whom all eyes followed with one consent,
The cheer of whose laugh, and whose pleasant word,
Hushed all murmurs of discontent.

Only last night, as we rode along,
Down the dark of the mountain gap,
To visit picket-guard at the ford,   10

---

*Henry Wadsworth Longfellow, "Killed at the Ford," *Atlantic Monthly*,
XVII (Apr., 1866) , 479. The poem was written January 14, 1866.

Little dreaming of any mishap,
He was humming the words of some old song:
"Two red roses he had on his cap
And another he bore at the point of his sword."

Sudden and swift a whistling ball
Came out of a wood, and the voice was still;
Something I heard in the darkness fall,
And for a moment my blood grew chill;
I spake in a whisper, as he who speaks
In a room where some one is lying dead;   20
But he made no answer to what I said.

We lifted him up to his saddle again,
And through the mire and the mist and the rain
Carried him back to the silent camp,
And laid him as if asleep on his bed;
And I saw by the light of the surgeon's lamp
Two white roses up his cheeks,
And one, just over his heart, blood-red!

And I saw in a vision how far and fleet
That fatal bullet went speeding forth,   30
Till it reached a town in the distant North,
Till it reached a house in a sunny street,
Till it reached a heart that ceased to beat
Without a murmur, without a cry;
And a bell was tolled, in that far-off town,
For one who had passed from cross to crown,
And the neighbors wondered that she should die. [479]

HERMAN MELVILLE

(1819–1891)

Melville was a careful observer of the war, following the progress of events in the Rebellion Record, *and even visiting the Virginia battlefront in the spring of 1864. In spite of his interest, he "never was a blind adherent." His doubts about the war are suggested by some of the poem titles in* Battle-Pieces and Aspects of the War: *"Misgivings," "The Conflict of Convictions," "Apathy and Enthusiasm," and "A Utilitarian View of the Monitor's Fight." As Hennig Cohen points out in his Introduction to* Battle-Pieces *(1963), while some of the seventy-odd poems are strongly nationalistic, others more skeptically treat the Civil War as part of the history of man at war, as a metaphor of man's conflict, or as chaos. Richard Harter Fogle in "Melville and the Civil War,"* Tulane Studies in English, *IX (1959), 61–89, shows how Melville considered the war a second fall of man and "an historic tragedy, full of meaning." According to Fogle, Melville's "great and brooding intelligence impels him to look on every side of his subject, and thus the epic strain in him is complicated and deepened by his painful awareness of lurking doom and the abyss he senses underneath life's surface."*

BALL'S BLUFF*

A Reverie

(October, 1861)

One noonday, at my window in the town,
  I saw a sight—saddest that eyes can see—

---

*The following poems are from Herman Melville, *Battle-Pieces and Aspects of the War* (New York: Harper & Brothers, 1866). In the Introduction to this

Young soldiers marching lustily
    Unto the wars,
With fifes, and flags in mottoed pageantry;
    While all the porches, walks, and doors
Were rich with ladies cheering royally.

They moved like Juny morning on the wave,
    Their hearts were fresh as clover in its prime
      (It was the breezy summer time),   10
      Life throbbed so strong,
How should they dream that Death in a rosy clime
    Would come to thin their shining throng?
Youth feels immortal, like the gods sublime. [28/29]

Weeks passed; and at my window, leaving bed,
    By night I mused, of easeful sleep bereft,
    On those brave boys (Ah War! thy theft) ;
      Some marching feet
Found pause at last by cliffs Potomac cleft;
    Wakeful I mused, while in the street   20
Far footfalls died away till none were left.

SHILOH

A Requiem

(April, 1862)

Skimming lightly, wheeling still,
    The swallows fly low
Over the field in clouded days,
    The forest-field of Shiloh—
Over the field where April rain
Solaced the parched ones stretched in pain
    Through the pause of night
That followed the Sunday fight
    Around the church of Shiloh—

---

volume, Melville says, "With few exceptions, the Pieces in this volume originated in an impulse imparted by the fall of Richmond."

The church so lone, the log-built one,   10
That echoed to many a parting groan
    And natural prayer
Of dying foemen mingled there—
Foemen at morn, but friends at eve—
    Frame or country least their care:
(What like a bullet can undeceive!)
    But now they lie low,
While over them the swallows skim,
    And all is hushed at Shiloh. [63]

GETTYSBURG

The Check

(July, 1863)

O pride of the days in prime of the months
    Now trebled in great renown,
When before the ark of our holy cause
        Fell Dagon down—
Dagon foredoomed, who, armed and targed,
Never his impious heart enlarged
Beyond that hour; God walled his power,
And there the last invader charged.

He charged, and in that charge condensed
    His all of hate and all of fire;   10
He sought to blast us in his scorn,
    And wither us in his ire.
Before him went the shriek of shells—
Aerial screamings, taunts and yells;
Then the three waves in flashed advance [84/85]
    Surged, but were met, and back they set:
Pride was repelled by sterner pride,
    And Right is a strong-hold yet.

Before our lines it seemed a beach
    Which wild September gales have strown   20

With havoc on wreck, and dashed therewith
    Pale crews unknown—
Men, arms, and steeds. The evening sun
Died on the face of each lifeless one,
And died along the winding marge of fight
    And searching-parties lone.

Sloped on the hill the mounds were green,
    Our centre held that place of graves,
And some still hold it in their swoon,
    And over these a glory waves.   30
The warrior-monument, crashed in fight,
Shall soar transfigured in loftier light,
    A meaning ampler bear;
Soldier and priest with hymn and prayer
Have laid the stone, and every bone
    Shall rest in honor there. [85]

THE HOUSE-TOP*

A Night Piece

(July, 1863)

No sleep. The sultriness pervades the air
And binds the brain—a dense oppression, such
As tawny tigers feel in matted shades,
Vexing their blood and making apt for ravage.
Beneath the stars the roofy desert spreads
Vacant as Libya. All is hushed near by.
Yet fitfully from far breaks a mixed surf
Of muffled sound, the Atheist roar of riot.
Yonder, where parching Sirius set in drought,
Balefully glares red Arson—there—and there.   10
The Town is taken by its rats—ship-rats
And rats of the wharves. All civil charms
And priestly spells which late held hearts in awe—

* This poem is a response to the New York draft riots of July 13–15, 1863.

Fear-bound, subjected to a better sway
Than sway of self; these like a dream dissolve,
And man rebounds whole æons back in nature. [86/87]
Hail to the low dull rumble, dull and dead,
And ponderous drag that shakes the wall.
Wise Draco comes, deep in the midnight roll
Of black artillery; he comes, though late;   20
In code corroborating Calvin's creed
And cynic tyrannies of honest kings;
He comes, nor parlies; and the Town, redeemed,
Gives thanks devout; nor, being thankful, heeds
The grimy slur on the Republic's faith implied,
Which holds that Man is naturally good,
And—more—is Nature's Roman, never to be scourged. [87]

IN THE PRISON PEN

(1864)

Listless he eyes the palisades
    And sentries in the glare;
'Tis barren as a pelican-beach—
    But his world is ended there.

Nothing to do; and vacant hands
    Bring on the idiot-pain;
He tires to think—to recollect,
    But the blur is on his brain.

Around him swarm the plaining ghosts
    Like those on Virgil's shore—   10
A wilderness of faces dim,
    And pale ones gashed and hoar.

A smiting sun. No shed, no tree;
    He totters to his lair—
A den that sick hands dug in earth
    Ere famine wasted there, [118/119]

Or, dropping in his place, he swoons,
　Walled in by throngs that press,
Till forth from the throngs they bear him dead—
　Dead in his meagreness.　　　　　　　　　　　　20

THE SURRENDER AT APPOMATTOX

(April, 1865)

As billows upon billows roll,
　On victory victory breaks;
Ere yet seven days from Richmond's fall
　And crowning triumph wakes
The loud joy-gun, whose thunders run
　By sea-shore, streams, and lakes.
　　　　The hope and great event agree
　　　　In the sword that Grant received from Lee.

The warring eagles fold the wing,
　But not in Cæsar's sway;　　　　　　　　　　10
Not Rome o'ercome by Roman arms we sing,
　As on Pharsalia's day,
But Treason thrown, though a giant grown,
　And Freedom's larger play.
　　　　All human tribes glad token see
　　　　In the close of the wars of Grant and Lee. [137]

A MEDITATION

How often in the years that close,
　When truce has stilled the sieging gun,
The soldiers, mounting on their works,
　With mutual curious glance have run
From face to face along the fronting show,
And kinsman spied, or friend—even in a foe.

What thoughts conflicting then were shared,
    While sacred tenderness perforce
Welled from the heart and wet the eye;
    And something of a strange remorse   10
Rebelled against the sanctioned sin of blood,
And Christian wars of natural brotherhood.

Then stirred the god within the breast—
    The witness that is man's at birth;
A deep misgiving undermined
    Each plea and subterfuge of earth;
They felt in that rapt pause, with warning rife,
Horror and anguish for the civil strife. [241/242]

Of North or South they recked not then,
    Warm passion cursed the cause of war: 20
Can Africa pay back this blood
    Spilt on Potomac's shore?
Yet doubts, as pangs, were vain the strife to stay,
And hands that fain had clasped again could slay.

How frequent in the camp was seen
    The herald from the hostile one,
A guest and frank companion there
    When the proud formal talk was done;
The pipe of peace was smoked even 'mid the war,
And fields in Mexico again fought o'er.   30

In Western battle long they lay
    So near opposed in trench or pit,
That foeman unto foeman called
    As men who screened in tavern sit:
"You bravely fight" each to the other said—
"Toss us a biscuit!" o'er the wall it sped.

And pale on those same slopes, a boy—
    A stormer, bled in noon-day glare;
No aid the Blue-coats then could bring,
    He cried to them who nearest were,   40

And out there came 'mid howling shot and shell
A daring foe who him befriended well. [242/243]

Mark the great Captains on both sides,
    The soldiers with the broad renown—
They all were messmates on the Hudson's marge,
    Beneath one roof they laid them down;
And, free from hate in many an after pass,
Strove as in school-boy rivalry of the class.

A darker side there is; but doubt
    In Nature's charity hovers there: 50
If men for new agreement yearn,
    Then old upbraiding best forbear:
"The South's the sinner!" Well, so let it be;
But shall the North sin worse, and stand the Pharisee?

O, now that brave men yield the sword,
    Mine be the manful soldier-view;
By how much more they boldly warred,
    By so much more is mercy due:
When Vicksburg fell, and the moody files marched out,
Silent the victors stood, scorning to raise a shout. [243]   60

JOHN GREENLEAF WHITTIER

(1807–1892)

In Whittier: Bard of Freedom *(1941)*, *Whitman Bennett says that Whittier was "the most effective literary man in direct personal influence on our political and social system that this country has ever produced." From the 1830s into the Civil War period Whittier was an active abolitionist who participated in antislavery organizations, wrote abolitionist essays and poetry, acted from 1845 to 1860 as contributing editor to the* National Era *(journal of the National and Foreign Anti-Slavery Society), and encouraged the free-soil settlement of Kansas. When the war broke out, though, he had doubts that Unionism was the highest good or that the war was necessary. As he wrote in a letter in November, 1861: "The sad war drags along. I long to see some compensation for its horrors, in the deliverance of the Slaves. Without this, it is the wickedest war of the nineteenth century." He was encouraged by the Emancipation Proclamation—although he, like many other abolitionists, desired more direct action. His real satisfaction and joy came, as he expresses in "Laus Deo!", with the passage of the constitutional amendment abolishing slavery.*

A WORD FOR THE HOUR*

The firmament breaks up. In black eclipse
Light after light goes out. One evil star,

*The following poems are from John Greenleaf Whittier, *Anti-Slavery Poems; Songs of Labor & Reform* (London: Macmillan and Co., 1889). "A Word for the Hour" was written January 16, 1861. "In War Time" was first published in the *Atlantic Monthly*, August, 1862, and was used as the dedication piece to Whittier's volume, *In War Time and Other Poems* (1864).

Luridly glaring through the smoke of war,
As in the dream of the Apocalypse,
Drags others down. Let us not weakly weep
Nor rashly threaten. Give us grace to keep
Our faith and patience; wherefore should we leap
On one hand into fratricidal fight,
Or, on the other, yield eternal right,
Frame lies of law, and good and ill confound?   10
What fear we? Safe on freedom's vantage-ground
Our feet are planted: let us there remain
In unrevengeful calm, no means untried
Which truth can sanction, no just claim denied,
The sad spectators of a suicide!
They break the links of Union: shall we light
The fires of hell to weld anew the chain
On that red anvil where each blow is pain? [218/219]
Draw we not even now a freer breath,
As from our shoulders falls a load of death   20
Loathsome as that the Tuscan's victim bore
When keen with life to a dead horror bound?
Why take we up the accursed thing again?
Pity, forgive, but urge them back no more
Who, drunk with passion, flaunt disunion's rag
With its vile reptile-blazon. Let us press
The golden cluster on our brave old flag
In closer union, and, if numbering less,
Brighter shall shine the stars which still remain. [219]

IN WAR TIME

Olor Iscanus queries: "Why should we
Vex at the land's ridiculous miserie?"
So on his Usk banks, in the blood-red dawn
Of England's civil strife, did careless Vaughan
Bemock his times. O friends of many years!
Though faith and trust are stronger than our fears,
And the signs promise peace with liberty,

Not thus we trifle with our country's tears
And sweat of agony. The future's gain
Is certain as God's truth; but, meanwhile, pain
Is bitter and tears are salt: our voices take
A sober tone; our very household songs
Are heavy with a nation's griefs and wrongs;
And innocent mirth is chastened for the sake
Of the brave hearts that nevermore shall beat,
The eyes that smile no more, the unreturning feet! [216]

LAUS DEO!

On hearing the bells ring on the passage of the constitutional amendment
abolishing slavery. The resolution was adopted by Congress, January 31, 1865.
The ratification by the requisite number of States was announced December 18,
1865.

It is done!
Clang of bell and roar of gun
Send the tidings up and down. [254/255]
How the belfries rock and reel!
How the great guns, peal and peal,
Fling the joy from town to town!

Ring, O bells!
Every stroke exulting tells
Of the burial hour of crime.
Loud and long, that all may hear,   10
Ring for every listening ear
Of Eternity and Time!

Let us kneel:
God's own voice is in that peal,
And this spot is holy ground.
Lord, forgive us! What are we,
That our eyes this glory see,
That our ears have heard the sound!

    For the Lord
  On the whirlwind is abroad;   20
In the earthquake He has spoken;
    He has smitten with His thunder
    The iron walls asunder,
And the gates of brass are broken!

    Loud and long
  Lift the old exulting song;
Sing with Miriam by the sea,
    He has cast the mighty down;
    Horse and rider sink and drown;
"He hath triumphed gloriously!"   30

    Did we dare,
  In our agony of prayer, [255/256]
Ask for more than He has done?
    When was ever His right hand
    Over any time or land
Stretched as now beneath the sun?

    How they pale,
  Ancient myth and song and tale,
In this wonder of our days,
    When the cruel rod of war   40
    Blossoms white with righteous law,
And the wrath of man is praise!

    Blotted out!
  All within and all about
Shall a fresher life begin;
    Freer breathe the universe
    As it rolls its heavy curse
On the dead and buried sin!

    It is done!
  In the circuit of the sun   50
Shall the sound thereof go forth.
    It shall bid the sad rejoice,

It shall give the dumb a voice,
It shall belt with joy the earth!

  Ring and swing,
 Bells of joy! On morning's wing
Send the song of praise abroad!
  With a sound of broken chains
  Tell the nations that He reigns,
Who alone is Lord and God! [256]   60

ENTHUSIASTS
South

Upon them, O sons of the mighty of yore,
And fatten the sands with their Sodomite gore!

William Gilmore Simms

Then gird your brave empress, O heroes! with
flame
Flashed up from the sword-points that cover
her breast!
She is guarded by Love and enhaloed by
Fame,
And never, stern foe! shall your footsteps be
pressed
Where her dead martyrs rest!

Paul Hamilton Hayne

BILL ARP (CHARLES H. SMITH)

(1826–1903)

Charles H. Smith was the most popular Southern humorist during the Civil War. As a lawyer in Rome, Georgia, Smith became acquainted with a Georgia cracker named Bill Earp, and used the name Arp—much to Earp's pleasure—to write humorous sketches in an illiterate dialect. Smith's anecdotes, begun in the first years of the war, first portrayed Bill Arp as a naïve Union sympathizer. Later, though, that role was dropped, and Smith satirized the North more straightforwardly. During these years Smith was also active in the military—first in the Georgia militia, then in the home guard, and later in the Army of Virginia; in 1864 he served as Judge Advocate of a Confederate Habeas Corpus Court.

Bill Arp was a counterpart to Artemus Ward. Both used their humor not only to entertain but also to articulate thoughts and feelings of the common people in their regions. A discussion of this aspect of Arp's writings is found in Anne M. Christie, "Bill Arp," Civil War History, *II (September, 1956), 103–19.*

from TO THE PUBLISHER*

. . . These letters may be worthy of preservation, as illustrative of a part of the war—as a [5/6] side-show to the Southern side of it—an index to our feelings and sentiments. . . .

*The following are from [Charles H. Smith], *Bill Arp, So Called. A Side Show of the Southern Side of the War* (New York: Metropolitan Record Office, 1866). The letters, here regularized in their spelling as Arp desired, were first written in an illiterate dialect (e.g., addressed to "Mr. Abe Linkhorn") and published in 1861–62 by the *Southern Confederacy* (Rome, Georgia).

For the sentiments that pervade these letters, I have no apology
to make. At the time they appeared in the press of the South, these
sentiments were the [6/7] silent echoes of our people's thoughts,
and this accounts in the main for the popularity with which they
were received. Of course they contain exaggerations, and prophecies
which were never fulfilled; but both sections were playing "brag" as
well as "battle," and though we could not compete with our oppo-
nents in the former, yet some of us did try to hold our own. At both
games we were whipped by overwhelming forces, and we have
given it up. Conquered, but not convinced, we have accepted the
situation, and have pledged ourselves to abide by it. . . . [7]

from A MESSAGE TO ALL FOLKS

Some folks say it was the Abolishonists who got up this fuss. *Some
say they didn't.* Some say it was politicians, and some it was a supernatural thing called *Manifest Destiny.* Some are of the opinion that
the *nigger* was at the bottom of it, and that ever since the Romans
carried the war into Africa, Africa has carried it everywhere else.
But, my fellow-citizens, it was caused exclusively by Gen. States
Rights going to sleep one day, and old Colonel Federalist come
along, and tried to cut his ham-string. I am for the General as long
as I am on his staff, and I am going to pitch into the Colonel on
every possible occasion. So now you understand what brought about
the war. [57]

[BILL ARP TO ABE LINCOLN]

ROME, GEO., April, 1861.

MR. LINCOLN—
    SIR: These are to inform you that we are all well, and hope
these lines may find you in *statu quo.* We received your proclamation, and as you have put us on very short notice, a few of us boys
have concluded to write you, and ask for a little more time. The
fact is, we are most obliged to have a few more days, for the way
things are happening, it is utterly impossible for us to disperse in
twenty days. Old Virginia, and Tennessee, and North Carolina are

continually aggravating us into tumults and carousments, and a body can't disperse until you put a stop to such unruly conduct on their part. I tried my darn'dst yesterday to disperse and retire, but it was no go; and besides, your marshal here ain't doing a darn'd thing—he don't read the riot-act, nor remonstrate, nor nothing, and ought to be turned out. If you conclude to do so, I am authorized to recommend to you Colonel Gibbons or Mr. McClung, who would attend to the business as well as most anybody. [18/19]

The fact is, the boys around here want watching, or they'll take something. A few days ago I heard they surrounded two of our best citizens because they were named Fort and Sumter. Most of them are so hot that they fairly siz when you pour water on them, and that's the way they make up their military companies here now—when a man applies to join the volunteers, they sprinkle him, and if he sizzes they take him, and if he don't they don't.

Mr. Lincoln, sir, privately speaking, I'm afraid I'll get in a tight place here among these bloods, and have to slope out of it, and I would like much to have your Scotch cap and cloak that you travelled in to Washington. I suppose you wouldn't be likely to use the same disguise again when you left, and therefore I would propose to swap. I am five feet five, and could get my plough breeches and coat to you in eight or ten days if you can wait that long. I want you to write to me immediately about things generally, and let us know where you intend to do your fighting. Your proclamation says something about taking possession of all the private property at "All Hazards." We can't find no such a place on the map. I thought it must be about Charleston, or Savannah, or Harper's Ferry, but they say it ain't anywhere down South. One man said it was a little factory on an island in Lake Champlain, where they make sand-bags. My opinion is, that sand-bag business won't pay, and it is a great waste of money. Our boys [19/20] here carry their sand in their gizzards, where it keeps better, and is always handy. I'm afraid your Government is giving you and your Kangaroo a great deal of unnecessary trouble, and my humble advice is, if things don't work better soon, you'd better grease it, or trade the darn'd old thing off. I'd take rails or any thing for it. If I could see you, I'd show you a sleight-of-hand trick that would change the whole concern into buttons quick. If you don't trade or do something else with it soon, it will spoil or die on your hands certain.

Give my respects to Bill Seward and the other members of the Kangaroo. What's Hannibal doing? I don't hear any thing from him now-a-days.

Yours, with care,

BILL ARP.

P.S.—If you can possibly extend that order to thirty days, do so. We have sent you a CHECK at Harper's Ferry (who keeps that darn'd old Ferry now? it's giving us a heap of trouble) , but if you positively won't extend, we'll send you a check, drawn by Jeff. Davis, Beauregard endorser, payable on sight anywhere. Yours,

B. A. [20/21]

CENTREVILLE, January 12, 1862.

MR. LINCOLN—

SIR: In the spring of the year I wrote you a letter from my native soil, asking for a little more time to disperse. I told you then that twenty days were not enough—that the thing could not be done in that brief interval. You can look back and see I was right. We tried our durndest to comply with your schedule, but as you kept calling for volunteers, our Cherokee Georgia Democrats kept coming out from under their clay roots. They shook themselves and spit fire, and wouldn't go back so long as the Whigs would read them the news about this fuss.

Mr. Abe Lincoln, sir, the spring has shed its fragrance, the summer is over and gone, the yellow leaves of autumn have covered the ground, old winter is slobbering his froth on the earth, but we have not been able to disperse as yet. Me and the boys started last May to see you personally, and ask for an extension of your brief furlough, but we got on a bust in old Virginia, about the 21st of July, and like to have got run over by a parcel of fellows running [21/22] from Bull Run to your city. After that we tried to get to you by the Potomac River, but Mr. Whiting said you were not running that machine *at these presents.* We next went to Mr. Harper's Ferry, to take the Baltimore Railroad, but we couldn't find the conductor, and cars seemed scarce, and the folks said you were not running that machine *much.* We thought, however, to take a deck passage on the canal, but a dam had broke and General Jackson said you were not running that machine, *scarcely any.* After all that we came back, and thought we'd get Captain Wilkes to ship us over, but Mr. Bennett sent us word that the captain had quit a seafaring life. Mr. Seward made him quit, to pacify an old English Bull that was bellowing about and pawing dirt in the air. Mr. Lincoln, sir, if that Bull is of the same stock as the one your folks saw here in July, he is dangerous, and will have a bad effect on your population. You had better circumscribe him before he hurts somebody.

Mr. Lincoln, sir, what are your factories doing now-a-days? I heard you had quit running their machines, owing to a thin crop of cotton. If you would put sweet oil on your factories, they wouldn't rust while standing idle. I was glad to hear that you had got enough cotton to do yours and Seward's families. The boys say you got enough to make as many shirts as Falstaff had in his company.

Mr. Lincoln, sir, how do you come on with your stone fleet—does it pay expenses—is it a safe investment—could [22/23] I get any stock in it at a fair price? Don't you think it is most too far to haul rocks, and won't it impoverish New England soil to take the rocks off of it?

Mr. Abe Lincoln, sir, the 18th is the anniversary of the day when Georgia tore herself frantically loose from the abolition dynasty—when she ripped her star from off the striped rag, and spread a new shirting to the breeze. We calculate to celebrate that day, and I am authorized to invite you and Bill Seward over to partake of our hospitalities. Where is Hamlin? I allow that he is dead, or I would ask him too. Let me know if you and Seward are coming, so we can fix up and swap a lie or two with you. Couldn't you all come along with Mack when he makes that advance he has been talking about so long? Bring your knitting with you when you come, and a clean shirt or two. Do you chaw tobacco? We have got some that is good. Ely chawed, and Mr. Davis gave him a whole warehouse at Richmond.

Mr. Lincoln, sir, I wish you would ask Banks to send me a codfish. Pole-cats are bad around here, and we want something to drive 'em away. If you bring Banks and Picayune Butler with you, you needn't bring the cod.

Yours, till death,

BILL ARP.

P. S.—Where is Fremont? I hear he has gone up a spout. [23/24]

December 2, 1862.

Mr. Lincoln—

Sir: A poet has said that "Time untied waiteth for no man." To my opinion it is untied now and hastens on to that eventful period which you have fixed when Africa is to be unshackled, when Niggerdom is to feel the power of your proclamation, when Uncle Tom is to change his base and evacuate his cabin, when all the emblems of darkness are to rush frantically forth into the arms of their deliverers, and with perfumed and scented gratitude embrace your Excellency and Madam Harriet Beecher Stowe! What a glorious day that is to be! What a sublime era in history! What a proud culmination and consummation and corruscation of your political hopes! After a few thousand have clasped you in their ebony arms it will be a fitting time, Mr. Lincoln, for you to lay yourself down and die. Human ambition can have no higher monument to climb. After such a work you might complete the immortal heroism of your character, by leaping from the topmost pinnacle of your glory upon the earth below. [24/25]

But alas for human folly—alas for all sublunary things—our people will not believe, these crazy rebels will not consider; Christmas is already here, only one more brief week to slide away before we must part, forever part, with all our negro heritage, and yet our stubborn people continue to buy and sell them, and the shorter the lease, the higher the price they are paying. What infatuation! I do verily believe they will keep up their old ways until next Wednesday night, just as though they did not have to give them all up the next morning before breakfast. Some say the stay law affects the niggers and will operate to make them stay at home—some say you have not got transportation nor rations for four millions of darkeys —some say your call is premature; but the majority are of the opinion that a little difficulty you met at Fredericksburg has interfered with your arrangements, and extended the time like a sine die.

Mr. Lincoln, sir, I forewarned you about crossing those sickly rivers. The Lee side of any shore is unhealthy to your population; keep away from those Virginia water courses, go around them or under them, but for the sake of economy don't try to cross them. It is too hard upon your burial squads and ambulance horses.

Mr. Lincoln, sir, when is this war to close? How much longer can you renew your note of ninety days which you said was time enough to settle this difficulty—do you pay the interest? How much territory have you [25/26] subjugated—what makes cotton sell at 67 cents a pound in your diggins—is it not awful scarce—what do your bony women do for stuffing and padding? I heard they had to use hay and saw-dust and such like, and I thought it must be very painful to their tender bosoms to have to resort to such scarce commodity; I would like to send you a bale, but Governor Brown would seize it. It is said by many that the war is about to close because of the Governor's late raid on leather—they say the war begun with a John Brown raid in Virginia, and will end with a Joe Brown raid in Georgia—I allow not, for I think the Governor only took that way of getting the State rid of its surplus, for he wanted to drive it into the adjoining States where things were scarcer. I would like to see you personally, Mr. Lincoln, and hear you talk and tell some of your funny anecdotes, like you told Governor Morehead. I laughed when I read them till the tears fairly rained from my eyelids—I know I could make my fortune, Mr. Lincoln, compiling your wit. May I be your Boswell, and follow you about?

But fare thee well, my friend, and, before you cross another Rubicon, I advise you, in the eloquent language of Mr. Burke, "consider, old cow, consider."

Yours, till death,

BILL ARP.

P.S.—Give my respects to Johnny Van Buren; I heard you and him were mighty thick and affectionate.

B. A. [26/27]

[October, 1862]

Mr. LINCOLN—

SIR: Is it not possible that you are using too much proclamation? More than eighteen months ago you published an edict, ordering the boys to retire and be peaceable, but they disretired and went to fighting. The effect was bad, very bad. Now you have proclaimed the negroes free after January, and I am afraid it will prove a fee-simple title for all time.

Every free negro will get in the cotton-patch now, sure; for the tarnal rebels do everything by contraries. Negroes have risen twenty per cent., and are growing darker and blacker every day. A big plantation now looks like the sun was in an eclipse. Your proclamation has entailed Africa upon us so strong that you can actually smell it. Tippio says (we call him Tip for short) that he is personally interested, and he thinks you had better make them free first and issue your proclamation afterwards. General Hunter tried it your way, and over-cropped himself. Tip got no free papers at all. [27/28]

Mr. Lincoln, sir, I am afraid you are taking in more ground than you can tend. You are trying to do too much at once. General Hunter tried your plan and couldn't work it over three States, so you had better practise on homœopathic doses. If you will begin on Dade County you can tell what your machine will do, as there is but one nigger there, and they keep him in a cage as a curiosity. If they will not accept your freedom, why, let them alone. It is useless to call them if they won't come. I once heard a fellow in a theatre say he could call spirits from the nasty deep, but the spirits never come and he got nary drink—so go it gently, Mr. Lincoln, but go it sure. The world, the flesh, and the devil are looking to you to extend the ægis of freedom over all creation—over things animate and inanimate—over bull bats and screech-owls, grub-worms and grindstones, niggers and alligators, and every thing that don't spill as the earth turns upside down. You will have a free fight, Mr. Lincoln, in doing all this, but never mind—pitch in—great is your reward.

Mr. Lincoln, sir, it is amazing to think what a big job you have undertaken. It is a big job, sure. Matthy Matties nor his daddy couldn't figure out how long it will take you to get through according to your feeble progress. The double rule of three won't touch it, nor tare and tret. Great Bethel! what a power of work! Had you not better sublet the contract to some European nations? Sure as you are born you will need a heap of *undertakers* [28/29] before you finish your overland march. If you could march like Jackson it would do, but you can't. Dr. Battey says that Jackson's troops take the gout if they rest twenty-four hours.

Mr. Lincoln, sir, our people get more stubborn every day. They go mighty near naked, and say they are saving their Sunday clothes to wear after we have whipped you. They just glory in living on half rations, and stewing salt out of their smoke-house dirt. They say they had rather fight you than feed you, and swear by the ghost of Calhoun they will eat roots and drink branch-water the balance of time before they will kernowly to your abolition dynasty. Chickahominy! what a job you have undertaken! Does Hannibal help you any? I hear tell that he just set in the corner of your office all day long, and never said a word but *nigger, nigger, nigger,* and that since your proclamation his face has turned darker and his hair more kinky.

Mr. Lincoln, sir, have you any late news from Mr. Harper's Ferry? I heard that Stone W. Jackson kept the parole for a few days, and that about fourteen thousand crossed over in twenty-four hours. He is a smart ferryman, sure. Do your folks know how to make it pay? It is a bad crossing, but I suppose it is a heap safer than Ball's Bluff or Sheppardstown. These are dangerous fords, Mr. Lincoln, sure, and I am afraid if your folks keep crossing such sickly rivers as the Potomac and Chickahominy, you will have all the scum of your population killed up, and you have to encroach on your good society. [29/30]

Mr. Lincoln, sir, your generals don't travel the right road to Richmond nohow. The way they have been trying to come is through a mighty Longstreet, over two powerful Hills, and across a tremendous Stonewall. It would be safer and cheaper for 'em to go around by the Rocky Mountains, if spending time in military excursions is their chief object.

But I must close this brief epistle. I feel very gloomy, Mr. Lincoln, about this destructive war, and have no heart to write much. As General Byron said, "I ain't now what I used to was, and my spirits are fluttering, faint, and low."

Yours, till death,

BILL ARP.

P. S.—How is Bill Seward? I heard that a mad dog bit him the other day, and the dog died immediately. Is it a fact?

B. A. [30]

JOHN ESTEN COOKE

(1830–1886)

John Esten Cooke was a novelist and historian of Virginia in the finest FFV tradition. Before the war he wrote novels such as The Virginia Comedians *(1854) and* Henry St. John *(1859) which idealized the Virginia past. After the war he wrote fictional accounts of his experiences as an officer in the Army of Northern Virginia. The first of these was* Surry of Eagle's Nest *(1866) and its sequel was* Mohun *(1869), from which the following selections are taken. Cooke also published collections of essays on military subjects,* Wearing of the Gray *(1867) and* Hammer and Rapier *(1870), and wrote biographies of Jackson and Lee.*

In his fiction Cooke exalted chivalry and emphasized romantic elements. As he said, "I prefer recalling the strong adventures, the brave voices, the gallant forces; even in the tremendous drama of 1861–65, I can find something besides blood and tears, even here and there some sunshine." On the other hand, he was also aware that "battle is a stern, not a poetical affair; the genius of conflict a huge, dirty, bloody, and very hideous figure,—not a melodramatic actor, spouting a part."

LEE'S "RAGGED REGIMENTS"*

It required a stout heart to laugh and sing, *con amore,* in the last days of that winter, and the first days of spring, 1864.

*The following selections are from John Esten Cooke, *Mohun; or, The Last Days of Lee and His Paladins* (New York: F. J. Huntington and Co., 1869).

194

Those very figures, "1864," tell the story, and explain this. Do they not, reader?

Each year of the war has its peculiar physiognomy.

1861—that is mirth, adventure, inexperience, bright faces, wreaths of flowers, "boxes" from home, and "honorable mention" in reports, if you only waved your sword and shouted "Hurrah!" Then you heard the brass bands playing, the drum gayly rolling, the bugles sending their joyous notes across the fields and through the forests—blooming fields, untouched forests!—and that music made the pulses dance. Gayly-clad volunteers marched gallantly through the streets; the crowds cheered; the new flags, shaped by fair hands, fluttered;—not a bullet had torn through them, not a rent was seen in the new uniforms. As the trains swept by with the young heroes on board, bevies of lovely girls cheered, waved handkerchiefs, and threw nosegays. Eyes were sparkling, lips smiling, cheeks glowing in '61. The youths had havelocks to ward off the sun; gaiters to keep out the dust; woollen belts to prevent rheuma-[140/141] tism; fanciful shirt bosoms, and pretty needle-cases and tobacco pouches of silk and velvet, decked with beads and gay needlework, by the dearest fingers in the world!

So they went to the wars—those stout and ruddy youths. Every one anxious to have his head taken off by a cannon ball, all for the honor and glory of it. They marched along cheering, as the white handkerchiefs waved; they proudly kept step to the tap of the drum, or moved briskly beside the cannon, or cantered by on their glossy and spirited horses.

The epoch was agitated, but joy coursed in every vein. And when the first successes came, those small affairs were greeted with "thunders of applause."

General Spoons marched to Bethel; took a look at the gray people; fired a gun or two before retreating—and a thousand Southern journalists shouted "Io, triumphe!—a grand victory!" The brave Del. Kemper fired a shot at the Federal train approaching Vienna, and the journalists cried, "we have driven back the whole Federal army!"

Then some real fighting came, and the applause was again tremendous. When the news of the first Manassas flashed over the wires, the Southern people stood upon their heads, and went wild. The war was ended—the affair was over—the brass bands, and rolling drums, and dazzling uniforms had speedily done the business. The power of the North was broken. She had run upon the breakers. The great hulk was lying stranded, the waves were beating her, and she was about to go to pieces.

Such was 1861—an era of mirth, inexperience, inflated views, brilliant pageants, gay adventures, ruddy cheeks, sparkling eyes and splendid banners, floating proudly in the sunshine of victory!

1862 came, and with it a new phase of the war. Sweat, dust, and blood had replaced the music and wreaths of roses. Faces, were not so ruddy—they began to look war-worn. The rounded cheeks had become gaunt. The bright uniforms were battle-soiled. Smoke had stained them, the bivouac dimmed them, the sun had changed the blue-gray to a sort of scorched yellow. Waving handkerchiefs still greeted the troops—as they greeted them to the end of the war. But few flowers were thrown now—their good angels looked on in silence, and prayed for them. [141/142]

They were no longer holiday soldiers, but were hardened in battle. They knew the work before them, and advanced to it with the measured tramp of veterans. They fought as well as soldiers have ever fought in this world. Did they not? Answer, Cold Harbor, Malvern Hill, Cedar Mountain, Manassas, Boonsboro', Sharpsburg, and Fredericksburg! And every battle, nearly, was a victory. In the lowlands and the mountains—in Virginia and Maryland—they bore aloft the banner of the South in stalwart hands, and carried it forward with unshrinking hearts, to that baptism of blood awaiting it. That was the great year for the South. The hour was dark—a huge foe fronted us—but wherever that foe was met, he seemed to reel before the mailed hand that buffeted his front. All frippery and decoration had long been stripped from the army. The fingers of war—real war—had torn off the gaudy trappings; and the grim lips had muttered, "What I want is hard muscle, and the brave heart—not tinsel!" The bands were seldom heard—the musicians were tending the wounded. The drums had ceased their jovial rattle, and were chiefly used in the "long roll," which said "Get ready, boys! they are coming!"

So in the midst of smoke and dust,—with yells of triumph, or groans of agony, in place of the gay cheering—passed that year of battles, 1862.

The South was no longer romantic and elated on the subject of the war. The soldiers no longer looked out for adventures, or for the glorious cannon-ball to carry off their heads, and make their names immortal. At home, the old men were arming, and the women sending words of cheer to their husbands and sons, and praying. In the camps, the old soldiers had forgotten the wreaths of roses. Their havelocks were worn out, and they no longer minded the sun. Gray flannel had replaced the "fancy" shirt bosoms; they carried tobacco in their pockets; and you saw them, seated on some log, busy sewing on buttons, the faces once so round and ruddy, now gaunt and stained with powder.

1863 came, and it was an army of veterans that struck Hooker at Chancellorsville. It was no longer a company of gay gallants marching by, amid music, waving scarfs, and showers of nosegays from fairy hands. It was a stormy wave of gaunt warriors, [142/143] in ragged clothes and begrimed faces, who clutched their shining muskets, rushed headlong over the breastworks, and, rolling through the blazing and crackling woods, swept the enemy at the point of the bayonet, with the hoarse and menacing cry, "Remember Jackson!" Gettysburg followed—never was grapple more fierce than that, as we have seen; and when the veterans of Lee were hurled back, the soil of the continent seemed to shake. They were repulsed and retreated, but as the lion retreats before the huntsman, glaring back, and admonishing him not to follow too closely, if he would consult his own safety. At Williamsport the wounded lion halted and turned—his pursuer did not assail him—and he crossed the Potomac, and descended to the Rapidan, to strike in turn that dangerous blow in October, when Meade was nearly cut off from Washington.

With that campaign of Bristoe, and the fiasco of Mine Run, the year 1863 ended.

It left the South bleeding, and what was worse,—discouraged. Affairs were mismanaged. The army had scarcely sufficient meat and bread to live on. The croakers, clad in black coats, and with snowy shirt bosoms, began to mutter under their breath, "It is useless to struggle longer!"—and, recoiling in disgust from the hard fare of "war times," began to hunger for the flesh-pots of Egypt. Manna was tasteless now; the task-master was better than the wilderness and the scant fare. Oh! to sit by the flesh-pots and grow fat, as in the days when they did eat thereof! Why continue the conflict? Why

waste valuable lives? Why think of still fighting when flour was a
hundred dollars a barrel, coffee twenty dollars a pound, cloth fifty
dollars a yard, and good whiskey and brandy not to be purchased at
any price? Could patriotism live amid trials like that? Could men
cling to a cause which made them the victims of Yankee cavalry?
Why have faith any longer in a government that was bankrupt—
whose promises to pay originated the scoffing proverb, "as worthless
as a Confederate note!" Meat and drink was the religion of the
croakers in those days. Money was their real divinity. Without meat
and drink, and with worthless money, the Confederacy, in their
eyes, was not the side to adhere to. It was unfortunate—down with
it! Let it be anathema-maranatha! [143/144]

The croakers said that—and the brave hearts whom they in-
sulted could not silence them. There were stout souls in black
coats—but the croakers distilled their poison, working busily in the
darkness. It was the croakers who bought up the supplies, and
hoarded them in garrets, and retailed them in driblets, thereby
causing the enormous prices which, according to them, foretold the
coming downfall. They evaded the conscript officers; grew fat on
their extortions; and one day you would miss them from their
accustomed haunts—they had flitted across the Potomac, and were
drinking their wine in New York, London, or Paris.

Meanwhile, three classes of persons remained faithful to the
death:—the old men, the army, and the women.

The gray-beards were taking down their old guns and swords,
and forming home-battalions, to fight the enemy to the death when
his cavalry came to lay waste the country.

The women were weaving homespun, knitting socks, nursing
the wounded, and praying. They had never ceased to pray, nor had
they lost the heart of hope. The croakers believed in success, and
their patron saint was Mammon. The women believed in the justice
of the cause, and in God. In 1861, they had cheered the soldiers,
and waved their handkerchiefs, and rained bouquets. In 1862, they
had sent brave words of encouragement, and bade their sons, and
brothers, and husbands fight to the end. In 1863, they repeated
that—sent the laggards back to the ranks—and when they were not
sewing, or nursing the sick, were praying. O women of Virginia, and
the great South to her farthest limits, there is nothing in all history
that surpasses your grand record! You hoped, in the dark days as in

the bright;—when bearded men shrunk, you fronted the storm unmoved! Always you hoped, and endured, and prayed for the land. Had the rest done their duty like the women and the army, the red-cross flag would be floating to-day in triumph!

The army—that was unshaken. Gettysburg had not broken its strength, nor affected its stout manhood. Lee's old soldiers believed in him after Gettysburg, in the winter of '63, as they had believed in him after Fredericksburg, in the winter of '62. They had confidence still in their great leader, and in their cause. The [144/145] wide gaps in their ranks did not dismay them; want of food did not discourage them; hunger, hardships, nakedness, defeat,—they had borne these in the past, they were bearing them still, they were ready to bear them in the future. War did not fright them—though the coming conflict was plainly going to be more bitter than any before. The great array of Grant on the north bank of the Rapidan did not depress them—had they not met and defeated at Fredericksburg and Chancellorsville a force as great, and could not they do it again?

So they lay in their camps on the Rapidan, in that cold winter of 1863—a little army of ragged and hungry men, with gaunt faces, wasted forms, shoeless feet; with nothing to encourage them but the cause, past victories, and Lee's presence. That was much; what was enough, however, was the blood in their veins; the inspiration of the great race of fighting men from whom they derived their origin. Does any one laugh at that? The winner will—but the truth remains.

That ragged and famished army came to a fighting race. It was starving and dying, but it was going to fight to the last.

When the cannon began to roar in May, 1864, these gaunt veterans were in line, with ragged coats, but burnished bayonets. When Lee, the gray cavalier, rode along their lines, the woods thundered with a cheer which said, "Ready!" [145]

[PICKETT'S CHARGE AT GETTYSBURG]

Lee's great blow at the enemy's left had failed. He had thrown his entire right wing, under Longstreet, against it. The enemy had been driven; victory seemed achieved;—but suddenly the blue lines had rallied, they had returned to the struggle, their huge masses had rolled forward, thrown Longstreet back in turn, and now the pale moon looked down on the battle-field where some of the bravest souls of the South had poured out their blood in vain.

Lee had accomplished nothing, and one of his great corps was panting and bleeding. It was not shattered or even shaken. The iron fibre would stand any thing almost. But the sombre result remained—Longstreet had attacked and had been repulsed.

What course would Lee now pursue? Would he retire? [87/88]

Retire? The army of Northern Virginia lose heart at a mere rebuff? Lee's veteran army give up the great invasion, after a mere repulse? Troops and commander alike shrunk from the very thought. One more trial of arms—something—an attack some-where—not *a retreat!*

That was the spirit of the army on the night of the second of July.

A flanking movement to draw the enemy out of their works, or a second attack remained.

Lee determined to attack.

Longstreet and Ewell had accomplished nothing by assailing the right and left of the enemy. Lee resolved now to throw a column against its centre—to split the stubborn obstacle, and pour into the gap with the whole army, when all would be over.

That was hazardous, you will say perhaps to-day, reader. And you have this immense argument to advance, that it failed. Ah! these arguments *after the event!* they are so fatal, and so very easy.

Right or wrong, Lee resolved to make the attack; and on the third of July he carried out his resolution.

If the writer of the South shrinks from describing the bloody repulse of Longstreet, much more gloomy is the task of painting that last charge at Gettysburg. It is one of those scenes which Lee's old soldiers approach with repugnance. That thunder of the guns which comes back to memory seems to issue, hollow and lugubrious, from a thousand tombs.

Let us pass over that tragedy rapidly. It must be touched on in these memoirs—but I leave it soon.

It is the third of July, 1863. Lee's line of battle, stretching along the crest of Seminary Ridge, awaits the signal for a new conflict with a carelessness as great as on the preceding day. The infantry are laughing, jesting, cooking their rations, and smoking their pipes. The ragged cannoneers, with flashing eyes, smiling lips, and faces blackened with powder, are standing in groups, or lying down around the pieces of artillery. Near the centre of the line a gray-headed officer, in plain uniform, and entirely unattended, has dismounted, and is reconnoitring the Federal position through a pair of field-glasses. [88/89]

It is Lee, and he is looking toward Cemetery Heights, the Mount St. Jean of the new Waterloo—on whose slopes the immense conflict is going to be decided.

Lee gazes for some moments through his glasses at the long range bristling with bayonets. Not a muscle moves; he resembles a statue. Then he lowers the glasses, closes them thoughtfully, and his calm glance passes along the lines of his army. You would say that this glance penetrates the forest; that he sees his old soldiers, gay, unshrinking, unmoved by the reverses of Longstreet, and believing in themselves and in him! The blood of the soldier responds to that thought. The face of the great commander suddenly flushes. He summons a staff officer and utters a few words in calm and measured tones. The order is given. The grand assault is about to begin.

That assault is going to be one of the most desperate in all history. Longstreet's has been fierce—this will be mad and full of headlong fury. At Round Top blood flowed—here the earth is going to be soaked with it. Gettysburg is to witness a charge recalling that of the six hundred horsemen at Balaklava. Each soldier will feel that the fate of the South depends on him, perhaps. If the wedge splits the tough grain, cracking it from end to end, the axe will enter after it—the work will be finished—the red flag of the South will float in triumph over a last and decisive field.

Pickett's division of Virginia troops has been selected for the hazardous venture, and they prepare for the ordeal in the midst of a profound silence. Since the morning scarce a gunshot has been heard. Now and then only, a single cannon, like a signal-gun, sends its growl through the hills.

Those two tigers, the army of Northern Virginia and the army of the Potomac, are crouching, and about to spring.

At one o'clock the moment seems to have arrived. Along the whole front of Hill and Longstreet, the Southern artillery all at once bursts forth. One hundred and forty-five cannon send their threatening thunder across the peaceful valley. From Cemetery Heights eighty pieces reply to them; and for more than an hour these two hundred and twenty-five cannon tear the air with their harsh roar, hurled back in crash after crash from the rocky ram- [89/ 90] parts. That thunder is the most terrible yet heard in the war. It stirs the coolest veterans. General Hancock, the composed and unexcitable soldier, is going to say of it, "Their artillery fire was most terrific; . . . it was the most terrific cannonade I ever witnessed, and the most prolonged. . . . It was a most terrific and appalling cannonade, one possibly hardly ever equalled."

For nearly two hours Lee continues this "terrific" fire. The Federal guns reply—shot and shell crossing each other; racing across the blue sky; battering the rocks; or bursting in showers of iron fragments.

Suddenly the Federal fire slackens, and then ceases. Their ammunition has run low, or they are silenced by the Southern fire. Lee's guns also cease firing. The hour has come.

The Virginians, under Pickett, form in double line in the edge of the woods, where Lee's centre is posted. These men are ragged and travel-worn, but their bayonets and gun-barrels shine like silver. From the steel hedge, as the men move, dart lightnings.

From the Cemetery Heights the enemy watch that ominous apparition—the gray line of Virginians drawn up for the charge.

At the word, they move out, shoulder to shoulder, at common time. Descending the slope, they enter on the valley, and move steadily toward the heights.

The advance of the column, with its battle-flags floating proudly, and its ranks closed up and dressed with the precision of troops on parade, is a magnificent spectacle. Old soldiers, hardened in the fires of battle, and not given to emotion, lean forward watching the advance of the Virginians with fiery eyes. You would say, from the fierce clutch of the gaunt hands on the muskets, that they wish to follow; and many wish that.

The column is midway the valley, and beginning to move more rapidly, when suddenly the Federal artillery opens. The ranks are swept by round shot, shell, and canister. Bloody gaps appear, but the line closes up, and continues to advance. The fire of the Federal artillery redoubles. All the demons of the pit seem howling, roaring, yelling, and screaming. The assaulting column is torn by a whirl-wind of canister, before which men fall in heaps mangled, stream-ing with blood, their bosoms torn to [90/91] pieces, their hands clutching the grass, their teeth biting the earth. The ranks, how-ever, close up as before, and the Virginians continue to advance.

From common time, they have passed to quick time—now they march at the double-quick. That is to say, they run. They have reached the slope; the enemy's breastworks are right before them; and they dash at them with wild cheers.

They are still three hundred yards from the Federal works, when the real conflict commences, to which the cannonade was but child's play. Artillery has thundered, but something more deadly succeeds it—the sudden crash of musketry. From behind a stone wall the Federal infantry rise up and pour a galling fire into the charging column. It has been accompanied to this moment by a body of other troops, but those troops now disappear, like dry leaves swept off by the wind. The Virginians still advance.

Amid a concentrated fire of infantry and artillery, in their front and on both flanks, they pass over the ground between themselves and the enemy; ascend the slope; rush headlong at the breastworks; storm them; strike their bayonets into the enemy, who recoil before them, and a wild cheer rises, making the blood leap in the veins of a hundred thousand men.

The Federal works are carried, and the troops are wild with enthusiasm. With a thunder of cheers they press upon the flying enemy toward the crest.

Alas! as the smoke drifts, they see what is enough to dishearten the bravest. They have stormed the first line of works only! Beyond, is another and a stronger line still. Behind it swarm the heavy reserves of the enemy, ready for the death-struggle. But the column can not pause. It is "do or die." In their faces are thrust the muzzles of muskets spouting flame. Whole ranks go down in the fire. The survivors close up, utter a fierce cheer, and rush straight at the second tier of works.

Then is seen a spectacle which will long be remembered with a throb of the heart by many. The thinned ranks of the Virginians are advancing, unmoved, into the very jaws of death. They go forward—and are annihilated. At every step death meets them. The furious fire of the enemy, on both flanks and in their [91/92] front, hurls them back, mangled and dying. The brave Garnett is killed while leading on his men. Kemper is lying on the earth maimed for life. Armistead is mortally wounded at the moment when he leaps upon the breastworks:—he waves his hat on the point of his sword, and staggers, and falls. Of fifteen field officers, fourteen have fallen. Three-fourths of the men are dead, wounded, or prisoners. The Federal infantry has closed in on the flanks and rear of the Virginians—whole corps assault the handful—the little band is enveloped, and cut off from succor—they turn and face the enemy, bayonet to bayonet, and die.

When the smoke drifts away, all is seen to be over. It is a panting, staggering, bleeding remnant only of the brave division that is coming back so slowly yonder. They are swept from the fatal hill—pursued by yells, cheers, cannon-shot, musket-balls, and canister. As they doggedly retire before the howling hurricane, the wounded are seen to stagger and fall. Over the dead and dying sweeps the canister. Amid volleys of musketry and the roar of cannon, all but a handful of Pickett's Virginians pass into eternity.

[92]

THE UNSEEN DEATH

The morning of the 6th of May was ushered in with thunder.

The battle of the preceding day had been a sort of "feeler"—now the real struggle came.

By a curious coincidence, Grant and Lee both began the attack and at the same hour. At five o'clock in the morning the blue and gray ranks rushed together, and opened fire on each other. Or rather, they fired when they heard each others' steps and shouts. You saw little in that jungle.

I have already spoken more than once of this sombre country—a land of undergrowth, thicket, ooze; where sight failed, and attacks had to be made by the needle, the officers advancing in front of the line with drawn—compasses!

The assaults here were worse than night-fighting; the combats strange beyond example. Regiments, brigades, and divisions stumbled on each other before they knew it; and each opened fire, guided alone by the crackling of steps in the bushes. There was something weird and lugubrious in such a struggle. It was not a conflict of men, matched against each other in civilized warfare. Two wild animals were prowling, and hunting each other in the jungle. When they heard each others' steps, they sprang and grappled. One fell, the other fell upon him. Then the conqueror rose up and went in pursuit of other game—the dead was lost from all eyes. [195/196]

In this mournful and desolate country of the Spottsylvania Wilderness, did the bloody campaign of 1864 begin. Here, where the very landscape seemed dolorous; here, in blind wrestle, as at midnight, did 200,000 men, in blue and gray, clutch each other—bloodiest and weirdest of encounters.

War had had nothing like it. Destruction of life had become a science, and was done by the compass.

The Genius of Blood, apparently tired of the old commonplace mode of killing, had invented the "Unseen Death," in the depths of the jungle.

On the morning of May 6th, Lee and Grant had grappled, and the battle became general along the entire line of the two armies. In these rapid memoirs I need only outline this bitter struggle—the histories will describe it.

Lee was aiming to get around the enemy's left, and huddled him up in the thicket—but in this he failed.

Just as Longstreet, who had arrived and taken part in the action, was advancing to turn the Federal flank on the Brock road, he was wounded by one of his own men; and the movement was arrested in mid career.

But Lee adhered to his plan. He determined to lead his column in person, and would have done so, but for the remonstrances of his men.

"To the rear!" shouted the troops, as he rode in front of them; "to the rear!"

And he was obliged to obey.

He was not needed.

The gray lines surged forward: the thicket was full of smoke and quick flashes of flame: then the woods took fire, and the scene of carnage had a new and ghastly feature added to it. Dense clouds of smoke rose, blinding and choking the combatants: the flames crackled, soared aloft, and were blown in the men's faces; and still, in the midst of this frightful array of horrors, the carnival of destruction went on without ceasing.

At nightfall, General Lee had driven the enemy from their front line of works—but nothing was gained.

What *could* be gained in that wretched country, where there was nothing but thicket, thicket! [196/197]

General Grant saw his danger, and, no doubt, divined the object of his adversary,—to arrest and cripple him in this tanglewood, where numbers did not count, and artillery could not be used.

There was but one thing to do—to get out of the jungle.

So, on the day after this weird encounter, in which he had lost nearly 20,000 men, and Lee about 8,000, Grant moved toward Spottsylvania.

The thickets of the Wilderness were again silent, and the blue and gray objects in the undergrowth did not move.

The war-dogs had gone to tear each other elsewhere. [197]

MY LAST RIDE WITH STUART

More than one stirring incident marked those days of desperate fighting, when, barricading all the roads, and charging recklessly, Stuart opposed, at every step, Grant's advance toward the Po.

But I can not describe those incidents. They must be left to others. The pen which has paused to record that exploit of Breathed, is drawn onward as by the hand of Fate toward one of those scenes which stand out, lugubrious and bloody, from the pages of history.

From the moment when Grant crossed the Rapidan, Stuart had met the horsemen of Sheridan everywhere in bitter conflict; and the days and nights had been strewed all over with battles.

Now, on the ninth of May, when the two great adversaries faced each other on the Po, a more arduous service still was demanded of the great sabreur. Sheridan had been dispatched to sever General Lee's communications, and, if possible, capture Richmond. The city was known to be well nigh stripped of troops, and a determined assault might result in its fall. Sheridan accordingly cut loose a heavy column, took command of it in [202/203] person, and descended like a thunderbolt toward the devoted city.

No sooner, however, had he begun to move, than Stuart followed on his track. He had no difficulty in doing so. A great dust-cloud told the story. That cloud hung above the long column of Federal cavalry, accompanied it wherever it moved, and indicated clearly to Stuart the course which his adversary was pursuing.

If he could only interpose, with however small a force, between Sheridan and Richmond, time would be given for preparation to resist the attack, and the capital might be saved. If he failed to interpose, Sheridan would accomplish his object—Richmond would fall.

It was a forlorn hope, after all, that he could arrest the Federal commander. General Sheridan took with him a force estimated at 9,000. Stuart's was, in all, about 3,000; Gordon, who was not in the battle at Yellow Tavern, included. That action was fought by Fitz Lee's division of 2,400 men all told. But the men and officers were brave beyond words; the incentive to daring resistance was enormous; they would do all that could be done.

Such was the situation of affairs on the 9th of May, 1864.

Stuart set out at full gallop on his iron gray, from Spottsylvania Court-House, about three o'clock in the day, and reached Chilesburg, toward Hanover Junction, just as night fell.

Here we found General Fitz Lee engaged in a hot skirmish with the enemy's rear-guard; and that night Stuart planned an attack upon their camp, but abandoned the idea.

His spirits at this time were excellent, but it was easy to see that he realized the immense importance of checking the enemy.

An officer said in his presence:—

"We won't be able to stop Sheridan."

Stuart turned at those words; his cheeks flushed; his eyes flamed, and he said:—

"No, sir! I'd rather die than let him go on!"

On the next morning, he moved in the direction of Hanover Junction; riding boot to boot with his friend General Fitz Lee. [203/204] I had never seen him more joyous. Some events engrave themselves forever on the memory. That ride of May 10th, 1864, was one of them.

Have human beings a presentiment, ever, at the near approach
of death? Does the shadow of the unseen hand ever reveal itself to
the eye? I know not, but I know that no such presentiment came to
Stuart; no shadow of the coming event darkened the path of the
great cavalier. On the contrary, his spirits were buoyant beyond
example, almost; and, riding on with General Fitz Lee, he sang in
his gallant voice his favorite ditties "Come out of the Wilderness!"
and "Jine the Cavalry!"

As he rode on thus, he was the beau ideal of a cavalier. His seat
in the saddle was firm; his blue eyes dazzling; his heavy mustache
curled with laughter at the least provocation. Something in this
man seemed to spring forward to meet danger. Peril aroused and
strung him. All his energies were stimulated by it. In that ride
through the May forest, to attack Sheridan, and arrest him or die,
Stuart's bearing and expression were superbly joyous and inspiring.
His black plume floated in the spring breeze, like some knight-
errant's; and he went to battle humming a song, resolved to conquer or fall.

Riding beside him, I found my eyes incessantly attracted to his
proud face; and now I see the great cavalier as then, clearly with the
eyes of memory. What a career had been his! what a life of battles!

As we went on through the spring woods, amid the joyous songs
of birds, all the long, hard combats of this man passed before me
like an immense panorama. The ceaseless scouting and fighting in
the Shenandoah Valley; the charge and route of the red-legged
"zouaves" at Manassas; the falling back to the Peninsula, and the
fighting all through Charles City; the famous ride around McClellan; the advance and combats on the Rapidan and Rappahannock,
after Cedar Mountain; the night attack on Catlett's, when he
captured Pope's coat and papers; the march on Jackson's flank, and
the capture of Manassas; the advance into Maryland; the fights at
Frederick, Crampton's, and Boonsboro', with the hard rear-guard
work, as Lee retired to Sharpsburg; his splendid handling of artillery on the left wing of the army [204/205] there; the retreat,
covered by his cavalry; the second ride around McClellan, and safe
escape from his clutches; the bitter conflicts at Upperville and
Barbee's, as Lee fell back; the hard fighting thereafter, on the banks
of the Rappahannock; the "crowding 'em with artillery," on the
night of Fredericksburg; the winter march to Dumfries; the des-

perate battle at Kelly's Ford; the falling back before Hooker; the battle of Chancellorsville, when he succeeded Jackson; the stubborn wrestle of Fleetwood; the war of giants below Upperville; the advance across Maryland into Pennsylvania, when the long march was strewed all over with battles, at Westminster, Hanover, Carlisle, Gettysburg, where he met and repulsed the best cavalry of the Federal army; the retreat from Gettysburg, with the tough affair near Boonsboro'; guarding the rear of the army as it again crossed the Potomac; then the campaign of October, ending with Kilpatrick's route at Buckland; the assault on Meade's head of column, when he came over to Mine Run; the bold attack on his rear there; and the hard, incessant fighting since Grant had come over to the Wilderness;—I remembered all these splendid scenes and illustrious services as I rode on beside Stuart, through the fields and forests of Hanover, and thought, "This is one of those great figures which live forever in history, and men's memories!"

To-day, I know that I was not mistaken, or laboring under the influence of undue affection and admiration. That figure has passed from earth, but still lives!

Stuart is long dead, and the grass covers him; but there is scarce a foot of the soil of Virginia that does not speak of him. He is gone, but his old mother is proud of him—is she not?

Answer, mountains where he fought—lowlands, where he fell—river, murmuring a dirge, as you foam through the rocks yonder, past his grave! [205]

GEORGE CARY EGGLESTON

(1839–1911)

*George Cary Eggleston is often paired with his brother Edward,
author of* The Hoosier School-Master. *Both were born in southeastern Indiana, but at the death of their father, George went
to Virginia to stay with relatives and Edward remained in the
Midwest. In Virginia, George made friends with the Richmond
literary group, which included John Esten Cooke. When war
broke out, he joined with his Virginian friends. He first served
in a cavalry unit under "Jeb" Stuart and later Fitzhugh Lee;
then he was transferred to artillery, where he became sergeant-
major of a battery which served as sharpshooters during the
siege of Petersburg. After the war Eggleston went to New York,
where he was a newspaper and periodical editor and also
literary adviser to Harper and Brothers. He wrote ten novels
(three of which treat antebellum Virginia), boys' stories, an
autobiography, and a two-volume* History of the Confederate
War (1910).

A Rebel's Recollections *intentionally minimizes the darker
aspect of war and exalts the chivalry and courage of the Southern soldier. Eggleston says in the Preface to the fourth edition
that he also is writing with the intent of helping forward the
reconciliation between North and South.*

from **THE MUSTERING***

That was an admirable idea of De Quincey's, formally to postulate
any startling theory upon which he desired to build an argument or

---

**The following selections are from George Cary Eggleston, *A Rebel's Recol-
lections* (New York and London: G. P. Putnam's Sons, 1905). Published in book
form in 1875, after being serialized in the *Atlantic Monthly.*

a story, and to insist that his readers should regard the postulate as proved, on pain of losing altogether what he had to say. The plan is a very convenient one, saving a deal of argument, and establishing in the outset a very desirable relation of mastery and subordination between writer and reader. Indeed, but for some such device I should never be able to get on at all with these sketches, fully to understand which, the reader must make of himself, for the time at least, a Confeder-[1/2] ate. He must put himself in the place of the Southerners and look at some things through their eyes, if he would understand those things and their results at all; and as it is no part of my purpose to write a defense of the Southern view of any question, it will save a good deal of. explanation on my part, and weariness on the part of the reader, if I follow De Quincey's example and do a little postulating to begin with. I shall make no attempt whatever to prove my postulates, but any one interested in these pages will find it to his advantage to accept them, one and all, as proved, pending the reading of what is to follow. After that he may relapse as speedily as he pleases into his own opinions. Here are the postulates:—

1. The Southerners honestly believed in the right of secession, not merely as a revolutionary, but as a constitutional right. They not only held that whenever any people finds the government under which it is [2/3] living oppressive and subversive of the ends for which it was instituted, it is both the right and the duty of that people to throw off the government and establish a new one in its stead; but they believed also that every State in the Union held the reserved right, under the constitution, to withdraw peaceably from the Union at pleasure.

2. They believed that every man's allegiance was due to his State only, and that it was only by virtue of the State's continuance in the Union that any allegiance was due to the general government at all; wherefore the withdrawal of a State from the Union would of itself absolve all the citizens of that State from whatever obligations they were under to maintain and respect the Federal constitution. In other words, patriotism, as the South understood it, meant devotion to one's State, and only a secondary and consequential devotion to the Union, existing as a result of the State's action in making itself a part of the Union [3/4] and terminable at any time by the State's withdrawal.

3. They were as truly and purely patriotic in their secession

and in the fighting which followed, as were the people of the North in their adherence to the Union itself. The difference was one of opinion as to what the duties of a patriot were, and not at all a difference in the degree of patriotism existing in the two sections.

4. You, reader, who shouldered your musket and fought like the hero you are, for the Union and the old flag, if you had been bred at the South, and had understood your duty as the Southerners did theirs, would have fought quite as bravely for secession as you did against it; and you would have been quite as truly a hero in the one case as in the other, because in either you would have risked your life for the sake of that which you held to be the right. If the reader will bear all this in mind we shall get on much better than we [4/5] otherwise could, in our effort to catch a glimpse of the war from a Southern point of view.

With all its horrors and in spite of the wretchedness it has wrought, this war of ours, in some of its aspects at least, begins to look like a very ridiculous affair, now that we are getting too far away from it to hear the rattle of the musketry; and I have a mind, in this chapter, to review one of its most ridiculous phases, to wit, its beginning. We all remember Mr. Webster's pithy putting of the case with regard to our forefathers of a hundred years ago: "They went to war against a preamble. They fought seven years against a declaration. They poured out their treasures and their blood like water, in a contest in opposition to an assertion." Now it seems to me that something very much like this might be said of the Southerners, and particularly of the Virginians, without whose pluck and pith there could have been no war at all [5/6] worth writing or talking about. They made war upon a catch-word, and fought until they were hopelessly ruined for the sake of an abstraction. And certainly history will not find it to the discredit of those people that they freely offered themselves upon the altar of an abstract principle of right, in a war which they knew must work hopeless ruin to themselves, whatever its other results might be. Virginia did not want to secede, and her decision to this effect was given in the election of a convention composed for the most part of men strongly opposed to secession. The Virginians believed they had both a moral and a constitutional right to withdraw voluntarily from a Union into which they had voluntarily gone, but the majority of them preferred to remain as they were. They did not feel themselves particularly aggrieved or threatened by the election of Mr. Lincoln, and so, while they never doubted that they had an unquestionable right to secede at will, they [6/7] decided by their votes not to do anything of the kind. This decision was given in the most unmistakable way, by heavy majorities, in an election which involved no other issue whatever. But without Virginia the States which had already passed ordinances of secession would have been wholly unable to sustain themselves. Virginia's strength in men, material, and geographical position was very necessary, for one thing, and her moral influence on North Carolina, Arkansas, and other hesitating States, was even more essential to the success of the movement. Accordingly every pospossible effort was made to "fire the heart" of the conservative old commonwealth. Delegations, with ponderous stump speeches in their mouths and parchment appeals in their hands, were sent from the seceding States to Richmond, while every Virginian who actively favored secession was constituted a committee of one to cultivate a public sentiment in favor of the movement. [7/14] . . . [Tells of noisy speech-makers whose vaporings were not taken seriously by the "real people."]

Meantime a terrible dread was brooding over the minds of the Virginian people. They were brave men and patriots, who would maintain their honor at any cost. They were ready to sacrifice their lives and their treasures in a hopeless struggle about an abstraction, should the time come when their sense of right and honor required the sacrifice at their hands. There was no cowardice and no hesitation to be expected [14/15] of them when the call should come. But they dreaded war, and most of them prayed that it might never be. They saw only desolation in its face. They knew it would lay waste their fields and bring want upon their families, however it might result in regard to the great political questions involved in it. And so they refused to go headlong into a war which meant for them destruction. Some of them, believing that there was no possibility of avoiding the struggle, thought it the part of wisdom to accept the inevitable and begin hostilities at once, while the North was still but poorly prepared for aggressive measures. But the majority of the Virginians were disposed to wait and to avoid war altogether, if that should prove possible. These said, "We should remain quiet until some overt act of hostility shall make resistance necessary." And these were called cowards and fogies by the brave men of the hustings already alluded to. [15/16]

There was still another class of men who were opposed to secession in any case. Of these, William C. Wickham, of Hanover, and Jubal Early will serve as examples. They thought secession unnecessary and imprudent in any conceivable event. They believed that it offered no remedy for existing or possible ills, and that it could result only in the prostration of the South. They opposed it, therefore, with all their might; not only as not yet called for, but as suicidal in any event, and not to be thought of at all. And yet these men, when the war came, believed it to be their duty to side with their State, and fought so manfully in behalf of the South as to make themselves famous military leaders.

Why, then, the reader doubtless asks, if this was the temper of the Virginians, did Virginia secede after all? I answer, because circumstances ultimately so placed the Virginians that they could not, without cowardice and dishonor, do otherwise; and [16/17] the Virginians are brave men and honorable ones. They believed, as I have said, in the abstract right of any State to secede at will. Indeed, this right was to them as wholly unquestioned and unquestionable as is the right of the States to establish free schools, or to do any other thing pertaining to local self-government. The question of the correctness or incorrectness of the doctrine is not now to the purpose. The Virginians, almost without an exception, believed and had always believed it absolutely, and believing it, they held of necessity that the general government had no right, legal or moral, to coerce a seceding State; and so, when the President called upon Virginia for her quota of troops with which to compel the return of the seceding States, she could not possibly obey without doing that which her people believed to be an outrage upon the rights of sister commonwealths, for which, as they held, there was no warrant in law or equity. [17/18]

She heartily condemned the secession of South Carolina and the rest as unnecessary, ill-advised, and dangerous; but their secession did not concern her except as a looker-on, and she had not only refused to be a partaker in it, but had also felt a good deal of indignation against the men who were thus endangering the peace of the land. When she was called upon to assist in reducing these States to submission, however, she could no longer remain a spectator. She must furnish the troops, and so assist in doing that which she believed to be utterly wrong, or she must herself withdraw from the Union. The question was thus narrowed down to this: Should Virginia seek safety in dishonor, or should she meet destruction in doing that which she believed to be right? Such a question was not long to be debated. Two days after the proclamation was published Virginia seceded, not because she wanted to secede,—not because she believed it wise,—but [18/19] because, as she understood the matter, the only other course open to her would have been cowardly and dishonorable.

Now, unless I am sadly mistaken, the Virginians understood what secession implied much more perfectly than did the rest of the Southern people. They anticipated no child's play, and having cast in their lot with the South, they began at once to get ready for war. From one end of the State to the other, every county seat became a drill field. The courts suspended their sessions, on the ground that it was not a proper time for the enforced collection of debts. Volunteer companies soon drained the militia organization of its men. Public opinion said that every man who did not embrace the very surest and earliest opportunity of getting himself mustered into actual service was a coward; and so, to withdraw from the militia and join a volunteer company, and make a formal tender of services to the State, became absolutely es-[19/20] sential to the maintenance of one's reputation as a gentleman.

from **THE MEN WHO MADE THE ARMY**

A newspaper correspondent has told us that the great leader of the German armies, Count Von Moltke, has never read anything—even a history—of our war, and that when questioned on the subject, he has said he could not afford to spend time over "the wrangling of two armed mobs." If he ever said anything of the kind, which is doubtful, his characterization of the two armies had reference, probably, to their condition during the first year or two of the struggle, when they could lay very little claim indeed to any more distinctively military title. The Southern army, at any rate, was simply a vast mob of rather ill-armed young gentlemen from the country. As I have said [29/30] in a previous chapter, every gentleman in Virginia, not wholly incapable of rendering service, enlisted at the beginning of the war, and the companies, unarmed, untrained, and hardly even organized, were sent at once to camps of instruction. Here they [30/31] were in theory drilled and disciplined and made into soldiers, by the little handful of available West-Pointers and the lads from the Military Institute at Lexington. In point of fact, they were only organized and taught the rudiments of the drill before being sent to the front as full-fledged soldiers; and it was only after a year or more of active service in the field that they began to suspect what the real work and the real character of the modern soldier is.

Our ideas of the life and business of a soldier were drawn chiefly from the adventures of Ivanhoe and Charles O'Malley, two worthies with whose personal history almost every man in the army was familiar. The men who volunteered went to war of their own accord, and were wholly unaccustomed to acting on any other than their own motion. They were hardy lovers of field sports, accustomed to out-door life, and in all physical respects excellent material of which to make an army. But they were [31/32] not used to control of any sort, and were not disposed to obey anybody except for good and sufficient reason given. While actually on drill they obeyed the word of command, not so much by reason of its being proper to obey a command, as because obedience was in that case necessary to the successful issue of a pretty performance in which they were interested. Off drill they did as they pleased, holding themselves gentlemen, and as such bound to consult only their own wills. Their officers were of themselves, chosen by election, and subject, by custom, to enforced resignation upon petition of the men. Only corporals cared sufficiently little for their position to risk any magnifying of their office by the enforcement of discipline. I make of them an honorable exception, out of regard for the sturdy corporal who, at Ashland, marched six of us (a guard detail) through the very middle of a puddle, assigning as his reason for doing so the fact that "It's [32/33] plagued little authority they give us corporals, and I mean to use that little, any how." Even corporals were elected, however, and until December, 1861, I never knew a single instance in which a captain dared offend his men by breaking a non-commissioned officer, or appointing one, without submitting the matter to a vote of the company. In that first instance the captain had to bolster himself up with written authority from head-quarters, and even then it required three weeks of mingled diplomacy and discipline to quell the mutiny which resulted.

With troops of this kind, the reader will readily understand, a feeling of very democratic equality prevailed, so far at least as military rank had anything to do with it. Officers were no better than men, and so officers and men messed and slept together on terms of entire equality, quarreling and even fighting now and then, in a gentlemanly way, but without a thought of allow- [33/ 34] ing differences of military rank to have any influence in the matter. The theory was that the officers were the creatures of the men, chosen by election to represent their constituency in the performance of certain duties, and that only during good behavior. And to this theory the officers themselves gave in their adhesion in a hundred ways. Indeed, they could do nothing else, inasmuch as they knew no way of quelling a mutiny.

There was one sort of rank, however, which was both maintained and respected from the first, namely, that of social life. The line of demarkation between gentry and common people is not more sharply drawn anywhere than in Virginia. It rests there upon an indeterminate something or other, known as family. To come of a good family is a patent of nobility, and there is no other way whatever by which any man or any woman can find a passage into the charmed circle of Virginia's peer- [34/35] age. There is no college of heralds, to be sure, to which doubtful cases may be referred, and there is no law governing the matter; but every Virginian knows what families are, and what are not good ones, and so mistakes are impossible. The social position of every man is sharply defined, and every man carried it with him into the army. The man of good family felt himself superior, as in most cases he unquestionably was, to his fellow-soldier of less excellent birth; and this distinction was sufficient, during the early years of the war, to override everything like military rank. . . . [35]

PAUL HAMILTON HAYNE
(1830–1886)

Born in Charleston, Hayne was a lifelong friend of Henry Tim-rod and a close associate with Simms. Before the war he helped launch Russell's Magazine, *a notable but short-lived literary journal, and published several volumes of verse. During the war Hayne served as an aide on Governor Pickens's staff until he had to retire because of physical frailty. His home burned during the bombardment of Charleston, and he moved to Groveton, near Augusta, Georgia, where at his "Copse Hill" he continued to write poetry.*

CHARLESTON AT THE CLOSE OF 1863*

What! still does the mother of treason uprear
    Her crest 'gainst the furies that darken her sea,
Unquelled by mistrust, and unblanched by a fear,
    Unbowed her proud head, and unbending her knee,
        Calm, steadfast and free!

Ay! launch your red lightnings! blaspheme in your wrath!
    Shock earth, wave, and heaven with the blast of your ire;
But she seizes your death-bolts yet hot from their path,
    And hurls back your lightnings and mocks at the fire
        Of your fruitless desire!   10

Ringed round by her brave, a fierce circlet of flame
    Flashes up from the sword-points that cover her breast;

*The following are from *Poems of Paul Hamilton Hayne* (Boston: D. Lothrop and Company, 1882). Both poems were probably written at the time of the events they discuss.

She is guarded by love, and enhaloed by fame, [78/79]
   And never, we swear, shall your footsteps be pressed,
     Where her dead heroes rest.

Her voice shook the tyrant, sublime from her tongue
   Fell the accents of warning! a prophetess grand—
On her soil the first life notes of liberty rung,
   And the first stalwart blow of her gauntleted hand
     Broke the sleep of her land.   20

What more? she hath grasped in her iron-bound will
   The fate that would trample her honors to earth;
The light in those deep eyes is luminous still
   With the warmth of her valor, the glow of her worth,
     Which illumine the earth.

And beside her a knight the great Bayard had loved,
   "Without fear or reproach," lifts her banner on high;
He stands in the vanguard majestic, unmoved,
   And a thousand firm souls when that chieftain is nigh,
     Vow " 'tis easy to die!"   30

Their words have gone forth on the fetterless air,
   The world's breath is hushed at the conflict! Before
Gleams the bright form of Freedom, with wreaths in her hair—
   And what though the chaplet be crimsoned with gore—
     We shall prize her the more!

And while Freedom lures on with her passionate eyes
   To the height of her promise, the voices of yore
From the storied profound of past ages arise,
   And the pomps of their magical music outpour
     O'er the war-beaten shore!   40

Then gird your brave empress, O heroes! with flame
   Flashed up from the sword-points that cover her breast!
She is guarded by Love and enhaloed by Fame,
   And never, stern foe! shall your footsteps be pressed
     Where her dead martyrs rest! [79]

VICKSBURG—A BALLAD

For sixty days and upwards,
    A storm of shell and shot
Rained round us in a flaming shower,
    But still we faltered not.
"If the noble city perish,"
    Our grand young leader said,
"Let the only walls the foe shall scale
    "Be ramparts of the dead!"

For sixty days and upwards,
    The eye of heaven waxed dim;   10
And e'en throughout God's holy morn,
    O'er Christian prayer and hymn,
Arose a hissing tumult,
    As if the fiends in air
Strove to engulf the voice of faith
    In the shrieks of their despair.

There was wailing in the houses,
    There was trembling on the marts,
While the tempest raged and thundered,
    'Mid the silent thrill of hearts;   20
But the Lord, our shield, was with us,
    And ere a month had sped,
Our very women walked the streets
    With scarce one throb of dread.

And the little children gambolled,
    Their faces purely raised,
Just for a wondering moment,
    As the huge bombs whirled and blazed,
Then turned with silvery laughter
    To the sports which children love,   30
Thrice-mailed in the sweet, instinctive thought
    That the good God watched above.

Yet the hailing bolts fell faster,
   From scores of flame-clad ships,
And about us, denser, darker,
   Grew the conflict's wild eclipse,
Till a solid cloud closed o'er us,
   Like a type of doom and ire,
Whence shot a thousand quivering tongues
   Of forked and vengeful fire.   40

But the unseen hands of angels
   Those death-shafts warned aside,
And the dove of heavenly mercy
   Ruled o'er the battle tide;
In the houses ceased the wailing,
   And through the war-scarred marts
The people strode, with step of hope,
   To the music in their hearts. [80]

WILLIAM GILMORE SIMMS

(1806–1870)

Born in Charleston, South Carolina, William Gilmore Simms
was undoubtedly the most prominent Southern man of letters
during the Civil War. In the antebellum years he had published
a good deal of verse and several novels, among them The
Yemassee (*1835*), The Partisan (*1835*), and Woodcraft (*1854*).
He was ardently pro-Southern and in 1856 tried in vain to
explain the Southern position to audiences in New York.

    Before the war began he was active in preparing for the
defense of Charleston Harbor. Also he wrote many editorials
for the Charleston Mercury. During the war Simms was faced
with successive tragedies. His home at Woodlands burned, his
wife died in 1863, he lost several children, and near the end of
the war stragglers connected with Sherman's army burned his
rebuilt house, destroying with it his library of 10,700 volumes.

from LETTER TO JOHN JACOB BOCKEE*

[Woodlands], December 12, 1860

My Dear Mr. B—:

    I thank you for your letter, and the kindly feelings which it so
well expresses. But you are wholly mistaken, equally in your
argument and your convictions. *Our safety* is much more important
to us than *any Union;* and, in the event of our future union with
other parties, we shall certainly look to our safety, with much more
circumspection than our fathers did, though they strove to guard
their people, with all their vigilance, against the danger equally of a

---

* From the *Charleston Mercury*, January 17, 1861, p. 1. The editor of the
Mercury at this time was the Southern "fire-eater" Robert Barnwell Rhett.

majority and of Federal usurpation. If fortunate in little else, we are now fortunate in an experience far superior to theirs; and we shall deserve the worst of fates, if we do not become wiser and safer for it. We have learned, for example, to value the Union, not according to the hopes of its beginning, but through the wrongs which now demand that we bring it to an early end.

Our case, I admit, is something different from yours—and so is our experience! You at the North may well put the most enormous estimate upon the *value of the Union.* *You* may well lift up your hands and call it *blessed!* You have fattened upon it for nearly eighty years; fattened and flourished, in a degree of prosperity unexampled in the history of nations. We can easily conceive the reluctance of your section to see it dissolved. The Union, as Daniel Webster once said before the Supreme Court, in reply to young Van Buren, has been the source of all your prosperity. It is your misfortune that, with the usual blind tendencies of all over-prosperous people, you have not sufficiently valued it yourselves. You have perilled it dozens of times, simply because of the insanity of your prosperity. You have, at length, destroyed it.

Understand me. I mean no harsh reflections upon *you,* individually. I do you the justice to believe that *you* would have saved it if you could, and in the only right way—by being just and honest to the South. It is our great regret that, in the measures which we have need to take for our own safety, we must necessarily compromise yours. But in the case of great states, or nations, and their vast and various issues, we are compelled to ignore all individual exceptions. I know that you have thousands, possibly millions, who are in the same category with yourself; who have been friendly to us, and were anxious to be just; but either you were not strong enough in numbers, or warm enough in zeal, or active enough in performance, to secure us justice, by keeping down the fanatical, the foolish, the base and the presumptuous of your section; and it is the law in morals and society, that men should be punished for the bad company they keep! You have not been able to secure us justice or safety, and we must now look out for ourselves. You have allowed our enemies—and I think your own—to triumph; and if you will permit me to say, *now,* your present mistake still consists in the desire, *rather to save the Union, than to do justice to the South.*

Why, my dear deluded friend, do you still desire to save the

Union? Of what sort of value, to a Christian man, is that sort of union which persists in keeping men in the same household, who hate and blaspheme each other? And can you be really a friend to the South—a wise one you certainly are not—when you desire *us,* the *minority* States, to submit to the uncontrolled legislation of a majority, which has not only proved faithless to all its pledges, but which has declared its determined purpose to subdue, rule and destroy the minority, and abrogate all its rights and securities?

Suffer me, my dear friend, to hint to you a few other matters. How is it that, in all the trespasses and exactions of the North, upon and from the South, you never wrote such a letter to the aggressors and the trespassers, in behalf of the South, as you now write to me in behalf of the Union? I never got from you a letter of indignation, when the North was taxing the sweat and labor of the South, even to its ruin, by protective tariffs, for the benefit and greed of the manufacturing monopolists of New England and Pennsylvania. I never heard from you—addressed either to me or to the enemies of my people—in anger, at the abrogation of the Fugitive Slave law by some twelve or fifteen of your States, your own among them! You never cried out your griefs, or your wrath, when our slaves were hurried from us by underground railroads—by wretches, exulting doubly when, robbing the master of his slaves, they succeeded in persuading them to murder him also; and, when the fugitives from justice were withheld, and the pursuing owners or officers were seized and mobbed, and maltreated, and doomed to the penitentiary—why was your voice silent? Nor do I know, or believe, when, violating the Missouri Compromise, the hostile and abolition North refused to the South their recognized rights south of the line of 36° 30′, that you even made your clamors heard in defence of Southern rights and privileges, and in the maintenance of a sacred stipulation. And yet, in that very conquest of Mexico and California, the South sent 46,000 volunteers into the field; the North but 22,000; and with a handsome proportion of the New England troops refusing to fight when they got to Vera Cruz, alleging, in the hour of battle, their conscientious scruples about the morals of war in general, and this war in particular! The battle fought, the victory won, the territory gained, their moral scruples all gave way, at the gathering of the spoils! They grasped the whole territory with the eagerness of a half starved parish boy, blessed with the unexpected sight of a sudden plum pudding within his reach! By a majority vote in Congress, they took it all—some 700 miles on the Pacific coast; and drove out the Southern slaveholders, who had fought the battle! As Edward said to Bruce, "Have I nothing to do but to win kingdoms for you?" And where were you, and other friends of the South, while this royal robbery went on? Not a voice was heard in opposition; and I do not find in any of the frequent friendly letters which I have had from you, that you even once allude to *our* wrongs at all, or in the language of indignation. You never seem to have foreseen that a fatal blow was given to this Union *then*—in that very hour—in that stroke of a policy so very cunning as to—cut its own throat!

I look in vain, my excellent friend, among all your excellent letters to me, to find one single expression of your horror at the John Brown raid in Virginia! Your indignation, I suppose, was so intense as to keep you dumb! I cannot, of course, suppose that you were indifferent! Oh! no; your expressions of love forbid that idea! So, too, I see not a word of your wrath and indignation, in any of these letters, at the burnings of our towns, and the poisoning of our fountains, in Texas, by creatures of the same kidney with the vulture Brown! And when Brown is made a martyr of in the North, and his day made a sacred record in the Northern calendar, I do not perceive that you covered your head with sackcloth and ashes, and wrote to me lamenting!

And when your people *did* rise, after a fashion, and at a very late hour—you among them—to oppose Abolitionism, you had neither the virtue, nor the wisdom, to take issue with the enemy by a manly justification of the South! You only moved *to save the Union*—in other words, *not to lose the keeping of that excellent milch cow,* whose dugs have yielded, for sixty years, so large a proportion of the milk and butter which have fattened your hungry people. You claimed nothing for the South—asserted nothing; asked nothing; had no purpose beyond the preservation of the Confederacy, *as it was;* the South being the victim still—the North the wolf.

I had no pathetic letters from you, touching any of the exactions, aggressions, usurpations, or atrocities of the North! I cannot find a single one in all my collection! and now that you do write of these things, I find that you have but one plea, one prayer, one entreaty—*to save the Union!* to keep the milch cow still within your pleasant pastures; to persuade the lamb not to use his heels, or his watch dogs; but to leave everything to the tender mercies of the wolf!

Ah! my friend, this is very terrible on the part of friendship! Is it malice? Is it mockery?

You now only write to the injured and the endangered party, entreating him to yield himself placidly to injury and danger; to submit to continued outrage and aggression! You do not write when you see *him* in danger. You only write and plead and pray, when you think that the Union, which is the instrument of *his* destruction—as it has been the agent of your bloated prosperity—is in danger! When you see that, driven to desperation by the incessant robberies, aggressions and atrocities of the North, the South is resolved at last to shake herself free from a union which is but the cloak and cowardly shelter, under cover of which her enemies aim the dagger at her breast, assail her midnight slumbers with pikes and fire, and poison the fountains where her women and children drink.

And is such a union desirable, worth preserving, profitable in morals or honorable to either party? What sort of union is it—and with what sort of brethren? It is not a union, surely, of God's joining; but a union of the Devil's joining—to use the strong language of Milton. Is it not a union with hell, and crime, and lust, and vice, and the most satanic ministry? Surely, as a Christian man, you cannot desire that such a union as this should continue, whether you argue from your section or from mine! If you have any esteem for yourselves or for us, it is surely undesirable to preserve it, unless by such miserable wretches as care not what the crime may be, so that they profit by it. A mercenary tradesman may be pleased to continue such a connection, but an honest, and virtuous, God-fearing man, never! . . .

As regards South Carolina, I have only now to say to you that, having *tried* co-operation in vain, she will now act for herself, precisely as if the great danger stood at her own doors only, and there were no Virginia, no other States to suffer in like manner with herself, and to share her dangers. *She will secede* as surely as the sun shines in heaven. She will rely upon the justice of her cause and the virtue of her people. She will invade nobody. She will aggress upon no rights of others. She has never done so. The South has never been the aggressor! We have never meddled in the internal affairs of the North. But we will no longer suffer aggression under the mask of "this blessed Union." We shall tear off the mask, and show the hideous faithlessness, cupidity, lying and selfishness that lurk beneath. And we shall do this, regardless of all consequences. For these we shall prepare ourselves as well as we can. We have arms, and know how to use them. We can send into the field sixty-five Palmetto Regiments—say sixty-five thousand men—born to the rifle, and on horseback. We may be isolated by our sister States, though I think not, for *their instincts* will teach them, in spite of all their politicians, that we are fighting *their* battles as well as our own. And on our own ground, in defence of our firesides, and in the assertion of ancestral rights, we shall deliver no blow in vain. We may be conquered, my friend, but we *will* be free!

In five days more South Carolina will have repealed the act which carried her into the Confederacy. And, suffer me to predict, in fifty days more, or less, all of the Cotton States will have withdrawn from a Confederacy which we now begin generally to believe is under the curse of Heaven! The madness that has possessed the Northern States, in their wild rage against their best customers, shows them to be under the doom of judicial blindness! Those whom God seeks to destroy, he first makes mad! Their ears shall not serve for hearing, nor their eyes for seeing; and they but recklessly rush upon their doom. In three months more, all the *Slave* States must follow the *Cotton* States, and withdraw from a Confederacy which would otherwise swallow them up! Nor these alone. The Southern States are welded together by the one grand cohesive institution of slavery; while New England, New York and Pennsylvania, are deadly rivals, in the same pursuits, for the trade of the South. It will not be easy to suppose that these States can blend together. They must tumble asunder; and it is doubtful which of the two, New York or Pennsylvania, will show most speed of foot in the endeavor to get into the folds of this Southern Confederacy. Meditate the argument for yourself, and see if, according to all reasoning policy, you can come to any other conclusion.

Nor should these things take you by surprise. Your people have been working, against all warnings, to this very consummation! Their purpose was avowed, to make the conflict an *irrepressible*

one! What did this mean? Simply that there should be no power
capable to repress or still the conflict, until the bitter end had been
reached of destroying negro slavery in the South, and reducing the
South to a provincial subjection under a wholly irresponsible majority of a section which, for forty years, has been incessant in its
hostilities. And they have at length reached a result which served to
make their full triumph easy, and to obtain all the fruits which they
promised themselves from it. With the Government of the United
States exclusively in their hands—the Treasury—Army—Navy—
Supreme Court, all,—the cry was already sent up, with demoniac
shoutings, "Væ Victis!" Woe to the conquered! Do we not hear
them? Are we deaf, as well as blind; base and cowardly, as well as
weak? Shall we not take their own assurances, as to what they
design; that design being in full harmony with all their past pro-
ceedings? Having consummated all their proposed plans, and
grasped all the necessary power, shall we doubt that our continuance in the Union is simply submission to our doom!

Ah! my old friend, I fear that you think us equally silly and
cowardly, as the Black Republicans seem to have done, if you can
suppose that a section possessing four millions of slaves—$400,000,-
000 of property—and able to send into the field two millions of
fighting men, all trained in a high spirit of liberty—trained to
arms—all proud of a brave and free ancestry—should tamely submit until the chains are riveted about their limbs, and the knives of
the butchers are at their throats! And, even if you could suppose so
meanly of us, it is yet a wonder that you should lower us still more
in human estimation, by supposing we could *love,* or desire to
cherish, a continued union with the people who have been de-
nouncing, reviling, robbing, and finally preparing such a doom for
us! In this Union, by cunning acts, protective tariffs, navigation,
and other such laws, and the perpetual appropriation of the greater
part of the annual revenue, we have been fleeced of our profits for
fifty years. In this Union we find neither profit nor honor. We are
reviled, as well as robbed, daily. When we ask for our rights under
the Constitution and its laws, we are threatened with fine and
imprisonment; and maltreated by the licensed mobs of the North
when we seek redress in person. The territory for which our money
has been paid, and for which our young men have bled, has been
wrested from us; and, not satisfied with this, and a thousand other
forms of wrong, robbery and aggression, it is now the loving labor

of these fraternal States of the North, whose Union is so precious in your sight, to annihilate the sources of prosperity in our actual possession, and deliver us, bound hand and foot, into the meshes of incendiarism. To bring about this unnatural achievement of brotherhood there needed but one crowning act, the election of a President by a section which disdained to ask the approval of the South—which sought to conciliate no support or sympathy in the South—which consulted neither our interests nor our desires—the election of a creature wholly unknown before, save, as it appears, a rail-splitter, in which few well trained Southern negroes cannot excel him; and for a Vice-President who, according to report, possesses no single quality in mind or manhood, so well marked as a streak of the negro in his blood. . . .

It is high time that the South should confine itself to its own rule. The Abolitionists have forced this rule upon them, and with its exercise, come independence and prosperity. We, in the South, have all the essential elements for establishing the greatest and most prosperous, and longest lived of all the republics of the earth! We are, indeed, in possession of the philosopher's stone. We reconcile the great problem now threatening all Europe, and all the North,—the struggle between capital and labor. Our labor is our capital. Exporting, now, some $300,000,000 annually (destined to indefinite increase) of the greatest staples of the world—that raw material which all the world consumes, and which we willingly leave to other nations to work up; we employ the world's labor to an enormous extent, and thus hold the world's tacit bond of good behavior and friendship. We have long furnished the freights to nine-tenths of the Atlantic shipping of the North, as all our exports are bulky, no less than valuable. The moment that the South shall discriminate between foreign and domestic bottoms, all that shipping must become ours; and so soon as we shall declare our ports free to the industrial energies and productions of all the world, we subject Northern manufactures, for the first time, to that wholesome competition with the industry of other countries, the absence of which has made her bloated in prosperity, and utterly insane in its enjoyments.

The Southern States are all welded together by the institution of African Slavery—an institution which has done more for philanthropy and humanity in one year than there ever has been achieved by all the professional philanthropists of Europe and America in one hundred years; and this labor, in our genial climate, can be applied to all the industrial arts—to the construction of railroads—to the working of mills—in brief, to all the provinces of toil. Our water power never freezes, and it is abundant; our labor never times itself to short or long hours, and never *strikes,* impatient to share more largely of the profits of the capitalists.

But what, my interesting friend, shall bind the States of the North—New York, Pennsylvania, and New England, together? What does New York ask at the hands of either Pennsylvania or New England? You are all deadly rivals of each other in commercial, mechanical, and manufacturing pursuits, for the trade of the South. So long as you had this, so vast a market and complete monopoly in your hands, you could *all* flourish, and it was a common cause with you to keep it in your hands, and keep the South in subjection. It was enough for all of you, and you have fattened upon it, till, like Jeshurun, you have kicked! This market gone, this monopoly lost, what is it that ye can yield to, or ask from, each other? What bond of union blends you in one? What is the tie? What the interest? You cannot sell to each other, for each possesses in abundance what the other has for sale! Was there ever a more brutal suicide than that of your States, thus driving from them, by constant persecution, their best customers, struggling to strangle the wondrous goose that laid for them all the golden eggs? And how you shudder, when, fastening your hands upon her throat, the goose becomes the eagle! Ah! my friend, God may forgive you—*we* may forgive you—but will you ever forgive yourselves?

There is something more in your epistle which remains to be noticed. You admit our wrongs—you denounce the trespasses of the Abolitionists, and you counsel us to seek our remedy. Where? How? On whom? On the ignorant farmers who sell us onions, cabbages, buckets, baskets, and the ordinary cargo of notions which are brought us in sloops and schooners from Connecticut, creeping along our shores, and slipping into our bays and inlets, wherever they can find a market for their prog! This, surely, my friend, would be a small business for any people, and how wretchedly inadequate as a remedy for that wholesale robbery, which, through the Union, has been spoiling the South for thirty years. For the wholesale appropriation of the resources of the country; for the entire usurpation of Canada; for the loss of thousands of slaves; for the abuse of justice; for the defiance of law; the violation of the

Constitution; for contumely and slander; for insurrections, poisonings and houseburnings; and as a security against the power of Lincoln and his satellites, in full possession of the Government—we are to reject or confiscate the onions and cabbages of Connecticut, and drive from our harbors their piddling little crafts and cargos. Verily, my friend, you do but jest! You might as well counsel us to an onslaught, sword in hand, upon their onion beds and cabbage fields! We are to expend our fury upon the ignorant tools, and suffer the cunning scoundrels who have beguiled them to their ruin, to escape. Would you yourself punish those poor devils, knowing as you well do who have been their teachers? These teachers are your leading citizens; your sense keepers,—preachers, editors,—men who profess to keep the intellect and consciences of your people in their hand; who direct their votes and judgments; and who know what the simple farmer[s] do not, that they inculcate crime, under the guise of philanthropy, and prompt incendiarism with the view to the usurpation of power. These must be made to feel rather than the farmers. But all will feel, good and bad alike, of that punishment which, in such a case as the present, must fail to discriminate. A people must suffer at large for the moral of their communities, for the crimes of their legislation, for the usurpations which they wink at, if they do not share. But our purpose is to punish none. We aim at no revenges. We simply seek escape for ourselves from worse evils. As we cannot live together in amity, we say to you, "let us part in peace. You take your course—we ours—each on his own ground." [1]

from LETTER TO JAMES LAWSON*

Woodlands, 20 August 1861.

. . . Oh! how your foolish [New York City] has been cutting its own throat. Only think of a people making war on their best customers. What suicide. Your *accounts* are not such as reach us of the events of the war. Our Government is not one to suppress reports of the action; to seize upon telegraphic despatches; to alter

*From *The Letters of William Gilmore Simms,* ed. Mary C. Simms Oliphant and T. C. Duncan Eaves (Columbia, 1955), Vol. IV. Reprinted by permission of the University of South Carolina Press.

reports for the press & telegraph—in brief to do what it pleases, in violation of Constitution, law & rights of the Citizen. Whether you will hear the truth until the war is ended, is very questionable. But you ought to be shrewd Scotchman enough to guess it for yourself, when, after all the mighty preparations of the North, they still tremble for the safety of Washington, & every step in Virginia has lost them blood & treasure. We do not exult in this. We wish for peace. We desire no war, but are prepared for the worst. We are resolved on Independence. We have been persecuted for 30 years & will stand it no longer—from our brethren. By this time your thinking men see the sort of game that is before them. Let them grow wise before it be too late. Every battle, thus far, has resulted in a Southern Victory.—Sumter, Bethel, Bull Run, Manassas, Harpers Ferry & Missouri,—all tell the same tale. Your Generals are cashiered. Your army demoralized. Your papers are at a loss where to cast the blame. They will be at no [373/374] loss before long. They will see that their cause is bad. We have now 200,000 men in the field, with 250,000 in preparation for it. We can feed our armies from the fields, without buying any thing but guns & ammunition. We shall make 4,500,000 bales of Cotton. We will look at the piles & if need be, burn them. We do not need to sell a bag. Of all this, you, among others, were well warned long ago. I do not blame *you* for this war. I know that you desired peace. We offered peace. But your people have sacrificed the country for the sake of a party that had no other object in view, than the monopoly of office. . . . [374/375]

. . . We shall have bread & meat in plenty, but possibly no money. I am already picking Cotton; and we shall pile it up in pyramids, with piles of light wood beneath it, ready to be fired as soon as your fierce Yankees penetrate the country. We shall admire daily the piles as they grow, and they will make a splendid conflagration, lighting up the country for miles, and showing the bright armour of the enemy on his march. But war is a sad subject for jesting upon & to us, old fellows, it is hateful. You & I might have adjusted the whole issue—i.e. if despotic powers for 24 hours had been given us. Love to Lyde & all.

Ever truly Yours

W. GILMORE SIMMS. [375]

ODE—"DO YE QUAIL?"*

I

Do ye quail but to hear, Carolinians,
The first foot-tramp of Tyranny's minions? [252/253]
Have ye buckled on armor, and brandished the spear,
But to shrink with the trumpet's first peal on the ear?
Why your forts now embattled on headland and height,
Your sons all in armor, unless for the fight?
Did ye think the mere show of your guns on the wall,
And your shouts, would the souls of the heathen appal?
That his lusts and his appetites, greedy as Hell,
Led by Mammon and Moloch, would sink at a spell;—   10
Nor strive, with the tiger's own thirst, lest the flesh
Should be torn from his jaws, while yet bleeding afresh.

II

For shame! To the breach, Carolinians!—
To the death for your sacred dominions!—
Homes, shrines, and your cities all reeking in flame,
Cry aloud to your souls, in their sorrow and shame;
Your greybeards, with necks in the halter—
Your virgins, defiled at the altar,—
In the loathsome embrace of the felon and slave,
Touch loathsomer far than the worm of the grave!   20
Ah! God! if you fail in this moment of gloom!
How base were the weakness, how horrid the doom!
With the fiends in your streets howling pæans,
And the Beast o'er another Orleans!

III

Do ye quail, as on yon little islet
They have planted the feet that defile it? [253/254]

*Both poems are from *War Poetry of the South,* ed. William Gilmore Simms (New York: Richardson & Company, 1866). "Fort Wagner" was first printed in the Charleston *Mercury,* August 1, 1863.

Make its sands pure of taint, by the stroke of the sword,
And by torrents of blood in red sacrifice pour'd!
Doubts are Traitors, if once they persuade you to fear,
That the foe, in his foothold, is safe from your spear!   30
When the foot of pollution is set on your shores,
What sinew and soul should be stronger than yours?
By the fame—by the shame—of your sires,
Set on, though each freeman expires;
Better fall, grappling fast with the foe, to their graves,
Than groan in your fetters, the slaves of your slaves.

IV

The voice of your loud exultation
Hath rung, like a trump, through the nation,
How loudly, how proudly, of deeds to be done,
The blood of the sire in the veins of the son!   40
Old Moultrie and Sumter still keep at your gates,
And the foe in his foothold as patiently waits.
He asks, with a taunt, by your patience made bold,
If the hot spur of Percy grows suddenly cold—
Makes merry with boasts of your city his own,
And the Chivalry fled, ere his trumpet is blown;
Upon them, O sons of the mighty of yore,
And fatten the sands with their Sodomite gore!

V

Where's the dastard that cowers and falters
In the sight of his hearthstones and altars? [254/255]   50
With the faith of the free in the God of the brave,
Go forth; ye are mighty to conquer and save!
By the blue Heaven shining above ye,
By the pure-hearted thousands that love ye,
Ye are armed with a might to prevail in the fight,
And an ægis to shield and a weapon to smite!
Then fail not, and quail not; the foe shall prevail not:
With the faith and the will, ye shall conquer him still.
To the knife—with the knife, Carolinians,
For your homes, and your sacred dominions. [255]   60

FORT WAGNER

I

Glory unto the gallant boys who stood
    At Wagner, and, unflinching, sought the van;
Dealing fierce blows, and shedding precious blood,
    For homes as precious, and dear rights of man!
They've won the meed, and they shall have the glory;—
    Song, with melodious memories, shall repeat
The legend, which shall grow to themes for story,
    Told through long ages, and forever sweet!

II

High honor to our youth—our sons and brothers,
    Georgians and Carolinians, where they stand!   10
They will not shame their birthrights, or their mothers,
    But keep, through storm, the bulwarks of the land!
They feel that they *must* conquer! Not to do it,
    Were worse than death—perdition! Should they fail,
The innocent races yet unborn shall rue it,
    The whole world feel the wound, and nations wail!

III

No! They must conquer in the breach or perish!
    Assured, in the last consciousness of breath, [323/324]
That love shall deck their graves, and memory cherish
    Their deeds, with honors that shall sweeten death!   20
They shall have trophies in long future hours,
    And loving recollections, which shall be
Green as the summer leaves, and fresh as flowers,
    That, through all seasons, bloom eternally!

IV

Their memories shall be monuments, to rise
    Next those of mightiest martyrs of the past;
Beacons, when angry tempests sweep the skies,
    And feeble souls bend crouching to the blast!

A shrine for thee, young Cheves, well devoted,
  Most worthy of a great, illustrious sire;—   30
A niche for thee, young Haskell, nobly noted,
  When skies and seas around thee shook with fire!

V

And others as well chonicled shall be!
  What though they fell with unrecorded name—
They live among the archives of the free,
  With proudest title to undying fame!
The unchisell'd marble under which they sleep,
  Shall tell of heroes, fearless still of fate;
Not asking if their memories shall keep,
  But if they nobly served, and saved, the State! [324/325]   40

VI

For thee, young Fortress Wagner—thou shalt wear
  Green laurels, worthy of the names that now,
Thy sister forts of Moultrie, Sumter, bear!
  See that thou lift'st, for aye, as proud a brow!
And thou shalt be, to future generations,
  A trophied monument; whither men shall come
In homage; and report to distant nations,
  A SHRINE, which foes shall never make a TOMB! [325]

from **SACK AND DESTRUCTION OF THE CITY
OF COLUMBIA, S.C.***

It has pleased God, in that Providence which is so inscrutable to
man, to visit our beautiful city with the most cruel fate which can
ever befall States or cities. He has permitted an invading army to
penetrate our country almost without impediment; to rob and
ravage our dwellings, and to commit three-fifths of our city to the
flames. Eighty-four squares, out of one hundred and twenty-four (?)
which the city contains, have been destroyed, with scarcely the

---

*From William Gilmore Simms, *Sack and Destruction of the City of Colum-
bia, S.C.* (Columbia, S.C.: Power Press of Daily Phoenix, 1865) .

exception of a single house. The ancient capitol building of the State—that venerable structure, which, for seventy years, has echoed with the eloquence and wisdom of the most famous statesmen—is laid in ashes; six temples of the Most High God have shared the same fate; eleven banking establishments; the schools of learning, the shops of art and trade, of invention and manufacture; shrines equally of religion, benovolence and industry; are all buried together, in one congregated ruin. Humiliation spreads her ashes over our homes and garments, and the universal wreck exhibits only one common aspect of despair. It is for us, as succinctly but as fully as possible, and in the simplest language, to endeavor to make the melancholy record of our wretchedness as complete as possible. [3/16] . . .

It may be well to remark that the discipline of the soldiers, upon their first entry into the city, was perfect and most admirable. There was no disorder or irregularity on the line of march, showing that their officers had them completely in hand. They were a fine looking body of men, mostly young and of vigorous formation, well clad and well shod, seemingly wanting in nothing. Their arms and accoutrements were in bright order. The negroes accompanying them were not numerous, and seemed mostly to act as drudges and body servants. They groomed horses, waited, carried burdens, and, in almost every instance under our eyes, appeared in a purely servile, and not a military, capacity. The men of the West treated them generally with scorn or indifference, sometimes harshly, and not unfrequently with blows.

But, if the entrance into town and while on duty, was indicative of admirable drill and discipline, such ceased to be the case the moment the troops were dismissed. Then, whether by tacit permission or direct command, their whole deportment underwent a sudden and rapid change. The saturnalia soon began. We have shown that the robbery of the persons of the citizens and the plunder of their homes commenced within one hour after they had reached the Market Hall. It continued without interruption throughout the day. Sherman, at the head of his cavalry, [16/17] traversed the streets everywhere—so did his officers. Subsequently, these officers were everywhere on foot, yet beheld nothing which required the interposition of authority. And yet robbery was going on at every corner—in nearly every house. Citizens generally applied for a guard at their several houses, and, for a time, these guards were allotted them. These might be faithful or not. In some cases, as already stated, they were, and civil and respectful; considerate of the claims of women, and never trespassing upon the privacy of the family; but, in numbers of cases, they were intrusive, insulting and treacherous—leaving no privacy undisturbed, passing without a word into the chambers and prying into every crevice and corner.

But the reign of terror did not fairly begin till night. In some instances, where parties complained of the misrule and robbery, their guards said to them, with a chuckle: "This is nothing. Wait till to-night, and you'll see h—ll."

Among the first fires at evening was one about dark, which broke out in a filthy purlieu of low houses, of wood, on Gervais street, occupied mostly as brothels. Almost at the same time, a body of the soldiers scattered over the Eastern outskirts of the city, fired severally the dwellings of Mr. Secretary Trenholm, General Wade Hampton, Dr. John Wallace, J. U. Adams, Mrs. Starke, Mr. Latta, Mrs. English, and many others. There were then some twenty fires in full blast, in as many different quarters, and while the alarm sounded from these quarters, a similar alarm was sent up almost simultaneously from Cotton Town, the Northermost limit of the city, and from Main street in its very centre, at the several stores or houses of O. Z. Bates, C. D. Eberhardt, and some others, in the heart of the most densely settled portion of the town; thus enveloping in flames almost every section of the devoted city. At this period, thus early in the evening, there were few shows of that drunkenness which prevailed at a late hour in the night, and only after all the grocery shops on Main street had been rifled. The men engaged in this were well prepared with all the appliances essential to their work. They did not need the torch. They carried with them, from house to house, pots and vessels containing combustible liquids, composed probably of phosphorous and other similar agents, turpentine, &c.; and, with balls of cotton saturated in this liquid, with which they also overspread floors and walls, they conveyed the flames with wonderful rapidity from dwelling to dwelling. Each had his ready box of Lucifer matches, and, with a scrape upon the walls, the flames began to rage. Where houses were closely contiguous, a brand from one was the means of conveying destruction to the other. [17/18]

The winds favored. They had been high throughout the day, and steadily prevailed from South-west by West, and bore the flames Eastward. To this fact we owe the preservation of the portions of the city lying West of Assembly street.

The work, begun thus vigorously, went on without impediment and with hourly increase throughout the night. Engines and hose were brought out by the firemen, but these were soon driven from their labors—which were indeed idle against such a storm of fire—by the pertinacious hostility of the soldiers; the hose was hewn to pieces, and the firemen, dreading worse usage to themselves, left the field in despair. Meanwhile, the flames spread from side to side, from front to rear, from street to street, and where their natural and inevitable progress was too slow for those who had kindled them, they helped them on by the application of fresh combustibles and more rapid agencies of conflagration. By midnight, Main street, from its Northern to its Southern extremity, was a solid wall of fire. By 12 o'clock, the great blocks, which included the banking houses and the Treasury buildings, were consumed; Janney's (Congaree) and Nickerson's Hotels; the magnificent manufactories of Evans & Cogswell—indeed, every large block in the business portion of the city; the old Capitol and all the adjacent buildings were in ruins. The range called the "Granite" was beginning to flame at 12, and might have been saved by ten vigorous men, resolutely working.

At 1 o'clock, the hour was struck by the clock of the Market Hall, which was even then illuminated from within. It was its own last hour which it sounded, and its tongue was silenced forevermore. In less than five minutes after, its spire went down with a crash, and, by this time, almost all the buildings within the precinct were a mass of ruins.

Very grand, and terrible, beyond description, was the awful spectacle. It was a scene for the painter of the terrible. It was the blending of a range of burning mountains stretched in a continuous series for more than a mile. Here was Ætna, sending up its spouts of flaming lava; Vesuvius, emulous of like display, shooting up with loftier torrents, and Stromboli, struggling, with awful throes, to shame both by its superior volumes of fluid flame. The winds were tributary to these convulsive efforts, and tossed the volcanic torrents hundreds of feet in air. Great spouts of flame spread aloft in canopies of sulphurous cloud—wreaths of sable, edged with sheeted lightnings, wrapped the skies, and, at short intervals, the falling tower and the tottering wall, avalanche-like, went down with thunderous sound, sending up at every crash great billowy showers of glowing fiery embers. [18/19]

Throughout the whole of this terrible scene the soldiers continued their search after spoil. The houses were severally and soon gutted of their contents. Hundreds of iron safes, warranted "impenetrable to fire and the burglar," it was soon satisfactorily demonstrated, were not "Yankee proof." They were split open and robbed, yielding, in some cases, very largely of Confederate money and bonds, if not of gold and silver. Jewelry and plate in abundance was found. Men could be seen staggering off with huge waiters, vases, candelabra, to say nothing of cups, goblets and smaller vessels, all of solid silver. Clothes and shoes, when new, were appropriated—the rest left to burn. Liquors were drank with such avidity as to astonish the veteran Bacchanals of Columbia; nor did the parties thus distinguishing themselves hesitate about the vintage. There was no idle discrimination in the matter of taste, from that vulgar liquor, which Judge Burke used to say always provoked within him "an inordinate propensity to sthale," to the choicest red wines of the ancient cellars. In one vault on Main street, seventeen casks of wine were stored away, which, an eye-witness tells us, barely sufficed, once broken into, for the draughts of a single hour—such were the appetites at work and the numbers in possession of them. Rye, corn, claret and Madeira all found their way into the same channels, and we are not to wonder, when told that no less than one hundred and fifty of the drunken creatures perished miserably among the flames kindled by their own comrades, and from which they were unable to escape. The estimate will not be thought extravagant by those who saw the condition of hundreds after 1 o'clock A.M. By others, however, the estimate is reduced to thirty; but the number will never be known. Sherman's officers themselves are reported to have said that they lost more men in the sack and burning of the city (including certain explosions) than in all their fights while approaching it. It is also suggested that the orders which Sherman issued at daylight, on Saturday morning, for the arrest of the fire, were issued in consequence of the loss of men which he had thus sustained.

One or more of his men were shot, by parties unknown, in some dark passages or alleys—it is supposed in consequence of some attempted outrages which humanity could not endure; the assassin taking advantage of the obscurity of the situation and adroitly mingling with the crowd without. And while these scenes were at their worst—while the flames were at their highest and most extensively raging—groups might be seen at the several corners of the streets, drinking, roaring, revelling—while the fiddle and accordeon were playing their popular airs among them. There was no cessation of the work till 5 A.M. on Saturday. [19/20]

A single thought will suffice to show that the owners or lodgers in the houses thus sacrificed were not silent or quiet spectators of a conflagration which threw them naked and homeless under the skies of night. The male population, consisting mostly of aged men, invalids, decrepits, women and children, were not capable of very active or powerful exertions; but they did not succumb to the fate without earnest pleas and strenuous efforts. Old men and women and children were to be seen, even while the flames were rolling and raging around them, while walls were crackling and rafters tottering and tumbling, in the endeavor to save their clothing and some of their most valuable effects. It was not often that they were suffered to succeed. They were driven out headlong.

Ladies were hustled from their chambers—their ornaments plucked from their persons, their bundles from their hands. It was in vain that the mother appealed for the garments of her children. They were torn from her grasp and hurled into the flames. The young girl striving to save a single frock, had it rent to fibres in her grasp. Men and women bearing off their trunks were seized, despoiled, in a moment the trunk burst asunder with the stroke of axe or gun-butt, the contents laid bare, rifled of all the objects of desire, and the residue sacrificed to the fire. You might see the ruined owner, standing woe-begone, aghast, gazing at his tumbling dwelling, his scattered property, with a dumb agony in his face that was inexpressibly touching. Others you might hear, as we did, with wild blasphemies assailing the justice of Heaven, or invoking, with lifted and clenched hands, the fiery wrath of the avenger. But the soldiers plundered and drank, the fiery work raged, and the moon sailed over all with as serene an aspect as when she first smiled upon the ark resting against the slopes of Ararat.

Such was the spectacle for hours on the chief business street of Columbia. [20]

HENRY TIMROD
(1828–1867)

Timrod was born at Charleston, South Carolina, and lived mainly in Charleston and Columbia throughout his life. He enlisted in March, 1862, as a clerk at regimental headquarters, but was compelled to leave military service soon afterward because of incipient tuberculosis. He then became a correspondent for the Charleston Mercury *and later an associate editor of the* South Carolinian *at Columbia, but his livelihood was destroyed when Columbia was burned. After his death in 1867, his friend Paul Hamilton Hayne edited and had published* The Poems of Henry Timrod *(1873).*

"The Cotton Boll" expresses Timrod's faith at the beginning of the war that "King Cotton" would make the South economically superior to the North and give the South the advantage in any conflict between the sections. As the war progressed, though, Timrod became more and more disheartened —as is suggested in "The Unknown Dead."

THE COTTON BOLL*

While I recline
At ease beneath
This immemorial pine,

*The following are from *The Collected Poems of Henry Timrod*, ed. Edd Winfield Parks and Aileen Wells Parks (Athens: The University of Georgia Press, 1965). Reprinted by permission of the University of Georgia Press. "The Cotton Boll" was first published in the *Charleston Mercury*, Sept. 3, 1861; "A Cry to Arms" was published in the *Mercury*, Mar. 4, 1862; "The Unknown Dead" was published in *Southern Illustrated News*, July 4, 1863; and the "Ode . . . at Magnolia Cemetery" was published in the *Charleston Daily Courier*, June 18, 1866.

Small sphere!
(By dusky fingers brought this morning here
And shown with boastful smiles),
I turn thy cloven sheath,
Through which the soft white fibres peer,
That, with their gossamer bands,
Unite, like love, the sea-divided lands,   10
And slowly, thread by thread,
Draw forth the folded strands,
Than which the trembling line,
By whose frail help yon startled spider fled
Down the tall spear-grass from his swinging bed,
Is scarce more fine;
And as the tangled skein [95/96]
Unravels in my hands,
Betwixt me and the noonday light,
A veil seems lifted, and for miles and miles   20
The landscape broadens on my sight,
As, in the little boll, there lurked a spell
Like that which, in the ocean shell,
With mystic sound,
Breaks down the narrow walls that hem us round,
And turns some city lane
Into the restless main,
With all his capes and isles!

Yonder bird
Which floats, as if at rest,   30
In those blue tracts above the thunder, where
No vapors cloud the stainless air,
And never sound is heard,
Unless at such rare time
When, from the City of the Blest,
Rings down some golden chime,
Sees not from his high place
So vast a cirque of summer space
As widens round me in one mighty field,
Which, rimmed by seas and sands,   40
Doth hail its earliest daylight in the beams

Of gray Atlantic dawns;
And, broad as realms made up of many lands,
Is lost afar
Behind the crimson hills and purple lawns
Of sunset, among plains which roll their streams
Against the Evening Star!
And lo!
To the remotest point of sight,
Although I gaze upon no waste of snow,   50
The endless field is white;
And the whole landscape glows,
For many a shining league away,
With such accumulated light
As Polar lands would flash beneath a tropic day!
Nor lack there (for the vision grows, [96/97]
And the small charm within my hands—
More potent even than the fabled one,
Which oped whatever golden mystery
Lay hid in fairy wood or magic vale,   60
The curious ointment of the Arabian tale—
Beyond all mortal sense
Doth stretch my sight's horizon, and I see,
Beneath its simple influence,
As if, with Uriel's crown,
I stood in some great temple of the Sun,
And looked, as Uriel, down!)
Nor lack there pastures rich and fields all green
With all the common gifts of God,
For temperate airs and torrid sheen   70
Weave Edens of the sod;
Through lands which look one sea of billowy gold
Broad rivers wind their devious ways;
A hundred isles in their embraces fold
A hundred luminous bays;
And through yon purple haze
Vast mountains lift their plumed peaks cloud-crowned;
And, save where up their sides the ploughman creeps,
An unhewn forest girds them grandly round,
In whose dark shades a future navy sleeps!   80

Ye Stars, which, though unseen, yet with me gaze
Upon this loveliest fragment of the earth!
Thou Sun, that kindlest all thy gentlest rays
Above it, as to light a favorite hearth!
Ye Clouds, that in your temples in the West
See nothing brighter than its humblest flowers!
And you, ye Winds, that on the ocean's breast
Are kissed to coolness ere ye reach its bowers!
Bear witness with me in my song of praise,
And tell the world that, since the world began,   90
No fairer land hath fired a poet's lays,
Or given a home to man!

But these are charms already widely blown!
His be the meed whose pencil's trace
Hath touched our very swamps with grace, [97/98]
And round whose tuneful way
All Southern laurels bloom;
The Poet of "The Woodlands," unto whom
Alike are known
The flute's low breathing and the trumpet's tone,   100
And the soft west wind's sighs;
But who shall utter all the debt,
O Land wherein all powers are met
That bind a people's heart,
The world doth owe thee at this day,
And which it never can repay,
Yet scarcely deigns to own!
Where sleeps the poet who shall fitly sing
The source wherefrom doth spring
That mighty commerce which, confined   110
To the mean channels of no selfish mart,
Goes out to every shore
Of this broad earth, and throngs the sea with ships
That bear no thunders; hushes hungry lips
In alien lands;
Joins with a delicate web remotest strands;
And gladdening rich and poor,
Doth gild Parisian domes,

Or feed the cottage-smoke of English homes,
And only bounds its blessings by mankind!   120
In offices like these, thy mission lies,
My Country! and it shall not end
As long as rain shall fall and Heaven bend
In blue above thee; though thy foes be hard
And cruel as their weapons, it shall guard
Thy hearth-stones as a bulwark; make thee great
In white and bloodless state;
And, haply, as the years increase—
Still working through its humbler reach
With that large wisdom which the ages teach—   130
Revive the half-dead dream of universal peace!

As men who labor in that mine
Of Cornwall, hollowed out beneath the bed
Of ocean, when a storm rolls overhead, [98/99]
Hear the dull booming of the world of brine
Above them, and a mighty muffled roar
Of winds and waters, yet toil calmly on,
And split the rock, and pile the massive ore,
Or carve a niche, or shape the arched roof;
So I, as calmly, weave my woof   140
Of song, chanting the days to come,
Unsilenced, though the quiet summer air
Stirs with the bruit of battles, and each dawn
Wakes from its starry silence to the hum
Of many gathering armies. Still,
In that we sometimes hear,
Upon the Northern winds, the voice of woe
Not wholly drowned in triumph, though I know
The end must crown us, and a few brief years
Dry all our tears,   150
I may not sing too gladly. To Thy will
Resigned, O Lord! we cannot all forget
That there is much even Victory must regret.
And, therefore, not too long
From the great burthen of our country's wrong
Delay our just release!

And, if it may be, save
These sacred fields of peace
From stain of patriot or of hostile blood!
Oh, help us, Lord! to roll the crimson flood   160
Back on its course, and, while our banners wing
Northward, strike with us! till the Goth shall cling
To his own blasted altar-stones, and crave
Mercy; and we shall grant it, and dictate
The lenient future of his fate
There, where some rotting ships and crumbling quays
Shall one day mark the Port which ruled the Western seas. [99]

A CRY TO ARMS

Ho! woodsmen of the mountain side!
    Ho! dwellers in the vales!
Ho! ye who by the chafing tide
    Have roughened in the gales!
Leave barn and byre, leave kin and cot,
    Lay by the bloodless spade;
Let desk, and case, and counter rot,
    And burn your books of trade.

The despot roves your fairest lands;
    And till he flies or fears,   10
Your fields must grow but armed bands,
    Your sheaves be sheaves of spears!
Give up to mildew and to rust
    The useless tools of gain;
And feed your country's sacred dust
    With floods of crimson rain!

Come, with the weapons at your call—
    With musket, pike, or knife;
He wields the deadliest blade of all
    Who lightest holds his life.   20
The arm that drives its unbought blows

With all a patriot's scorn,
Might brain a tyrant with a rose,
  Or stab him with a thorn.

Does any falter? let him turn
  To some brave maiden's eyes,
And catch the holy fires that burn
  In those sublunar skies.
Oh! could you like your women feel,
  And in their spirit march,   30
A day might see your lines of steel
  Beneath the victor's arch.

What hope, O God! would not grow warm
  When thoughts like these give cheer? [108/109]
The Lily calmly braves the storm,
  And shall the Palm-tree fear?
No! rather let its branches court
  The rack that sweeps the plain;
And from the Lily's regal port
  Learn how to breast the strain!   40

Ho! woodsmen of the mountain side!
  Ho! dwellers in the vales!
Ho! ye who by the roaring tide
  Have roughened in the gales!
Come! flocking gaily to the fight,
  From forest, hill, and lake;
We battle for our Country's right,
  And for the Lily's sake! [109]

THE UNKNOWN DEAD

The rain is plashing on my sill,
But all the winds of Heaven are still;
And so it falls with that dull sound
Which thrills us in the church-yard ground,

When the first spadeful drops like lead
Upon the coffin of the dead.
Beyond my streaming window-pane,
I cannot see the neighboring vane,
Yet from its old familiar tower
The bell comes, muffled, through the shower. 10
What strange and unsuspected link
Of feeling touched, has made me think—
While with a vacant soul and eye
I watch that gray and stony sky—
Of nameless graves on battle-plains
Washed by a single winter's rains,
Where, some beneath Virginian hills,
And some by green Atlantic rills,
Some by the waters of the West,
A myriad unknown heroes rest. 20
Ah! not the chiefs who, dying, see
Their flags in front of victory,
Or, at their life-blood's noble cost
Pay for a battle nobly lost,
Claim from their monumental beds
The bitterest tears a nation sheds.
Beneath yon lonely mound—the spot
By all save some fond few forgot—
Lie the true martyrs of the fight, [126/127]
Which strikes for freedom and for right. 30
Of them, their patriot zeal and pride,
The lofty faith that with them died,
No grateful page shall farther tell
Than that so many bravely fell;
And we can only dimly guess
What worlds of all this world's distress,
What utter woe, despair, and dearth,
Their fate has brought to many a hearth.
Just such a sky as this should weep
Above them, always, where they sleep; 40
Yet, haply, at this very hour,
Their graves are like a lover's bower;
And Nature's self, with eyes unwet,

Oblivious of the crimson debt
To which she owes her April grace,
Laughs gayly o'er their burial place. [127]

ODE

SUNG ON THE OCCASION OF DECORATING
THE GRAVES OF THE CONFEDERATE DEAD, AT
MAGNOLIA CEMETERY, CHARLESTON, S.C., 1866

Sleep sweetly in your humble graves,
    Sleep, martyrs of a fallen cause!—
Though yet no marble column craves
    The pilgrim here to pause.

In seeds of laurels in the earth,
    The garlands of your fame are sown; [129/130]
And, somewhere, waiting for its birth,
    The shaft is in the stone.

Meanwhile, your sisters for the years
    Which hold in trust your storied tombs,   10
Bring all they now can give you—tears,
    And these memorial blooms.

Small tributes, but your shades will smile
    As proudly on these wreaths to-day,
As when some cannon-moulded pile
    Shall overlook this Bay.

Stoop, angels, hither from the skies!
    There is no holier spot of ground,
Than where defeated valor lies
    By mourning beauty crowned. [130]   20

DOUBTERS
South

. . . If war was ever right, then Christ
was always wrong. . . .

Sidney Lanier

. . . The taking of that unoffending life
seemed such a wanton thing. And it
seemed an epitome of war; that all war
must be just that—the killing of strangers
against whom you feel no personal animosity; strangers whom, in other circumstances, you would help if you found
them in trouble, and who would help
you if you needed it.

Mark Twain

SIDNEY LANIER
(1842–1881)

A native of Macon, Georgia, Sidney Lanier attended Ogle-thorpe University and then planned to study in Germany in preparation for college teaching. His plans were interrupted by the war, though, and in April, 1861, he joined the Macon Volunteers. He was in battle at Chickahominy and Malvern Hill, and later in the war served as a signal officer on blockade runners. While doing the latter he was captured and impris-oned at Point Lookout, Maryland, for four months. His health was impaired as a result, and he was never fully to recover. After the war Lanier practiced law in his father's office and then went to Baltimore, where he played the flute in the Pea-body Orchestra. In Baltimore he also was a lecturer in English literature at Johns Hopkins University.

Although Lanier's literary reputation rests mainly on his poetry such as "The Symphony" and "The Marshes of Glynn," he was also the author of a novel (Tiger-Lilies) and of critical studies of English verse and the English novel. Tiger-Lilies, from which "The Flower of War" is taken, was begun during the war and finished in March, 1867. It is not mainly a war novel, although it does contain some battle scenes and descrip-tions of war prisons. Lanier was also writing some poetry while in prison, but none of it concerns the war. Perhaps this was because his sensitive spirit was repelled by what he later called the "drunken, rude barbarity" of the war years.

[THE FLOWER OF WAR]*

The early spring of 1861 brought to bloom, besides innumerable violets and jessamines, a strange, enormous, and terrible flower.

This was the blood-red flower of war, which grows amid thunders; a flower whose freshening dews are blood and hot tears, whose shadow chills a land, whose odors strangle a people, whose giant petals droop downward, and whose roots are in hell.

It is a species of the great genus, sin-flower, which is so conspicuous in the flora of all ages and all countries, and whose multifarious leafage and fruitage so far overgrow a land that the violet, or love-genus, has often small chance to show its quiet blue.

The cultivation of this plant is an expensive business, and it is a wonder, from this fact alone, that there should be so many fanciers of it. A most profuse and perpetual manuring with human bones is absolutely necessary to keep it alive, and it is well to have these powdered, which can be easily done by hoofs of cavalry-horses and artillery-wheels, not to speak of the usual [115/116] method of mashing with cannon-balls. It will not grow, either, except in some wet place near a stream of human blood; and you must be active in collecting your widows' tears and orphans' tears and mothers' tears to freshen the petals with in the mornings.

It requires assiduous working; and your labor-hire will be a large item in the expense, not to speak of the amount disbursed in preserving the human bones alive until such time as they may be needed, for, I forgot to mention, they must be fresh, and young, and newly-killed.

It is, however, a hardy plant, and may be grown in any climate, from snowy Moscow to hot India.

It blooms usually in the spring, continuing to flower all summer until the winter rains set in: yet in some instances it has been known to remain in full bloom during a whole inclement winter, as was shown in a fine specimen which I saw the other day,

---

*From Sidney Lanier, *Tiger-Lilies* (New York: Hurd and Houghton, 1867). *Tiger-Lilies*, ed. Garland Greever, is Vol. V in *The Centennial Edition of the Works of Sidney Lanier* (Baltimore, 1945).

grown in North America by two wealthy landed proprietors, who combined all their resources of money, of blood, of bones, of tears, of sulphur and what not, to make this the grandest specimen of modern horticulture, and whose success was evidenced by the pertinacious blossoms which the plant sent forth even amid the hostile rigors of snow and ice and furious storms. It is supposed by some that seed of this American specimen (now dead) yet remain in the land; but as for this author (who, with many friends, suffered from the unhealthy odors of the plant), he could find it in his heart to wish fervently that these seed, if there be verily any, might perish in the germ, utterly out of sight and life and memory and out of the remote hope of resurrec- [116/117] tion, forever and ever, no matter in whose granary they are cherished!

But, to return.

It is a spreading plant, like the banyan, and continues to insert new branch-roots into the ground, so as sometimes to overspread a whole continent. Its black-shadowed jungles afford fine cover for such wild beasts as frauds and corruptions and thefts to make their lair in; from which, often, these issue with ravening teeth and prey upon the very folk that have planted and tended and raised their flowery homes!

Now, from time to time, there have appeared certain individuals (wishing, it may be, to disseminate and make profit upon other descriptions of plants) who have protested against the use of this war-flower.

Its users, many of whom are surely excellent men, contend that they grow it to protect themselves from oppressive hailstorms, which destroy their houses and crops.

But some say the plant itself is worse than any hailstorm; that its shades are damp and its odors unhealthy, and that it spreads so rapidly as to kill out and uproot all corn and wheat and cotton crops. Which the plant-users admit; but rejoin that it is cowardly to allow hailstorms to fall with impunity, and that manhood demands a struggle against them of some sort.

But the others reply, fortitude is more manly than bravery, for noble and long endurance wins the shining love of God; whereas brilliant bravery is momentary, is easy to the enthusiastic, and only dazzles the admiration of the weak-eyed since it is as often shown on one side as the other. [117/118]

But then, lastly, the good war-flower cultivators say, our preachers recommend the use of this plant, and help us mightily to raise it in resistance to the hailstorms.

And reply, lastly, the interested other-flower men, that the preachers should preach Christ; that Christ was worse hailed upon than anybody, before or since; that he always refused to protect himself, though fully able to do it, by any war-banyan; and that he did, upon all occasions, not only discourage the resort to this measure, but did inveigh against it more earnestly than any thing else, as the highest and heaviest crime against Love—the Father of Adam, Christ, and all of us.

Friends and horticulturists, cry these men, stickling for the last word, if war was ever right, then Christ was always wrong; and war-flowers and the vine of Christ grow different ways, insomuch that no man may grow with both! [118/119]

But these sentiments, even if anybody could have been found patient enough to listen to them, would have been called sentimentalities, or worse, in the spring of 1861, by the inhabitants of any of those States lying between Maryland and Mexico. An afflatus of war was breathed upon us. Like a great wind, it drew on and blew upon men, women, and children. Its sound mingled with the solemnity of the church-organs and arose with the earnest words of preachers praying for guidance in the matter. It sighed in the half-breathed words of sweethearts conditioning impatient lovers with war-services. It thundered splendidly in the impassioned appeals of orators to the people. It whistled through the streets, it stole in to the firesides, it clinked glasses in bar-rooms, it lifted the gray hairs of our wise men in conventions, it thrilled through the lectures in college halls, it rustled the thumbed book-leaves of the school-rooms.

This wind blew upon all the vanes of all the [119/120] churches of the country, and turned them one way—toward war. It blew, and shook out, as if by magic, a flag whose device was unknown to soldier or sailor before, but whose every flap and flutter made the blood bound in our veins.

Who could have resisted the fair anticipations which the new war-idea brought? It arrayed the sanctity of a righteous cause in the brilliant trappings of military display; pleasing, so, the devout and the flippant which in various proportions are mixed elements in all men. It challenged the patriotism of the sober citizen, while it inflamed the dream of the statesman, ambitious for his country or for himself. It offered test to all allegiances and loyalties; of church, of state; of private loves, of public devotion; of personal consanguinity; of social ties. To obscurity it held out eminence; to poverty, wealth; to greed, a gorged maw; to speculation, legalized gambling; to patriotism, a country; to statesmanship, a government; to virtue, purity; and to love, what all love most desires—a field wherein to assert itself by action.

The author devoutly wishes that some one else had said what is here to be spoken—and said it better. That is: if there was guilt in any, there was guilt in nigh all of us, between Maryland and Mexico; that Mr. Davis, if he be termed the ringleader of the rebellion, was so not by virtue of any instigating act of his, but purely by the unanimous will and appointment of the Southern people; and that the hearts of the Southern people bleed to see how their own act has resulted in the chaining of Mr. Davis, who was as innocent as they, and in the pardon of those who were as guilty as he! [120/121]

All of us, if any of us, either for pardon or for punishment: this is fair, and we are willing.

MARK TWAIN (SAMUEL L. CLEMENS)
(1835–1910)

Samuel L. Clemens was reared in Missouri, a state which during the Civil War was torn asunder by divided loyalties and guerrilla warfare. He was piloting a steamboat on the Mississippi River when the hostilities began, but he returned to St. Louis in June, 1861, and debated for a while whether to join with the Union or with the Confederacy. Finally siding with the Confederacy, he was a soldier for two weeks. He left for a variety of reasons, among which were saddle sores, a lack of enthusiasm for the Southern cause, and a distaste for war and violence. It also is possible that he left as a direct result of the shooting of the stranger, although A. B. Paine says in Mark Twain: A Biography *that the incident actually never occurred.*

During the rest of the war, Sam Clemens was in Nevada and California, where he had at first gone ostensibly as secretary to his brother Orion, who was to be secretary to the territorial governor of Nevada. Orion was a Union man and perhaps swayed his brother's feelings. At least by late 1862 Sam was reconstructed as a Union man. His feelings on the sectional differences were nevertheless ambivalent, partly because of his changing attitudes toward slavery and race (discussed in Arlin Turner, "Mark Twain and the South: An Affair of Love and Anger," The Southern Review, *IV, N.S. [April, 1968], 493–519). Other causes of ambivalence might have been his having a nephew killed fighting for the Confederacy, his later esteem for Ulysses S. Grant, or his ties with Northern journalists, businessmen, and literary groups.*

[SIR WALTER SCOTT AND THE SOUTH]*

[Sir Walter Scott] did measureless harm; more real and lasting harm, perhaps, than any other individual that ever wrote. Most of the world has now outlived good part of these harms, though by no means all of them; but in our South they flourish pretty forcefully still. Not so forcefully as half a generation ago, perhaps, but still forcefully. There, [467/468] the genuine and wholesome civilization of the nineteenth century is curiously confused and commingled with the Walter Scott Middle-Age sham civilization and so you have practical, common-sense, progressive ideas, and progressive works, mixed up with the duel, the inflated speech, and the jejune romanticism of an absurd past that is dead, and out of charity ought to be buried. But for the Sir Walter disease, the character of the Southerner—or Southron, according to Sir Walter's starchier way of phrasing it—would be wholly modern, in place of modern and mediæval mixed, [468/469] and the South would be fully a generation further advanced than it is. It was Sir Walter that made every gentleman in the South a Major or a Colonel, or a General or a Judge, before the war; and it was he, also, that made these gentlemen value these bogus decorations. For it was he that created rank and caste down there, and also reverence for rank and caste, and pride and pleasure in them. Enough is laid on slavery, without fathering upon it these creations and contributions of Sir Walter.

Sir Walter had so large a hand in making Southern character, as it existed before the war, that he is in great measure responsible for the war. It seems a little harsh toward a dead man to say that we never should have had any war but for Sir Walter; and yet something of a plausible argument might, perhaps, be made in support of that wild proposition. The Southerner of the American revolution owned slaves; so did the Southerner of the Civil War: but the former resembles the latter as an Englishman resembles a Frenchman. The change of character can be traced rather more easily to Sir Walter's influence than to that of any other thing or person. [469]

---

*From Mark Twain, *Life on the Mississippi* (Boston: James R. Osgood and Company, 1883). Reprinted by permission of Harper & Row, Publishers.

from THE PRIVATE HISTORY OF A CAMPAIGN THAT FAILED*

You have heard from a great many people who did something in the war; is it not fair and right that you listen a little moment to one who started out to do something in it, but didn't? Thousands entered the war, got just a taste of it, and then stepped out again, permanently. These, by their very numbers, are respectable, and are therefore entitled to a sort of voice,—not a loud one, but a modest one; not a boastful one, but an apologetic one. They ought not to be allowed much space among better people—people who did something—I grant that; but they ought at least to be allowed to state why they didn't do anything, and also to explain the process by which they didn't do anything. Surely this kind of light must have a sort of value.

Out West there was a good deal of confusion in men's minds during the first months of the great trouble—a good deal of unsettledness, of leaning first this way, then that, then the other way. It was hard for us to get our bearings. I call to mind an instance of this. I was piloting on the Mississippi when the news came that South Carolina had gone out of the Union on the 20th of December, 1860. My pilot-mate was a New Yorker. He was strong for the Union; so was I. But he would not listen to me with any patience; my loyalty was smirched, to his eye, because my father had owned slaves. I said, in palliation of this dark fact, that I had heard my father say, some years before he died, that slavery was a great wrong, and that he would free the solitary negro he then owned if he could think it right to give away the property of the family when he was so straitened in means. My mate retorted that a mere impulse was nothing—anybody could pretend to a good impulse; and went on decrying my Unionism and libeling my ancestry. A month later the secession atmosphere had considerably thickened on the Lower Mississippi, and I became a rebel; so did he. We were together in

*From Mark Twain, "The Private History of a Campaign That Failed," *The Century Magazine*, XXXI (Dec., 1885) , 193–204. This was a humorous contribution to an otherwise serious group of articles on "Battles and Leaders of the Civil War." Reprinted by permission of Harper & Row, Publishers.

New Orleans, the 26th of January, when Louisiana went out of the Union. He did his full share of the rebel shouting, but was bitterly opposed to letting me do mine. He said that I came of bad stock—of a father who had been willing to set slaves free. In the following summer he was piloting a Federal gun-boat and shouting for the Union again, and I was in the Confederate army. I held his note for some borrowed money. He was one of the most upright men I ever knew; but he repudiated that note without hesitation, because I was a rebel, and the son of a man who owned slaves.

In that summer—of 1861—the first wash of the wave of war broke upon the shores of Missouri. Our State was invaded by the Union forces. They took possession of St. Louis, Jefferson Barracks, and some other points. The Governor, Claib Jackson, issued his proclamation calling out fifty thousand militia to repel the invader.

I was visiting in the small town where my [193/194] boyhood had been spent—Hannibal, Marion County. Several of us got together in a secret place by night and formed ourselves into a military company. One Tom Lyman, a young fellow of a good deal of spirit but of no military experience, was made captain; I was made second lieutenant. We had no first lieutenant; I do not know why; it was long ago. There were fifteen of us. By the advice of an innocent connected with the organization, we called ourselves the Marion Rangers. I do not remember that any one found fault with the name. I did not; I thought it sounded quite well. . . . [194/195] . . .

We waited for a dark night, for caution and secrecy were necessary; then, toward midnight, we stole in couples and from various directions to the Griffith place, beyond the town; from that point we set out together on foot. Hannibal lies at the extreme southeastern corner of Marion County, on the Mississippi River; our objective point was the hamlet of New London, ten miles away, in Ralls County.

The first hour was all fun, all idle nonsense and laughter. But that could not be kept up. The steady trudging came to be like work; the play had somehow oozed out of it; the stillness of the woods and the somberness of the night began to throw a depressing influence over the spirits of the boys, and presently the talking died out and each person shut himself up in his own thoughts. During the last half of the second hour nobody said a word.

Now we approached a log farm-house where, according to report, there was a guard of five Union soldiers. Lyman called a halt; and there, in the deep gloom of the overhanging branches, he began to whisper a plan of assault upon that house, which made the gloom more depressing than it was before. It was a crucial moment; we realized, with a cold suddenness, that here was no jest—we were standing face to face with actual war. We were equal to the occasion. In our response there was no hesitation, no indecision: we said that if Lyman wanted to meddle with those soldiers, he could go ahead and do it; but if he waited for us to follow him, he would wait a long time.

Lyman urged, pleaded, tried to shame us, but it had no effect. Our course was plain, our minds were made up: we would flank the farm-house—go out around. And that is what we did.

We struck into the woods and entered upon a rough time, stumbling over roots, getting tangled in vines, and torn by briers. At last we reached an open place in a safe region, and sat down, blown and hot, to cool off and nurse our scratches and bruises. Lyman was annoyed, but the rest of us were cheerful; we had flanked the farm-house, we had made our first military movement, and it was a success; we had nothing to fret about, we were feeling just the other way. Horse-play and laughing began again; the expedition was become a holiday frolic once more.

Then we had two more hours of dull trudging and ultimate silence and depression; then, about dawn, we straggled into New London, soiled, heel-blistered, fagged with our little march, and all of us except Stevens in a sour and raspy humor and privately down on the war. We stacked our shabby old shot-guns in Colonel Ralls's barn, and then went in a body and breakfasted with that veteran of the Mexican war. Afterwards he took us to a distant meadow, and there in the shade of a tree we listened to an old-fashioned speech from him, full of gunpowder and glory, full of that adjective-piling, mixed metaphor, and windy declamation which was regarded as eloquence in that ancient time and that remote region; and then he swore us on the Bible to be faithful to the State of Missouri and drive all invaders from her soil, no matter whence they might come or under what flag they might march. This mixed us considerably, and we could not make out just what service we were embarked in; but Colonel Ralls, the practiced politician and phrase-juggler, was not similarly in doubt; he knew quite clearly that he had invested us in the cause of the Southern Confederacy. He closed the solemnities by belting around me the sword which his neighbor, Colonel Brown, had worn at Buena Vista and Molino del Rey; and he accompanied this act with another impressive blast.

Then we formed in line of battle and marched four miles to a shady and pleasant piece of woods on the border of the far-reaching expanses of a flowery prairie. It was an enchanting region for war— our kind of war.

We pierced the forest about half a mile, and took up a strong position, with some low, rocky, and wooded hills behind us, and a purling, limpid creek in front. Straightway half the command were in swimming, and the other half fishing. The ass with the French name gave this position a romantic title, but it was too long, so the boys shortened and simplified it to Camp Ralls.

We occupied an old maple-sugar camp, whose half-rotted troughs were still propped against the trees. A long corn-crib served for sleeping quarters for the battalion. On our left, half a mile away, was Mason's farm and house; and he was a friend to the cause. . . . [195/198] . . .

We had some horsemanship drill every forenoon; then, afternoons, we rode off here and there in squads a few miles, and visited the farmers' girls, and had a youthful good time, and got an honest good dinner or supper, and then home again to camp, happy and content.

For a time, life was idly delicious, it was perfect; there was nothing to mar it. Then came some farmers with an alarm one day. They said it was rumored that the enemy were advancing in our direction, from over Hyde's prairie. The result was a sharp stir among us, and general consternation. It was a rude awakening from our pleasant trance. The rumor was but a rumor—nothing definite about it; so, in the confusion, we did not know which way to retreat. Lyman was for not retreating at all, in these uncertain circumstances; but he found that if he tried to maintain that attitude he would fare badly, for the command were in no humor to put up with insubordination. So he yielded the [198/199] point and called a council of war—to consist of himself and the three other officers; but the privates made such a fuss about being left out, that we had to allow them to be present. I mean we had to allow them to remain, for they were already present, and doing the most of the talking too. The question was, which way to retreat; but all were so flurried that nobody seemed to have even a guess to offer. Except Lyman. He explained in a few calm words, that inasmuch as the enemy were approaching from over Hyde's prairie, our course was simple: all we had to do was not to retreat *toward* him; any other direction would answer our needs perfectly. Everybody saw in a moment how true this was, and how wise; so Lyman got a great many compliments. It was now decided that we should fall back on Mason's farm.

It was after dark by this time, and as we could not know how soon the enemy might arrive, it did not seem best to try to take the horses and things with us; so we only took the guns and ammunition, and started at once. The route was very rough and hilly and rocky, and presently the night grew very black and rain began to fall; so we had a troublesome time of it, struggling and stumbling along in the dark; and soon some person slipped and fell, and then the next person behind stumbled over him and fell, and so did the rest, one after the other; and then Bowers came with the keg of powder in his arms, whilst the command were all mixed together, arms and legs, on the muddy slope; and so he fell, of course, with the keg, and this started the whole detachment down the hill in a body, and they landed in the brook at the bottom in a pile, and each that was undermost pulling the hair and scratching and biting those that were on top of him; and those that were being scratched and bitten scratching and biting the rest in their turn, and all saying they would die before they would ever go to war again if they ever got out of this brook this time, and the invader might rot for all they cared, and the country along with him—and all such talk as that, which was dismal to hear and take part in, in such smothered, low voices, and such a grisly dark place and so wet, and the enemy may be coming any moment.

The keg of powder was lost, and the guns too; so the growling and complaining continued straight along whilst the brigade pawed around the pasty hillside and slopped around in the brook hunting for these things; consequently we lost considerable time at this; and then we heard a sound, and held our breath and listened, and it seemed to be the enemy coming, though it could have been a cow, for it had a cough like a cow; but we did not wait, but left a couple of guns behind and struck out for Mason's again as briskly as we could scramble along in the dark. But we got lost presently among the rugged little ravines, and wasted a deal of time finding the way again, so it was after nine when we reached Mason's stile at last; and then before we could open our mouths to give the countersign, several dogs came bounding over the fence, with great riot and noise, and each of them took a soldier by the slack of his trousers and began to back away with him. We could not shoot the dogs without endangering the persons they were attached to; so we had to look on, helpless, at what was perhaps the most mortifying spectacle of the civil war. There was light enough, and to spare, for the Masons had now run out on the porch with candles in their hands. The old man and his son came and undid the dogs without difficulty, all but Bowers's; but they couldn't undo his dog, they didn't know his combination; he was of the bull kind, and seemed to be set with a Yale time-lock; but they got him loose at last with some scalding water, of which Bowers got his share and returned thanks. Peterson Dunlap afterwards made up a fine name for this engagement, and also for the night march which preceded it, but both have long ago faded out of my memory. [199/201] . . .

We staid several days at Mason's; and after all these years the memory of the dullness, the stillness and lifelessness of that slumberous farm-house still oppresses my spirit as with a sense of the presence of death and mourning. There was nothing to do, nothing to think about; there was no interest in life. The male part of the household were away in the fields all day, the women were busy and out of our sight; there was no sound but the plaintive wailing of a spinning-wheel, forever moaning out from some distant room,—the most lonesome sound in nature, a sound steeped and sodden with homesickness and the emptiness of life. The family went to bed about dark every night, and as we were not invited to intrude any new customs, we naturally followed theirs. Those nights were a hundred years long to youths accustomed to being up till twelve. We lay awake and miserable till that hour every time, and grew old and decrepit waiting through the still eternities for the clock-strikes. This was no place for town boys. So at last it was with something very like joy that we received news that the enemy were on our track again. With a new birth of the old warrior spirit, we sprang to our places in line of battle and fell back on Camp Ralls.

Captain Lyman had taken a hint from Mason's talk, and he
now gave orders that our camp should be guarded against surprise
by the posting of pickets. I was ordered to place a picket at the forks
of the road in Hyde's prairie. Night shut down black and threatening. I told Sergeant Bowers to go out to that place and stay till
midnight; and, just as I was expecting, he said he wouldn't do it. I
tried to get others to go, but all refused. Some excused themselves
on account of the weather; but the rest were frank enough to say
they wouldn't go in any kind of weather. This kind of thing sounds
odd now, and impossible, but there was no surprise in it at the time.
On the contrary, it seemed a perfectly natural thing to do. There
were scores of little camps scattered over Missouri where the same
thing was happening. These camps were composed of young men
who had been born and reared to a sturdy independence, and who
did not know what it meant to be ordered around by Tom, Dick,
and Harry, whom they had known familiarly all their lives, in the
village or on the farm. It is quite within the probabilities that this
same thing was happening all over the South. . . . [201/202] One
might justly imagine that we were hopeless material for war. And so
we seemed, in our ignorant state; but there were those among us
who afterward learned the grim trade; learned to obey like machines; became valuable soldiers; fought all through the war, and
came out at the end with excellent records. One of the very boys
who refused to go out on picket duty that night, and called me an
ass for thinking he would expose himself to danger in such a fool-
hardy way, had become distinguished for intrepidity before he was
a year older.

I did secure my picket that night—not by authority, but by
diplomacy. I got Bowers to go, by agreeing to exchange ranks with
him for the time being, and go along and stand the watch with him
as his subordinate. We staid out there a couple of dreary hours in
the pitchy darkness and the rain, with nothing to modify the
dreariness but Bowers's monotonous growlings at the war and the
weather; then we began to nod, and presently found it next to
impossible to stay in the saddle; so we gave up the tedious job, and
went back to the camp without waiting for the relief guard. We
rode into camp without interruption or objection from anybody,
and the enemy could have done the same, for there were no sentries.
Everybody was asleep; at midnight there was nobody to send out

another picket, so none was sent. We never tried to establish a watch at night again, as far as I remember, but we generally kept a picket out in the daytime.

In that camp the whole command slept on the corn in the big corn-crib; and there was usually a general row before morning, for the place was full of rats, and they would scramble over the boys' bodies and faces, annoying and irritating everybody; and now and then they would bite some one's toe, and the person who owned the toe would start up and magnify his English and begin to throw corn in the dark. The ears were half as heavy as bricks, and when they struck they hurt. The persons struck would respond, and inside of five minutes every man would be locked in a death-grip with his neighbor. There was a grievous deal of blood shed in the corn-crib, but this was all that was split while I was in the war. No, that is not quite true. But for one circumstance it would have been all. I will come to that now.

Our scares were frequent. Every few days rumors would come that the enemy were approaching. In these cases we always fell back on some other camp of ours; we never staid where we were. But the rumors always turned out to be false; so at last even we began to grow indifferent to them. One night a negro was sent to our corn-crib with the same old warning: the enemy was hovering in our neighborhood. We all said let him hover. We resolved to stay still and be comfortable. It was a fine warlike resolution, and no doubt we all felt the stir of it in our veins—for a moment. We had been having a very jolly time, that was full of horse-play and school-boy hilarity; but that cooled down now, and presently the fast-waning fire of forced jokes and forced laughs died out altogether, and the company became silent. Silent and nervous. And soon uneasy—worried—apprehensive. We had said we would stay, and we were committed. We could have been persuaded to go, but there was nobody brave enough to suggest it. An almost noiseless movement presently began in the dark, by a general but unvoiced impulse. When the movement was completed, each man knew that he was not the only person who had crept to the front wall and had his eye at a crack between the logs. No, we were all there; all there with our hearts in our throats, and staring out toward the sugar-troughs where the forest foot-path came through. It was late, and there was a deep woodsy stillness everywhere. There was a veiled moonlight, which was only just strong enough to enable us to mark the general shape of objects. Presently a muffled sound caught our ears, and we recognized it as the hoof-beats of a horse or horses. And right away a figure appeared in the forest path; it could have been made of smoke, its mass had so little sharpness of outline. It was a man on horseback; and it seemed to me that there were others behind him. I got hold of a gun in the dark, and pushed it through a crack between the logs, hardly knowing what I was doing, I was so dazed with fright. Somebody said "Fire!" I pulled the trigger. I seemed to see a hundred flashes and hear a hundred reports, then I saw the man fall down out of the saddle. My first feeling was of surprised gratification; my first impulse was an apprentice-sportsman's impulse to run and pick up his game. Somebody said, hardly audibly, "Good—we've got him!—wait for the rest." But the rest did not come. We waited—listened—still no more came. There was not a sound, not the whisper of a leaf; just perfect stillness; an uncanny kind of stillness, which was all the more uncanny on account of the damp, earthy, late-night smells now ris- [202/203] ing and pervading it. Then, wondering, we crept stealthily out, and approached the man. When we got to him the moon revealed him distinctly. He was lying on his back, with his arms abroad; his mouth was open and his chest heaving with long gasps, and his white shirt-front was all splashed with blood. The thought shot through me that I was a murderer; that I had killed a man—a man who had never done me any harm. That was the coldest sensation that ever went through my marrow. I was down by him in a moment; helplessly stroking his forehead; and I would have given anything then—my own life freely—to make him again what he had been five minutes before. And all the boys seemed to be feeling in the same way; they hung over him, full of pitying interest, and tried all they could to help him, and said all sorts of regretful things. They had forgotten all about the enemy; they thought only of this one forlorn unit of the foe. Once my imagination persuaded me that the dying man gave me a reproachful look out of his shadowy eyes, and it seemed to me that I could rather he had stabbed me than done that. He muttered and mumbled like a dreamer in his sleep, about his wife and his child; and I thought with a new despair, "This thing that I have done does not end with him; it falls upon *them* too, and they never did me any harm, any more than he."

In a little while the man was dead. He was killed in war; killed in fair and legitimate war; killed in battle, as you may say; and yet he was as sincerely mourned by the opposing force as if he had been their brother. The boys stood there a half hour sorrowing over him, and recalling the details of the tragedy, and wondering who he might be, and if he were a spy, and saying that if it were to do over again they would not hurt him unless he attacked them first. It soon came out that mine was not the only shot fired; there were five others,—a division of the guilt which was a grateful relief to me, since it in some degree lightened and diminished the burden I was carrying. There were six shots fired at once; but I was not in my right mind at the time, and my heated imagination had magnified my one shot into a volley.

The man was not in uniform, and was not armed. He was a stranger in the country; that was all we ever found out about him. The thought of him got to preying upon me every night; I could not get rid of it. I could not drive it away, the taking of that unoffending life seemed such a wanton thing. And it seemed an epitome of war; that all war must be just that—the killing of strangers against whom you feel no personal animosity; strangers whom, in other circumstances, you would help if you found them in trouble, and who would help you if you needed it. My campaign was spoiled. It seemed to me that I was not rightly equipped for this awful business; that war was intended for men, and I for a child's nurse. I resolved to retire from this avocation of sham soldiership while I could save some remnant of my self-respect. These morbid thoughts clung to me against reason; for at bottom I did not believe I had touched that man. The law of probabilities decreed me guilt-less of his blood; for in all my small experience with guns I had never hit anything I had tried to hit, and I knew I had done my best to hit him. Yet there was no solace in the thought. Against a diseased imagination, demonstration goes for nothing.

The rest of my war experience was of a piece with what I have already told of it. We kept monotonously falling back upon one camp or another, and eating up the country. I marvel now at the patience of the farmers and their families. They ought to have shot us; on the contrary, they were as hospitably kind and courteous to us as if we had deserved it. In one of these camps we found Ab Grimes, an Upper Mississippi pilot, who afterwards became famous

as a dare-devil rebel spy, whose career bristled with desperate
adventures. The look and style of his comrades suggested that they
had not come into the war to play, and their deeds made good the
conjecture later. They were fine horsemen and good revolver-shots;
but their favorite arm was the lasso. Each had one at his pommel,
and could snatch a man out of the saddle with it every time, on a
full gallop, at any reasonable distance.

In another camp the chief was a fierce and profane old black-
smith of sixty, and he had furnished his twenty recruits with
gigantic home-made bowie-knives, to be swung with the two hands,
like the *machetes* of the Isthmus. It was a grisly spectacle to see that
earnest band practicing their murderous cuts and slashes under the
eye of that remorseless old fanatic.

The last camp which we fell back upon was in a hollow near
the village of Florida, where I was born—in Monroe County. Here
we were warned, one day, that a Union colonel was sweeping down
on us with a whole regiment at his heels. This looked decidedly
serious. Our boys went apart and consulted; then we went back and
told the other companies present that the war was a disappointment
to us and we were going to disband. They were getting ready,
themselves, to fall back on some place or other, and were only [203/
204] waiting for General Tom Harris, who was expected to arrive
at any moment; so they tried to persuade us to wait a little while,
but the majority of us said no, we were accustomed to falling back,
and didn't need any of Tom Harris's help; we could get along
perfectly well without him—and save time too. So about half of our
fifteen, including myself, mounted and left on the instant; the
others yielded to persuasion and staid—staid through the war.

An hour later we met General Harris on the road, with two or
three people in his company—his staff, probably, but we could not
tell; none of them were in uniform; uniforms had not come into
vogue among us yet. Harris ordered us back; but we told him there
was a Union colonel coming with a whole regiment in his wake, and
it looked as if there was going to be a disturbance; so we had
concluded to go home. He raged a little, but it was of no use; our
minds were made up. We had done our share; had killed one man,
exterminated one army, such as it was; let him go and kill the rest,
and that would end the war. I did not see that brisk young general
again until last year; then he was wearing white hair and whiskers.

In time I came to know that Union colonel whose coming frightened me out of the war and crippled the Southern cause to that extent—General Grant. I came within a few hours of seeing him when he was as unknown as I was myself; at a time when anybody could have said, "Grant?—Ulysses S. Grant? I do not remember hearing the name before." It seems difficult to realize that there was once a time when such a remark could be rationally made; but there *was,* and I was within a few miles of the place and the occasion too, though proceeding in the other direction.

The thoughtful will not throw this war-paper of mine lightly aside as being valueless. It has this value: it is a not unfair picture of what went on in many and many a militia camp in the first months of the rebellion, when the green recruits were without discipline, without the steadying and heartening influence of trained leaders; when all their circumstances were new and strange, and charged with exaggerated terrors, and before the invaluable experience of actual collision in the field had turned them from rabbits into soldiers. If this side of the picture of that early day has not before been put into history, then history has been to that degree incomplete, for it had and has its rightful place there. There was more Bull Run material scattered through the early camps of this country than exhibited itself at Bull Run. And yet it learned its trade presently, and helped to fight the great battles later. I could have become a soldier myself, if I had waited. I had got part of it learned; I knew more about retreating than the man that invented retreating. [204]

QUESTIONS AND TOPICS

The following questions and topics are meant to be suggestive rather than exhaustive, with the same applying to the names of authors accompanying some questions. Although the topics are divided into categories, there are not necessarily clear-cut divisions between them. For example, an observation ("an act of recognizing and noting a fact") differs in degree rather than kind from an attitude ("a feeling or emotion toward a fact or state").

A. ATTITUDES

1. ENTHUSIAM OR DOUBT IN AMERICAN AUTHORS CONTEMPORANEOUS WITH THE WAR. (See the Preface for ideas on this topic.) Compare and contrast the different forms patriotism takes. Try to discover various motivations for enthusiasm. How are doubt and pessimism justified? What conflicts of convictions occurred as the war progressed?

2. THE NATURE OF WAR. What is war, and how is it defined? Is it a step upward in man's evolution, a defense of home and of liberty, a conflict of ideologies, a struggle for power, or simply manslaughter? How can it result in good? (See especially Emerson and Whitman.) Is it worth the price? (Compare Emerson and Brownson with Hawthorne and Dickinson.) How are authors' attitudes toward war related to the degree of their participation in it? (See Appendix A.)

3. ROMANTICISM AND IDEALISM VERSUS REALISM. Find examples of, and account for, romantic views of the war (e.g., Southern

chivalry) . Contrast war plans and purposes with the realistic weaknesses and foibles of the men conducting the war. Examine the nature of the idealism found at the beginning of the war. (Eggleston says the Virginians "made war upon a catch-word.") What is concealed or glossed over in some accounts of the war? Discuss other oppositions related to this topic: ideologies versus pragmatism, transcendentalism versus realism, and thinking versus action.

4. CHANGES OF ATTITUDES DURING THE COURSE OF THE WAR. Discuss the change from beliefs in courage and honor to acceptance of expediency. Note the alternating hope or disappointment as the war progressed. Observe the contrast between the anticipation of great things to come from the war (see Stedman and Whitman) and the later realization of what the war brought about. What trends in thinking are discoverable in the selections from Adams, Emerson, Lincoln, and Whitman?

5. RELIGION AND WAR. To what degree did each side maintain it had the support of Providence? What doubts are cast on this? How and why was war considered by some a chastisement or purgation of the nation? To what extent was the Civil War considered a holy war? Contrast humanitarian views (war as an evil resulting from man's choices) with antihumanitarian views (war as mainly in the hands of Providence) .

6. NORTHERN CONCEPTS OF SOUTHERNERS, AND VICE VERSA. What stereotyped views did each side hold of the other? How did these views change in the course of the war?

7. CALLS TO ARMS AND ATTITUDES AT THE OUTBREAK OF THE WAR. What appeals were made to men of fighting age? What were the aims and motives of men going to war? What were the responses of older authors (e.g., Emerson and Longfellow) to the outbreak of the war?

8. CONCEPTS OF THE NEGRO. How did Northern and Southern writers view the Negro? What were some of their motivations for helping him?

9. FOREIGN RESPONSES TO THE AMERICAN CIVIL WAR AND ANSWERS TO PEOPLE IN OTHER COUNTRIES. (See especially Adams, Emerson's letter to Cabot, Hawthorne's letter to Bennoch, and Stedman's letter to his mother.)

10. RESPONSES TO KEY EVENTS IN THE WAR. Discuss, for example, the election of Lincoln (see Arp, Emerson, and Simms) , Chancellorsville (see Whitman) , Fort Wagner (see Emerson and Simms) ,

Gettysburg (see Adams, Arp, Cooke, James, Lincoln, Melville, and Whitman), Appomattox (see Melville), and the death of Lincoln (see Adams and Whitman).

11. RESULTS OF THE WAR. What results were anticipated and how did they coincide with what actually happened? What hopes for peace did authors have during the war? In Southern writers what conflicts were there between old traditional views and current realizations? To what degree did the North succeed in its war aims?

B. ISSUES AND CAUSES OF THE WAR

1. UNIONISM VERSUS SECESSION. How important was Unionism or secession in Northern or Southern motivation? Compare the arguments given for each side, and discuss the answers presented to these arguments.

2. SLAVERY. To what degree was slavery the cause of the Civil War? What differences are there between the views of those who saw slavery from the outside and those who saw it from the inside? (Compare Emerson and Higginson.) What was the impact of the Emancipation Proclamation?

3. ECONOMIC AND POLITICAL QUESTIONS. To what degree was economic competition between the sections a cause of the Civil War? (See Brownson, Simms, and Timrod.) Discuss states' rights versus federalism as a cause of the war. Do the same for oligarchy versus democracy. How was the war seen as the completion of the Revolutionary War? (See especially Holmes.)

4. THE QUESTION OF IRREPRESSIBLE CONFLICT. The phrase "irrepressible conflict" comes from a speech by William H. Seward on October 25, 1858, when he said that the United States "must and will, sooner or later, become either entirely a slave-holding nation, or entirely a free-labor nation." In regard to this question see especially the contrasting opinions of Holmes and Simms.

5. IMPORTANCE OF SUMTER. How did the firing on Fort Sumter serve to rouse the North in support of Lincoln? (See Adams, Arp, Holmes, Parker, Ward, and Whitman.)

6. RESPONSIBILITY FOR THE WAR. Which side, if either, was more responsible for the war, and why? In what ways was responsibility avoided?

7. THE WAR AS A TEST AND VINDICATION OF DEMOCRACY. How and why was the war a test of democracy? (See especially Lincoln and Whitman.) Discuss the question of the supremacy of institutions versus anti-institutionalism as related to the war. In what ways was the process of national identification tied up with the war?

C. OBSERVATIONS

1. PAGEANTRY AND MILITARY GLAMOUR VERSUS HARSH REALITIES AND CHAOS. (See also the topic on romanticism versus realism.) Compare and contrast the observations of Cooke, Dickinson, Hawthorne, Melville, Twain, and Ward. Also examine the contrast between Whitman's "Cavalry Crossing a Ford" and his notes on Chancellorsville or the letter to his mother.

2. LIFE OF A SOLDIER. How were soldiers recruited and molded into fighting men? (See Cooke, Eggleston, Stedman, Twain, and Ward.) What problems were encountered? Contrast the relation of soldiers and officers in regard to the aristocracy of the South or the democracy of the North. Discuss the process of the merging of the individual soldier into the mass army.

3. THE NATURE OF BATTLE. Discuss the contrast between the glory of battle and the ignominy of death. In what ways is battle dehumanizing? What part do obedience and discipline play in it? In spite of his grotesque stories about it, Bierce at times thought war was a "purgative and bracing institution." De Forest said he did not like war, "except in some expansive moments when this or that stirring success filled me with excitement." Account for this ambivalence.

4. DEATH AT WAR. Discuss the Civil War as individual suffering and death versus national tragedy. Examine and compare the various kinds of responses to death. What kind of reconciliation is made between humanitarianism and the brutality of war?

5. EFFECTS OF THE WAR. Consider the other negative effects of war, such as suffering of the wounded (see James and Whitman), miseries of prison (see Melville and Hawthorne), sorrows of family and friends at home, distresses of defeat, and destruction of homes and cities.

D. LITERARY AESTHETICS

1. LITERARY TRANSFORMATION OF EXPERIENCE. Since literary art is essentially the ordering of experience, how did American authors create or perceive some semblance of order in a war which was often chaotic? In what ways did this chaos limit their art? How did distance in time from the close of the war qualify a writer's response? (For this and the following topics, it will be helpful to refer to Appendix B.)

2. CHARACTERISTIC RHETORIC USED IN DISCUSSING THE WAR. What are some common elements in the rhetoric used by Northern writers to describe the South, and vice versa? What is the significance and purpose of the Biblical rhetoric? (See Bryant, Brownson, Holmes, Simms, and Whittier.) Why were Northern Unionists often confined to the rhetoric of orthodoxy?

What are the purposes of allusions to the Homeric and Roman wars, invasions by Goths and Huns, the Commonwealth war, and the American Revolutionary War?

What kinds of imagery are frequently employed? Notice particularly disease, animal, and machine imagery. Be aware of how an image, such as Lanier's "blood-red flower of war," affects the author's tone and meaning.

3. POINT OF VIEW OR PERSPECTIVE. How is a writer's view restricted by his frame of reference (including native region, religion, associates, etc.) ? Contrast works written during the war with those written many years afterward.

4. DIFFERENCES IN STYLE AND LEVEL OF APPEAL. Contrast the effects and purposes of different genres, such as letters versus public oratory or essays versus fiction. What makes an author's style effective? (Discover, for example, why Lincoln's style is more effective than Brownson's.) Examine the means of persuasion found in the oratory.

5. TONE AND THEMES. To what degree were these authors aware of a mythic import of the war? How do they regard the Civil War as related to the whole history of man? How do they see it as drama? Compare the tone and effect of the elegies by Longfellow, Lowell, and Timrod.

6. KINDS AND APPEAL OF HUMOR. (See Arp, Twain, and Ward.)

TOPICS FOR OUTSIDE STUDY

1. Whitman and Simms predicted a great literature would arise from the war, and both Whitman and Howells planned to write significant works on it. Neither accomplished his aim, though; in fact, we have no great imaginative work on the war coming from the authors most intimately associated with it. Attempt to account for this.

2. Discuss the changing responses of American authors to Lincoln during the war years, and compare these with the responses following his death. The one sketch in this anthology which deals with Lincoln's death is simply a representative response. One should also look at Whitman's "When Lilacs Last in the Dooryard Bloom'd," stanza VI of Lowell's "Harvard Commemoration Ode," R. H. Stoddard's "Abraham Lincoln: An Horatian Ode," and responses by Emerson, Bryant, and Hawthorne.

3. Examine the responses of persons in the Concord literary circle to the last days and death of John Brown.

4. Discuss the Civil War as depicted in novels such as Stephen Crane's *The Red Badge of Courage;* Harold Frederic's *The Copperhead;* S. W. Mitchell's *In War Time;* George W. Cable's *Kincaid's Battery;* Winston Churchill's *The Crisis;* Ellen Glasgow's *The Battle-Ground;* Mary Johnston's *The Long Roll;* MacKinlay Kantor's *Andersonville;* Stark Young's *So Red the Rose;* Andrew Lytle's *The Long Night;* Margaret Mitchell's *Gone with the Wind,* Clifford Dowdey's *Bugles Blow No More;* Hervey Allen's *Action at Aquila;* and William Faulkner's *The Unvanquished.*

5. Examine the responses to the Civil War of American authors not included in this anthology, such as Louisa May Alcott, Henry Howard Brownell, Bret Harte, John Pendleton Kennedy, Joseph Kirkland, Petroleum V. Nasby, Richard Henry Stoddard, Bayard Taylor, and George Ticknor.

6. Examine in more depth the responses to the war of authors in this anthology. Some topics of this nature might be:

a. Compare De Forest's account of the attack on Port Hudson with the report of the commanding Union officer found in *The War of the Rebellion* . . . *Official Records,* Ser. 1, Vol. XXVI, Part 1, pp. 132ff.

b. Outline the changing views of the Southern soldier in John Esten Cooke's Civil War novels.

c. Compare Henry Adams's views on the war with those of his father and brother as found in *A Cycle of Adams Letters.*

d. Examine the relationship between the abolitionism of New England intellectuals and their support of Lincoln before and after the Emancipation Proclamation.

e. Evaluate Whitman's poem "The Wound-Dresser" in light of his letters to his mother collected in *The Wound Dresser.*

APPENDIX A

CATEGORIES BY PARTICIPANTS AND OBSERVERS

NAME	AGE APRIL 12, 1861	RESIDENCE OR MILITARY PARTICIPATION	PAGE
I. Participants: North			
Ambrose Bierce	20	9th Indiana Infantry	127
J. W. De Forest	34	12th Conn. Volunteers	134
T. W. Higginson	37	1st S.C. Volunteers	31
II. Participants: South			
Bill Arp (C. H. Smith)	34	Army of North Virginia	185
J. E. Cooke	30	Army of Northern Virginia (J. E. B. Stuart's staff)	194
G. C. Eggleston	21	1st Virginia Cavalry; Artillery in Longstreet's Corps	210
P. H. Hayne	31	On the staff of General Pickens (S.C.)	218
Sidney Lanier	19	Macon (Georgia) Volunteers	253
Mark Twain (S. L. Clemens)	25	Marion (Missouri) Rangers (few weeks) ; Nevada and California	258
III. Observers: North			
Henry Adams	23	London, England	117
Orestes Brownson	57	Elizabeth, N.J.	3
W. C. Bryant	66	Roslyn, L.I., N.Y.	10
Emily Dickinson	30	Amherst, Mass.	145
R. W. Emerson	57	Concord, Mass.	15
Nathaniel Hawthorne	56	Concord, Mass.	148
O. W. Holmes	51	Boston, Mass.	38
Henry James	18	Newport, R.I., and Boston, Mass.	158
Abraham Lincoln	52	Washington, D.C.	47

H. W. Longfellow	54	Cambridge, Mass.	165
J. R. Lowell	42	Cambridge, Mass.	59
Herman Melville	41	Pittsfield, Mass., and New York, N.Y.	170
Francis Parkman	37	Boston and Jamaica Pond, Mass.	75
E. C. Stedman	27	Washington, D.C., and New York, N.Y.	83
Artemus Ward (C. F. Browne)	27	New York, N.Y.; lecture tours	87
Walt Whitman	42	Brooklyn, N.Y., and Washington, D.C.	92
J. G. Whittier	54	Amesbury, Mass.	178

IV. Observers: South

| W. G. Simms | 55 | Charleston and near Columbia, S.C. | 222 |
| Henry Timrod | 33 | Charleston and Columbia, S.C. (Brief military service) | 242 |

APPENDIX B

Categories by Genres

I. FICTION

II. POETRY

III. ESSAYS

VIII. JOURNAL ENTRIES

IX. LETTERS

APPENDIX C

A BRIEF CHRONOLOGY OF THE CIVIL WAR

20 Dec. 1860 — Secession of South Carolina from the Union, followed in January and February, 1861, by Mississippi, Florida, Alabama, Georgia, Louisiana, and Texas.

12 Apr. 1861 — Fort Sumter in Charleston Harbor fired upon by Confederate shore batteries, beginning hostilities of the Civil War.

15 Apr. 1861 — Lincoln's call for 75,000 three-month volunteers.

21 July 1861 — Battle of First Manassas (Bull Run), Va., ending in rout of Union forces.

16 Feb. 1862 — Surrender of Fort Donelson, Tenn., to Union forces under Gen. U. S. Grant.

6–7 Apr. 1862 — Battle of Shiloh, Tenn., with no real victor, but heavy casualties on both sides.

26 Apr. 1862 — Occupation of New Orleans after Farragut's Union fleet ran the forts below New Orleans.

9 Mar. 1862 — Battle between the *Monitor* and the *Merrimac* (which on 8 Mar. had sunk the *Cumberland* off Hampton Roads).

26 June–
2 July 1862 — Seven Days' Battles in which Lee's forces attempted to drive McClellan's army off the Peninsula.

28–31 Aug. 1862 — Battle of Second Manassas (Bull Run) resulting in the defeat of the Union forces under Gen. John Pope.

17 Sept. 1862 — Battle of Antietam (Sharpsburg, Md.), with this bloodiest day of fighting in the war ending in a draw. Considered by French and British governments a Union victory, and kept them from recognizing the Confederacy.

22 Sept. 1862   Lincoln's Preliminary Emancipation Proclamation.

13 Dec. 1862   Union forces under Maj. Gen. Burnside defeated at Fredericksburg.

1 Jan. 1863   Lincoln's Emancipation Proclamation freeing slaves in areas still in rebellion.

2–4 May 1863   Defeat of Hooker's army at Chancellorsville; "Stonewall" Jackson mistaken for a Union soldier and killed by his own men.

22 May–
4 July 1863   Siege of Vicksburg, ending in its surrender to Grant.

1–3 July 1863   Battle of Gettysburg, ultimately becoming a Union victory with Lee's retirement to Virginia. The most significant battle of the war.

19–20 Sept. 1863   Battle of Chickamauga; Federals defeated, fled into Chattanooga, Tenn.

23–25 Nov. 1863   Battle of Chattanooga, with Federal forces under Grant defeating Confederate forces under Bragg.

5–6 May 1864   Battle of the Wilderness followed by Battle of Spotsylvania (8–12 May), as Grant began his attempt to decimate Lee's army.

15 June 1864–
2 Apr. 1865   Siege of Petersburg by Grant.

7 May–
2 Sept. 1864   Sherman's march through Georgia, with significant battles at Resaca, New Hope Church, and Kenesaw Mountain; eventually resulting in the fall of Atlanta.

14 Nov.–
22 Dec. 1864   Sherman's march to the sea, ending in the fall of Savannah.

16 Jan.–
21 Mar. 1865   Sherman's drive through the Carolinas.

9 Apr. 1865   Lee's surrender to Grant at Appomattox Courthouse. This followed Lee's inability to join forces with Johnston after the evacuation of Petersburg and Richmond.

14 Apr. 1865 Assassination of President Lincoln by John Wilkes Booth.

26 Apr.–
 26 May 1865 Surrender of Confederate Generals Johnston, Taylor, and Smith.

SELECTED BIBLIOGRAPHY

Aaron, Daniel. "The Epic Is Yet to Be Written," *American Heritage,* IX (Oct., 1958), 112–16. Compares the responses of authors who fought in the war and those who did not. Useful in clarifying the romantic realism of Whitman and Melville.

Abel, Darrel. "The American Renaissance and the Civil War: Concentric Circles," *The Emerson Society Quarterly,* 44 (III Quarter, 1966), 86–91. Sees the Civil War and the American Renaissance as both part of "the process of American identification and assumption of a national character."

Albrecht, Robert C. "The Theological Response of the Transcendentalists to the Civil War," *New England Quarterly,* XXXVIII (Mar., 1965), 21–34. Says the Transcendentalists returned to the rhetoric of orthodoxy to explain the war.

Browne, Francis F., ed. *Bugle-Echoes: A Collection of the Poetry of the Civil War, Northern and Southern.* New York: Frederick A. Stokes, 1886.

Fredrickson, George M. *The Inner Civil War: Northern Intellectuals and the Crisis of the Union.* New York: Harper and Row, 1965. An excellent study in which the author studies the correlation between Northern intellectuals' "response to events and the transformation in thought and values which took place during the war."

Lively, Robert A. *Fiction Fights the Civil War.* Chapel Hill: University of North Carolina Press, 1957. A thorough survey of Civil War novels to the present.

Nevins, Allan, et al. *Civil War Books: A Critical Bibliography.* 2 vols. Baton Rouge: Louisiana State University Press, 1967–68. This thorough bibliography of Civil War books contains annotated listings in fifteen categories, but excludes fiction and poetry.

Pressly, Thomas J. *Americans Interpret Their Civil War.* Princeton: Princeton University Press, 1954. A study in the historiography of the war. Shows various and changing views on the causes and nature of the Civil War.

Randall, J. G., and David Donald. *The Civil War and Reconstruction.* 2nd ed. Boston: D. C. Heath, 1961. A highly respected, standard history of the Civil War.

Rubin, Louis D., Jr. "The Image of an Army: The Civil War in Southern Fiction," in *Virginia in History and Tradition,* ed. R. C. Simonini, Jr. Farmville, Virginia: Longwood College, 1958. Discusses Southern novels as chiefly being written to show the impact of war on the social pattern.

Spiller, Robert E., et al. *Literary History of the United States.* New York: The Macmillan Company, 1960. Contains critical biographies of major literary figures as well as essays on literary history of the 1860s. A handy bibliography of American literature is the *LHUS Bibliography*, 3rd ed. revised (New York, 1963). For additional biographies see James D. Hart, *The Oxford Companion to American Literature*, 4th ed. (New York, 1965), or the *Dictionary of American Biography*.

Steinmetz, Lee, ed. *The Poetry of the American Civil War.* Lansing: Michigan State University Press, 1960. Contains an excellent bibliography of books on war poetry.

Wilson, Edmund. *Patriotic Gore: Studies in the Literature of the American Civil War.* New York: Oxford University Press, 1962. The best-known criticism of literature of the war. Especially good on Higginson, Lanier, poetry of the war, Cable, Bierce, De Forest, James, and Adams.